THE UNIVERSITY CO
RIPON AND YORK

Interpreting the Field

CRP-K

Interpreting the Field

Accounts of Ethnography

Edited by

DICK HOBBS

and

TIM MAY

CLARENDON PRESS · OXFORD
1993

Oxford University Press, Walton Street, Oxford OX2 6DP
Oxford New York Toronto
Delhi Bombay Calcutta Madras Karachi
Kuala Lumpur Singapore Hong Kong Tokyo
Nairobi Dar es Salaam Cape Town
Melbourne Auckland Madrid
and associated companies in
Berlin Ibadan

Oxford is a trade mark of Oxford University Press

Published in the United States
by Oxford University Press Inc., New York

British Library Cataloguing in Publication Data
Data available

Library of Congress Cataloging in Publication Data
Interpreting the field: accounts of ethnography/edited by Dick
Hobbs and Tim May.
p. cm.
1. Sociology—Methodology. 2. Ethnology—Methodology. I. Hobbs,
Dick. II. May, Tim, 1957–
HM24.I577 1993
305.8—dc20 93–21752
ISBN 0–19–825841–0

1 3 5 7 9 10 8 6 4 2

Typeset by Cambrian Typesetters Frimley, Surrey
Printed in Great Britain
on acid-free paper by
Biddles Ltd., Guildford and Kings Lynn

Contents

Foreword

TALKING A GOOD FIGHT:
Authenticity and Distance in the Ethnographer's Craft

GEOFFREY PEARSON

ONE thing should be made clear about this book at the outset; this is not a 'research methods' text. That is to say, it is not a book which aims to tell you 'how to do it'. There are many research methods texts and manuals on the market, some specifically concerned with qualitative methodologies and ethnographic approaches (e.g. Ellen, 1984; Burgess, 1991; Spradley, 1980). Others are concerned with how to read and evaluate ethnographic research (Hammersley, 1990 and 1992), while a book such as Paul Atkinson's *The Ethnographic Imagination* (1990) approaches ethnography almost in the manner of a literary critic, dealing with the 'poetics' of the ethnographic text and such like. What *Interpreting the Field* offers is a variety of accounts by people who have undertaken ethnographic field research of one kind or another, which describe the difficulties which can (and do) arise when researchers attempt to 'immerse' themselves in other people's lives. The book also makes it clear that ethnography is a messy business, something which you would not always gather from many of the 'research methods' texts which deal with the subject. Published accounts of fieldwork are invariably cleansed of the 'private' goings-on between researcher and researched. When the lid is taken off, however, this can be something of a shock. There can be no better example of this than when the private diaries of Bronislaw Malinowski were first published amidst great controversy in the 1960s, revealing his irritation and disdain for the New Guinea life around him, even at the point when he was pioneering social anthropology's attention to the close details of language and local meaning.

In their different ways, the essays in this book are concerned with how to establish 'closeness' and 'authenticity' in social scientific accounts of other people's lives. This common thread runs through the otherwise quite different projects and subjects which are described—involving research into football hooligans, East End villains and detectives, drug dealers, probation officers, police officers, mining communities amidst the great coal strike of 1984–5, the women's peace camp at Greenham Common against nuclear war and cruise-missiles, and the campaign to identify and combat racism in the labour movement. And once having established 'closeness', a further commanding preoccupation of the ethnographer's task is how to make that available in a textual form to a very different kind of audience.

In introducing and discussing these chapters, I will sometimes refer to other ethnographic studies which exemplify or amplify this or that point. Most of the cases which I use will be concerned with either drugs or crime, simply because this is the area of research with which I am most familiar. Mine is therefore a 'personal' commentary, which seems fitting for a volume such as this. As Tim May and others points out in their contributions, although ethnographic accounts have often been sanitized in such a way that the words 'I' and 'me' do not appear, the researcher-as-subject is always there, even if it is only as a silent, hopefully unobtrusive, but nevertheless significant and looming presence. The ethnographer is never a neutral channel of communication, and to pretend to be is a deception. This is the underlying theme of this book. The researcher, however carefully disguised in either fieldwork comportment or textual display, is always the elephant in the room.

What is Ethnography?

Ethnography is often said to be a way of 'telling it like it is', looking at the social world of the subject as it is seen 'from the inside', telling stories as people might tell these stories themselves. But immediately, it is not (and never can be) that. This is a simplified view of the relations between subject–object, self and other. If one were able to tell the story as it is told 'from the inside', in the short-hand expression of anthropologists this would be to 'go native'. Going native means that one is no longer a member of one's own culture, but of the 'other'; therefore no longer able to communicate the story 'back home'. Dick Hobbs quotes a nice one-liner from Clifford Geertz about 'Being There' and 'Being Here'. To paraphrase: you are able to write the research report because you've been 'There'; we are able to read, quote, understand and criticize you because you're 'Here'. Being an ethnographer is to be in two places at the same time.

Ethnography can depend upon a number of methods. It can involve gathering information by moving closely among people, sometimes quite literally 'living among people', and observing their everyday lives. In some ethnographic studies this 'participant-observation' method, which is also central to the practices of anthropology, is the key-stone of the claim to authenticity. In other forms of study, in-depth interviews are the means by which to gather detailed life-histories and life-stories which could never be obtained simply by 'hanging around' and 'watching the action'. Not uncommonly, different methods are mixed together: interviews might, for example, offer the background to the direct observation provided by fieldwork which acts as foreground; or more informal fieldwork observations might be used to flesh out a study which rests largely on detailed interviews, in the way of 'incidents' and 'excerpts' from daily life.

Different studies in this book lean in different ways, sometimes violating what might be methodological taboos for some commentators. Because there are those who would argue for one version or another of methodological purity: arguing on the one hand that participant–observation is the only true route towards authenticity, while others view field research as merely 'hanging about' and privilege the in-depth interview as the valid means by which to secure a grounded subjectivity in ethnographic research. On any balanced view, however, flexibility is the not-quite-golden rule, adapting methods to circumstances.

There is always, for example, the consideration of worker safety. Some environments are simply too risky for field researchers to hang about, unless they have already established some presence within the field among key informants and negotiated both credibility and 'back up' (cf. Williams *et al.*, 1992). There is also the consideration of the safety of those who are researched, which can take a number of forms. There is the question of confidentiality and protecting the identity of informants in the published record of research, and a number of the chapters in this book illustrate these kinds of difficulties. In one guide to the ethical conduct of ethnographic research Davis (1984, p. 318) suggests that 'probably no solution is

perfect' and that while each anthropologist will attempt to 'camouflage' the identity of research subjects, 'it is always sensible to
consider whether or not it is essential to publish difficult information
at all'. In extreme circumstances, research subjects are of course
quite capable of providing their own 'camouflage'. In a pilot study
among high-level drug dealers who had been imprisoned, Peter
Reuter and John Haaga (1989) in the USA found that the suspicion
attached to agreeing even to be interviewed on a confidential basis—
namely, that this might be seen by fellow inmates as a means by
which to inform ('grass up') on others, with the consequent threat of
violent reprisal—was such that the refusal-rate among potential
interviewees was so high as to jeopardize the viable nature of the
interview sample. The possibility of participant-observation as an
alternative method was not even considered

Under different circumstances, Marsha Rosenbaum in her classic
study *Women on Heroin* (1981) opted for semi-structured interviews
as the core method, as opposed to field observation, in view of the
fact that women were less likely to be fully active participants in the
'street scene' because of the risks to women drug users. The point is
well taken, and more recent research among drug-using prostitutes
in Brooklyn illustrates the daily hazards of violence and sexual
brutality which they face (Maher and Curtis, 1992). In Avril
Taylor's research among women drug injectors in Glasgow, however,
this was not experienced as a problem—which probably speaks to
the differences between Europe and North America in terms of the
accessibility of the streets to women, rather than any fundamental
difference in terms of scientific method (Taylor, 1991 and 1993).
Differences in method in ethnographic research will, if one is true to
ethnographic principle, often result from differences in culture, the
interpretations and uses of social space, etc., rather than differences
in scientific philosophy.

This does not make these differences any less formidable or
important. In Angela McRobbie's pioneering work on the notion of
'youth culture' as applied to young women and girls, for example,
she drew attention to the ways in which their social life was
differently organized than that of boys and young men (McRobbie,
1991). Boys, for example, tend to hang around in gangs and among a
group of 'mates'—thus making for a relatively easy application of the
participant-observation methods in the study of male youth cultures.
Where girls are concerned, however, McRobbie suggested both that

their lifestyles were more focused on the home and also that the more tightly knit one-to-one 'best-friend' relationship was a central means by which girls explored and enacted the 'culture of feminity'. So that whereas in studying the 'view from the boys', the researcher can hang around the pool-table or the street-corner (hopefully unobtrusively) and watch the social world unfold, where the girls' 'best-friend' relations are concerned participant–observer research is a no-go area: two's company, three's a crowd.

For these kinds of reasons, there can be few if any hard-and-fast rules for the successful conduct of ethnographic research, other than a commitment to the maintenance, sustenance, and adequacy of one's information-base and the veracity of one's attempts to render this accessible to a wider audience. If ethnographers are sometimes sceptical about what counts as 'technique' and 'skill' in research, this is not to be mistaken for sloppiness, but is in the nature of the enterprise. This is an area of research where practice does not necessarily make perfect:

> Every field situation *is* different and initial luck in meeting good informants, being in the right place at the right time and striking the right note in relationships may be just as important as skill in technique. Indeed, many successful episodes in the field do come about through good luck as much as through sophisticated planning, and many unsuccessful episodes are due as much to bad luck as to bad judgement. These cannot be anticipated in advance. Simply having done fieldwork is no guarantee of being able to handle new fieldwork any better. (Sarsby, 1984, p. 96)

Authenticity and Distance

One central preoccupation in ethnographic research, whatever specific form it takes, is how to establish and maintain 'access' and 'rapport'. If this sometimes involves luck, it will also often involve a key informant who can act as 'sponsor' and 'gate-keeper' to the world of others. Because no matter how close the researcher might come to be in the quest for authenticity, he or she does not (and as a researcher cannot) fully belong to that other world. This vital opposition of authenticity and distance is at the heart of ethnography. In what follows I will explore how this recurring theme is viewed and handled in different ways by the authors of this book.

In the first chapter, Gary Armstrong describes some of his

experiences doing football research in the city of Sheffield among the hooligan element who supported Sheffield United FC, otherwise known as the 'Blades'. In common with some of the other contributors to this volume, Armstrong claims a version of privileged access to this way of life in view of his own background as someone who was born in Sheffield and was a United supporter. He admits that he was never a fully committed member of the 'hooligan' element, and that his inclinations were always to run rather than stand and fight. Even so, sitting among Blade's fans with 'note-pad and pint' he felt able to construct and maintain a more authentic form of access than would have been available to an 'outsider'. Some of his informants were clearly suspicious of his motives, however, and it was rumoured in their circle that he might be a police spy. No doubt Armstrong's ability to 'blend in' and to 'talk their language' enabled him to weather this storm which could otherwise have blown his research off course. His own position, as I read it, would involve a much stronger argument than this: namely, that his already existing 'near-membership' and 'street cred' is what made his reserch possible in the first place.

If Armstrong stresses closeness in his search for authenticity, Tim May emphasizes distance and difference between 'subject' and 'object' in his research on organizational aspects of the probation service. Covert research on organizations is impossible, of course, unless one is already a member of that organization. One example of this would be Simon Holdaway's under-cover research while living and working as a police officer, although one clear limitation of such an approach is that it is questionable whether Holdaway could have continued to work as a policeman after the publication of his book (Holdaway, 1983).

Otherwise, it is necessary to negotiate access and the approach adopted by May to this process is characteristic of the self-reflexive emphasis of *Interpreting the Field*. The problems of negotiating access are not just regarded as an inconvenience which has to be overcome in order to make contact with 'data'. The negotiations themselves are data. They tell us, for example, about how the organization relates to its external environment (cf. Pearson *et al.*, 1992; Sampson *et al.*, 1991). Also, how it attempts to absorb non-members into its own way of looking at and interpreting the world. To be absorbed into and accepted by an organization, May suggests, does not therefore mean that this offers any privileged access to 'the truth'. On the contrary, it is distance and difference which are the touchstone of authenticity, so that May's view is that to feel an uneasy tension in the research role is quite appropriate. Indeed, May wishes to allow these feelings into the 'truth equation'. Too often 'bracketed' along with the pronouns 'I' and 'me' in sanitized versions of the research process, feelings should be allowed back into accounts of research as a sign of strength rather than weakness, and as a means to combat false versions of 'objectivity'.

A different kind of tension between 'subject' and 'object' is evident in Penny Green's account of her research within mining communities during the coal strike of 1984–5. This was a dispute which involved conflicts not only between the miners and the government, but also between those miners on strike and those who continued to work—leading to conflicts between different factions within and between mining communities, and within families. Admitting that her research was 'partisan' and that she sided with the striking miners, rather than with the working miners, Green nevertheless attempted to research the impact of the strike and the policing of the strike on both sides of the mining community. This was of course an industrial dispute with enormous repercussions within the labour movement, so that what might appear at one level as 'feelings' between striking and working miners were also representative of deeply political and historical forces. One might, for example, see the coal strike as a significant moment in the distancing of relations between the Trade Unions and the Labour Party, given that the issue of 'one-person-one-vote' remains such a lively issue. Green describes how, although she told her research subjects that she was interested 'in the whole community' and believed that they were 'unaware of my partisanship', she nevertheless experienced a reticence and lack of confidence among those working miners whom she contacted and interviewed. This seems hardly surprising given that such a degree of deceit was involved in these contacts with working miners, although Green seems reluctant to admit to the likely impact of unspoken cues and non-verbal communication which are inescapable within a face-to-face interview. Would it have been more appropriate for her to have 'declared her hand' with interviewees, possibly resulting in some interesting and illuminating forms of argument and self-justification in her dealings with working miners? An equally interesting question would then also be what would the outcomes of this research have looked like if it had been conducted by a researcher who was equally committed to the defence of non-striking miners in terms of their access to democratic process in the conduct of the strike?

Where Clive Norris is concerned, he offers an amiably sceptical view that *all* participant-observation research involves deceit. Addressing the social relations of fieldwork as an ethical consideration, with specific reference to participant–observation research on police work, his account of police research emerges as a tangled and sometimes contradictory set of commitments, rather than the one-sided partisanship which Green professes. The versions of his research strategy which Norris says that he gives to the researched, when they query his motives and actions, are in his own words 'not untrue, but they are veiled'. 'They construct the research role', he adds, 'so as to make it understandable and acceptable to the researched.' Norris calls into question the notion of 'trust' in fieldwork since 'the concept of trust implies mutuality of interest and an equality of dependency' which 'to a major degree . . . is inherently absent in the fieldwork role and, therefore, has to be manufactured'. He also discusses in some detail the ethical dilemmas of engaging in police research when this involves 'turning a blind eye' to instances of police misconduct. What, he asks, should be one's responsibilities as a citizen in these circumstances? One might wonder, however, whether or not police research is any different in this respect from fieldwork among people who routinely break the law such as thieves or drug dealers?

Jane Fountain's account of field research among cannabis dealers approaches ethical issues such as these through methodological questions of gathering and making sense of 'data'. She had stumbled across drug dealing through a couple of friends whom she met and who turned out to be regular cannabis dealers at the retail level.[1]

---

[1] This accidental discovery of key informants is not without precedent. In her study of upper-level drug dealing in California, Patricia Adler (1985, p. 12) describes how as a graduate student in a new town, anxious to make friends, she and her husband stumbled across her first major trafficker in the form of a neighbour: 'We started spending much of our free time over at his house, talking, playing board games late into the night, and smoking marijuana together. We were glad to find someone from whom we could buy marijuana in this new place . . . We noticed right away, however, that there was something unusual about his use and knowledge of drugs; while he always had a plentiful supply and was fairly expert about marijuana and cocaine, when we tried to buy a small bag of marijuana from him he had little idea of the going price. This incongruity piqued our curiosity . . . We wondered if he might be dealing in larger quantities.'

They became her gate-keepers (at one point she began to think of them as 'research assistants') to a wider network of cannabis users and dealers, among whom she combined overt and covert research methods. In an honest discussion of the moral difficulties of covert methods of research, she admits to feelings of guilt because of the sometimes intrusive nature of this approach, while avoiding the primness of some commentary on the matter (cf. Bulmer, 1982). There can be no doubt that little headway would be made in many research enterprises if an overt declaration of identity were always required—'Please go on, don't mind me, I'm only a researcher taking notes, and what did you say the profit was from that half-ounce transaction?'—and that unless such research is to be abandoned or outlawed, then a bluff moral pragmatism is necessary.

It makes interesting reading to compare Clive Norris on the police and Jane Fountain on dope dealers in this tricky area of field research ethics and the maintenance of rapport. Norris was sometimes mistaken for a CID officer (he admits to occasionally adopting a dress-style of flannels, blazer, white shirt, and tie in order to 'blend in') and Fountain often no doubt passed as either a user or a dealer. Gary Armstrong's difficulty of being suspected as a police informer is therefore not the only case of 'mistaken identity' experienced in the field. Indeed, in another telling moment, Penny Green had been mistaken for Arthur Scargill's research officer. Perhaps these kinds of experiences are the inevitable consequence of field research, where the researcher is constructing a calculated and pretended identity which attempts to bridge 'authenticity' and 'distance'.

For research on the women's peace camp against nuclear weapons at Greenham Common, Sasha Roseneil did not have to pretend to be anyone other than herself. Indeed, she argues that feminist research of the type she envisages can move beyond the knower–known, subject–object relations of research into a different realm of shared equality. Some will undoubtedly question the epistemological validity (indeed, the very possibility) of such a stance. However, Roseneil's claim to a heightened authenticity through her passionate involvement in the struggle at the Greenham Common women's peace camp is ultimately not one which wishes to collapse and erase the question of 'distance' to zero. Rather, although Roseneil claims the status of 'complete member' in her research as a result of living at the camp for some time, hers is a more general appeal that research should position the knowing subject's experience centrally within the field of vision. It is thus a theoretical stance which, while it has been adopted and enlarged by feminist writers, has a close affinity with Gadamer's philosophy of science which she acknowledges and is also reflected in the recognition embodied in Wittgenstein's much earlier quip in the *Tractatus*: 'From nothing in the field of sight can it be concluded that it is seen from an eye' (1922, p. 151).

It is against this 'invisibility' of the knowing subject that all of the chapters in this book are working, although undoubtedly Roseneil pushes this kind of approach much further than some would wish it to go, and she herself wonders whether her extreme emphasis on the subjective aspect of research might have gone 'beyond the pale' of academic acceptability. I would certainly not share such a view. The issues which her account raises—epistemological, methodological, ethical, political—would require a chapter to themselves. But there is one further aspect of distance which is perhaps all that can be entered here: which is to acknowledge the limits of legitimate commentary and interpretation available to a man in response to such a rootedly women's event as the Greenham peace camp and its associated meanings. I do not mean to imply by this some universal epistemological or interpretative blockage between the sexes. Rather that participation in the means of working, sharing, and acting together at Greenham Common was understood and felt by so many women as such a profoundly empowering set of experiences, precisely as a consequence of the radical exclusion of men.

In a retrospective view of her research on racism and political marginalization within the Labour Party, H. L. Ackers provides a very different kind of account of a woman gaining and maintaining access to the 'field'. She is particularly concerned to describe some of the experiences of obstruction, suspicion, and sexual harrassment which she encountered. At the time she viewed these simply as things which she had to 'put up with' as 'part of the job' of being a woman attempting ethnography in a predominantly male environment. Accordingly, whereas Roseneil placed her subjective experiences at the core of the research process, Ackers felt the need to purge these 'private' matters from what she intended as an objective and 'public' document. However, she kept detailed field notes and diaries of these day-to-day events and experiences which she would now see as fundamental in the workings of institutional racism, intertwined with stereotyped sexuality. She also comments on the ways in which different possible support systems—the academic community and the process of research supervision, the conceptual framework of her intellectual 'discipline' as a social geographer, friends, and family—each failed in different ways to provide the kinds of props and bolt-holes which she needed from time to time. Her account is thus not only a reminder of the all-too-human dimensions of research and the requirements of research supervision. It also leads her to conclude that 'ethnography was certainly not about "going native" '. Rather, she experienced it as a feeling of 'loneliness and a sense of isolation' and as 'a perpetual reminder that I fitted nowhere'.

Conclusion: Betraying the Field?

Anthropologists who visit distant and unfamiliar places in order to undertake fieldwork often experience 'homesickness' and a variety of problems with both physical and mental health (Sarsby, 1984, pp. 104–5). Ethnographers who do fieldwork in their own backyards sometimes feel confused. The problem of field research is not just about negotiating access, getting in, staying in, surviving, and then getting out more-or-less intact. There is also the requirement to carry the narrative 'back home', refashioning the fieldwork experience in a textual form which while it is accessible to a different audience (its academic readership) remains true to where it came from. It is a problem of multiple identities: 'Being There' and 'Being Here' in Geertz's words. Each of the studies in *Interpreting the Field* in their different ways searches for a version of 'authenticity'. But in each case, it is a claim hedged about with the limitations and hesitancy of 'distance'. What is being described is the complexity of the relationship between author–subject–object–audience–text.

Dick Hobbs explores this final aspect of authenticity and distance in the context of how to write about the lives of working-class villains and entrepreneurs from London's East End. A Cockney, he could 'speak like a native' but the demands of an academic audience and of publishers meant that this was not enough. The text must accomplish a dual task. It must reflect the authenticity of the 'street', while resonating with the quite different rhythms of the seminar and library. Severely tried by these difficulties, ultimately Hobbs seems to be saying, it does not matter whether the 'man-in-the-street' understands the text or recognizes himself in it. 'The text', he says, 'is influenced at every stage of its production up to and beyond publication by the rules specific to the intellectual, political, and economic milieu within which the writer performs.' 'Fieldwork is a crucial part of this process,' he adds later, 'but not *the* most crucial.' If so, then is ethnography invariably and ultimately an act of 'betrayal'?

While I believe that Hobbs is right to question the quasi-machismo element which sometimes clings to the 'cult of field-work'—as if 'getting one's hands dirty' in the field were a heroic venture, or some kind of fashion-statement to complement the care-worn office life of university teachers—I cannot quite agree with his over-deterministic emphasis on the conditions of textual production. Indeed, nor would his own richly nuanced account of the dialogue between fieldwork and text appear to support this. In my view, the ethnographic text cannot 'betray' the experience of the field since the vital opposition of authenticity *and* distance means that the experience of fieldwork is never quite as 'real' as it is sometimes supposed to be.[2] The ethnographer does not have to be a competent burglar, or prostitute, or policeman, or miner in order to deliver competent enthnographies of work, life, and crime. He or she does not have to be 'one of them'. It is an old adage of social research that you do not need to be Caesar in order to understand Caesar; indeed, it might even be a handicap. Admittedly, certain attributes will exclude the ethnographer sometimes from quite vital places, plots and conversations. A woman researcher can no more be a 'fly on the wall' to men's conversations in the 'happy hour' of the pub, than a man can 'infiltrate' the quiet confidences of 'women's talk', or whites watch unobtrusively at a black blues party. Even so, these limits are not about being truly competent actors. What is required of an ethnographer is neither full membership nor competence, but the ability to give voice to that experience, and to *bridge* between the experiences of actors and audiences, 'authenticity' and 'distance'. Just as a boxing commentator does not need to slug it out over twelve rounds to bring a fight to life, so the ethnographer must remain content to 'talk a good fight'.

---

[2] One issue not discussed here as much as one might wish is the question of language within ethnography. That is to say, what can be learned about cultures and subcultures from their improvised languages, slang, and argot; what can be both revealed and also cloaked about social reality and human experience in the use of words (cf. Pearson, 1987 and 1992; Mieczkowski, 1986 and 1990).

References

ADLER, P. A. (1985), *Wheeling and Dealing: An Ethnography of an Upper-Level Drug Dealing and Smuggling Community*, New York: Columbia University Press.

ATKINSON, P. (1990), *The Ethnographic Imagination: Textual Constructions of Reality*, London: Routledge.

BULMER, M. (ed.) (1982), *Social Research Ethics: An Examination of the Merits of Covert Participant-Observation*, London: Macmillan.

BURGESS, R. (1991), *In the Field: An Introduction to Field Research*, London: Routledge.

DAVIS, J. (1984), 'Data into Text', in R. F. Ellen (ed.), *Ethnographic Research: A Guide to General Conduct*, ASA Research Methods in Social Anthropology, 1, London: Academic Press.

ELLEN, R. F. (ed.) (1984), *Ethnographic Research: A Guide to General Conduct*, ASA Research Methods in Social Anthropology, 1, London: Academic Press.

HAMMERSLEY, M. (1990), *Reading Ethnographic Research*, London: Longman.

—— (1992), *What's Wrong with Ethnography?*, London: Routledge.

HOLDAWAY, S. (1983), *Inside the British Police*, Oxford: Blackwell.

McROBBIE, A. (1991), *Feminism and Youth Culture*, London: Macmillan.

MAHER, L. and CURTIS, R. (1992), 'Women on the Edge of Crime: Crack Cocaine and the Changing Contexts of Street-Level Sex Work in New York City', *Crime, Law and Social Change*, vol. 18.

MALINOWSKI, B. (1989), *A Diary in the Strict Sense of the Term*, London: Athlone.

MIECZKOWSKI, T. (1986), 'Monroe in a Cadillac: Drug Argot in Detroit', *International Journal of Comparative and Applied Criminal Justice*, vol. 10, no. 1.

—— (1990), 'Crack Lingo in Detroit', *American Speech*, vol. 65, no. 3.

PEARSON, G. (1987), *The New Heroin Users*, Oxford: Blackwell.

—— (1992), 'The Role of Culture in the Drug Question', in M. Lader, G. Edwards and D. C. Drummond (eds.), *The Nature of Alcohol and Drug Related Problems*, Society for the Study of Addiction Monograph no. 2, Oxford: Oxford University Press.

—— BLAGG, H., SMITH, D., SAMPSON, A., and STUBBS, P. (1992), 'Crime, Community and Conflict: The Multi-Agency Approach', in D. Downes (ed.), *Unravelling Criminal Justice*, London: Macmillan.

REUTER, P. and HAAGA, J. (1989), *The Organisation of High-Level Drug Markets: An Exploratory Study*, Santa Monica: RAND.

ROSENBAUM, M. (1981), *Women on Heroin*, New Jersey: Rutgers University Press.

SAMPSON, A., SMITH, D., PEARSON, G., BLAGG, H., and STUBBS, P. (1991), 'Gender Issues in Inter-Agency Relations: Police, Probation and Social Services', in P. Abbott and C. Wallace (eds.), *Gender, Power and Sexuality*, London: Macmillan.

SARSBY, J. (1984), 'The Fieldwork Experience', in R. F. Ellen (ed.), *Ethnographic Research: A Guide to General Conduct*, ASA Research Methods in Social Anthropology, 1, London: Academic Press.

SPRADLEY, J. P. (1980), *Participant Observation*, London: Holt, Rhinehart and Winston.

TAYLOR, A. (1993) *Women Drug Users: An Ethnography of a Female Injecting Community*, Oxford: Clarendon Press.

WILLIAMS, T., DUNLAP, E., JOHNSON, B. D., and HAMID, A. (1992), 'Personal Safety in Dangerous Places', *Journal of Contemporary Ethnography*, vol. 21, no. 3.

WITTGENSTEIN, L. (1922), *Tractatus Logico-Philosophicus* (1990 edn.), London: Routledge.

PART I

Field-Work

1

'Like that Desmond Morris?'

GARY ARMSTRONG*

In an attempt to redress gaps in our knowledge this study attempted a specific anthropological case study of a group of football hooligans. These were supporters of Sheffield United FC, nicknamed 'The Blades' due to their being founded by cutlers of the city's renowned steel industry. Borrowing this nickname all supporters of the club and also the Hooligan Element call themselves and each other Blades. For clarity I used this title when referring to the hooligans, and 'Unitedites' when referring to club supporters. Blades know they are hooligans, but do not refer to themselves or others by this term except in jest and ridicule. Instead they are into 'It' and their opponents are 'them'—better known as 'their boys' if from another town or city and 'the Pigs' when they are supporters of city rival Sheffield Wednesday, whose fans adopted the nickname of 'the Owls'. Against both opposition teams the Blades play an elaborate 'game'. Each week can bring a win, loss, or a draw. Blades are forever in pursuit of 'a good result'; this, however, can change with the opposition and the time of day. Whilst when facing Their Boys the match day provides the venue, when the opposition are fans of Sheffield Wednesday the venue is more flexible. When discussing them Blades prefer the term 'Pigs' to Owls, who in turn prefer 'Pigs' to Blades. This hostility extends beyond words and has resulted in violence since the mid-1960s, and reached an unprecedented level of frequency on the streets of the city centre at weekend nights from 1986 onwards. Two streets in particular, London Road, and West Street, each with a dozen pubs, were claimed as their 'patch' by Blades and Owls respectively.

The events which took place a few days before Christmas 1990 provided the Blades with a dishonourable defeat and a mutually recognized draw. Friday night had seen a late-night trespass by

* Criminology Department, University of Westminster.

twenty Owls onto the Blades' 'patch'. However, only five Blades were around at the time; their spirited resistance left one, Bobby, concussed in hospital minus a front tooth and Blades accusing the Pigs of despicable bullying. The following day United's visitors, Nottingham Forest, brought forty lads who managed to avoid the police and 'front' a few Blades after the game. Police arrived and prevented a battle as Blades ran to join their colleagues. Peacefully accompanying the Forest fans to their transport, two Blades received an admission that Forest were not claiming a 'result' because of the police. A suggestion was made that Blades arrive at a certain place in Nottingham when they played the return fixture four months later. Aware they were being followed by plain-clothes 'undercover' police (only they wore ear-muffs with collars up to conceal the ear-piece and radio wire), thirty Blades decided to have some fun. Walking in silence with definite purpose, the group took a dead-end route in the bus station then turned around and walked back. The three police continued their walk and moments later faced the brick wall, to the amusement of the group now watching and sniggering. Later, Blades were pushed and abused by police as they walked to pubs and the anthropologist was told by one of the two policemen who had followed the group at home and away for three years: 'Fuck off, Armstrong . . . hangin' about wi this bleedin' shower.' The weekend events had made fascinating ethnography, had sown the seeds of retribution in two arenas, and had provided the most unequivocal advice in the six-year research period.

The question of how to research a phenomenon such as football hooliganism concerns the question of the status of fieldwork data once it is accepted that scientific enquiry does not proceed by any simple process of induction from 'facts' (Armstrong and Harris 1991). This problem is not a new one, but it seems to be in urgent need of serious discussion since it appears that some academics are convinced that analysis of any social situation is dependent on a 'correct' understanding of the macro, social structure. Consequently, data are relevant only as a source of 'apt illustration' of basic theoretical positions. Such an approach may lead to serious misunderstandings of the nature of the issue under consideration; it inevitably involves stereotyping (ibid.). However, if it is to be accepted that research data provide a yardstick against which hypotheses must be measured, then clearly we have to be very sure that these data are indeed not just apt illustrations; that they are collected and presented with as much objectivity as possible and in such a way as to represent as many facets as possible of the situation that is under study. This is a task that inevitably presents very severe difficulties in situations where, for whatever reason, it is hard to get satisfactory answers to all the questions that need to be asked. It is because any attempt to study the football hooligan raises all these issues that it is a task that involves a real intellectual as well as a practical challenge.

A study of football hooligans, based on 'ethnographic' information (the basis of this research), must meet three major criteria. Most crucially, it must answer a Structural-Marxist challenge that says that the British football hooligan is essentially to be understood as linked to the response of Capital to a crisis in the 'capitalist hegemony' in Britain (Taylor 1982); from this viewpoint the main significance of hooligan behaviour is political: it is both a manifestation of fascist thuggery and a means of frightening people into taking right-wing positions (see also Robins and Cohen 1978; Robins 1984). Simultaneously, the research must convince mainstream sociologists that its approach to the problem and the quality of the information it will collect will be such as to add a new dimension to those studies of football fans that do seek to base themselves primarily on empirical evidence (see Harrington 1968; Trivizas 1980; Critcher 1979; and the Leicester University research team of Dunning *et al.* 1984, 1987, 1989, 1990). Thirdly, it must answer the constructs of the media and police (Phillips 1987; Appleby 1990, 1991; Home Affairs Committee 1991), not helped by pathetic claims of sociologists (see Dunning *et al.* 1990) which impose hierarchical structures and a high level of organization and conspiracy on the various hooligan gatherings. (For a challenge to this view see Armstrong and Harris 1991 and Armstrong *et al.* 1991). Research has to look beyond what some would see as common-sense assumptions.

Bearing the above in mind, I hereby declare my interests, which are in 'meaning' and 'motivation' located within a neo-Weberian perspective of *Verstehende* sociology—trying to think oneself into the situations of the people one is interested in, remembering how Evans-Pritchard (1951) stated that the anthropologist's fundamental aim was to investigate classifications, in this case the 'Hooligan'. This combined approach involves recognizing social and historical phenomena as beyond any single or simple identifying cause and trying to make sense from the social actors' viewpoint. As an end-product I attempted what Van Maanen (1988, p. 103) terms the 'impressionistic' style of ethnography, whereby the unfamiliar is presented to an audience 'seated ringside', whilst concomittantly trying to ascertain what are the actors' intentions and conscious choices within the class structure they are part of. This has been acknowledged by Leach (1954), Bordieu (1977), and Abrams, who suggests that the relationship of action and structure is 'a matter of process in time' and that such research must show the actor making decisions in complex circumstances (1982, pp. xiv–xv).

The starting-point for the analysis was what Goffman (1974, p. 564) described as ordinary, actual behaviour. Similarly Mary Douglas (1970, p. 12) stated that the only valid evidence comes from systematic observation of everyday life. Added to this was the approach Malinowski (1922, p. 18) evocatively described for researchers, who ideally should seek the 'imponderabilities of everyday life' which require detailed accounts of people over long time-periods in a variety of settings. This was for him the only way to illustrate how people handle the choices they face, and ties in with Turner's idea of 'optation' (1957, pp. 142–3), whereby an individual selects from a variety of possibilities. That said, however, the immediate problems was that Blades rarely sat round being highly articulate about the motives for their behaviour and the meanings of incidents they were involved in. Human motivation is not always easy to ascertain. We cannot always rely on the actors' explanations in these cases, so that the only course for the investigator is to try to present a 'rounded' picture of those involved so that the person may be seen in a proper context. This was the purpose of the study. It will, therefore, be asked how I got at their meanings. The answer is, by the standard techniques of good ethnographies—by watching and listening to Blades interacting with one another and with me, and by striving to make explicit to myself the common understandings which Blades as a group shared.

Social-science work on Britain is remarkably poor in good ethnography. The excellent works of Patrick (1973), Parker (1974), Gill (1977), Willis (1977), Corrigan (1979), Pryce (1979), Fielding (1981), and Hobbs (1989) stand out as unusual amidst surveys, questionnaires, interviews, and superficial impressionistic analysis. While often spoken of, participant-observation is, as Parker (1974) noted, 'rarely attempted and even less frequently successfully completed' (p. 15). This has been true particularly in the case of research into football hooliganism. Just as significant is the fact that the term has come to be a cliché, without definition (cf. McCall and Simmonds 1969 and Bulmer 1982). There have been a number of studies that purport to be based on detailed observations of hooligans, but on closer inspection are not all they claim to be. So many claim to be 'doing participant-observation' when all they are doing is standing at a distance pretending to be 'with the Lads' and therefore sociologically 'Right On'.

Most previous researchers have had comparatively restricted contacts with the individual actors; indeed, some had none at all. The earliest attempt at going out amongst the research subjects came from social psychologist Peter Marsh and his team (1978a, b), who observed events on the terraces at matches, usually from the distance of the stand, at times using a video recorder to reproduce the dynamics of incidents. They also spoke to young supporters at matches and at school. However, details on the time-scale and possible problems the research may have encountered are omitted, as is any attempt to present the social background of the participants or to tell the reader how they spend most of their time when not acting as football hooligans. The book was an important work but was not followed in style by later researchers. Writing both before and after Marsh, criminologist Ian Taylor makes no mention of ever having attended a football match. His early (1971) theory is clearly not of the kind that could be based on empirical data drawn from such a milieu; his stance did not require empirical research, or for that matter historical validity. We gain the impression that Taylor attended a few games of Sheffield Wednesday, watched a few more on television, and from this research produced his theory. Researchers Pratt and Salter (1984) disappeared from the debate after one paper, which on close scrutiny did not live up to its claims of participant-observation.

Another author, heavily involved in 'Youth and Community' studies, is Dave Robins (1984; see also Robins and Cohen 1978). His attitudes, and the kind of relationships he made with the fans, are revealed in his description of a time when, in his words: 'Some eleven year old "kamikaze" Chelsea fans attacked West Ham supporters, who retaliated' (p. 15). He says he cried out, presumably in the middle of this mayhem: 'This is crazy . . . over there' (p. 16), and pointed to the 'posh' seats of the director's box. Apart from raising the moral question of whether a researcher ought to try to urge violence against a particular group, what was Robins's competence in understanding his fans if he thought such words at such a time would have had the slightest effect? His own evidence showed that the teenagers he talked to seem to have been unimpressed by his attempts to get them interested in 'heroic, armed workers taking over key points in the city in the struggle for socialism' (p. 126). Again, he writes: 'I started a discussion group around the issue of "Why Football Violence?" Sitting around the tape recorder the mood was usually relaxed and sophisticated' (p. 13). Later he says: 'For the most part I avoided interviews with a more disturbed and psychopathic element in the ends. This is not for reasons of personal safety, but because I was concerned with locating the rise of soccer aggro within the experience of the main stream of working class youth' (p. 16). In saying this he is assuming what he should have set out to prove. He does not tell us how he decided who was a psychopath, or disturbed. Moreover, in using the word 'mainstream' he implies that the majority of the working class are an undifferentiated mass. Also, I would argue that, no matter how 'sophisticated' the audience, a tape-recorder is no substitute for direct observation of the actual behaviour of 'hooligans'.

The most prolific writers on the subject, and those with most funding from various concerned bodies, are the Leicester University researchers under the leadership of Eric Dunning, a sociologist. Significantly the most detailed material evidence so far presented by these sociologists is, as they note themselves, journalistic, being derived from a television documentary. This evidence was then used by them to support their position that the fans are of the lower working class—but this is surely not really an adequate basis for the construction of a theory (a fact acknowledged to me privately by the producer, but not by the sociologists). If ever there was an example of what the anthropologist Edmund Leach (1961, pp. 2–5) classified as academic 'Butterfly collecting', this was it.

Because their whole theory (see Dunning *et al.*, 1984 and 1987) is apparently based on observations at only *six* football matches, one might ask why, when they already had set out their theory on the phenomenon in earlier writings (cf. Dunning and Elias (1986)), they needed to send a researcher to any games at all. They note (1989) that a 'trained participant observer' can provide rich information of a 'more realistic kind than that to which we have been accustomed hitherto . . .' (p. xiii), and that the task in regard to football hooliganism is eased considerably because of the small number of fans who fit that label, helped by knowledge of the context and situation and the sorts of fans likely to take part in such events—so far so good. Their researcher, Williams, from the accounts given in the books (1984 and 1989) went nowhere near the hooligans, while his undercover research was amongst fans whom he had never met before (or was ever to meet again), in three different countries. Whilst travelling 'undercover' with Aston Villa fans on an official supporters' club coach, stewarded by two policemen, Williams tells of 4,000 others who travelled independently to avoid such control. What 'trouble' occurred was blamed on 600 youths accused of being outsiders masquerading as Villa fans. The sociologist cannot enlighten us as to the identity of a single one of them. Later (1986) Williams attempts a more detailed analysis of these people, who are characterized by 'Rambo-like xenophobia . . . anti-intellectualism and page three sexism' (p. 17), council-estate dwellers dressed like 'clones', who consider 'Paki-bashing' a sport. It is ironical that the researcher later (Dunning *et al.*, 1988) criticizes the impressionistic and sensational descriptions of the tabloid press, Later, (1990), we are presented with brief ethnography published, strangely enough, ten years after the research, which once again tells us nothing, yet conveniently fits their theories. Further afield, European researchers have not explored the participants deeply. In Belgium Waldergrave and Van Limbergen (1987) supplemented their observation with paid informants, and the Dutch academics Vanderbrug and Miejs (1988) paid fans to complete questionnaires.

This, then, is the state of 'participant' academic research by *the* 'experts' on the subject. In fact, in over twenty-five years of debate (and hysteria) on the subject, we have only two very good descriptive accounts of hooligan events, one by Allan (1989), a self-confessed hooligan, the other by Ward (1989) who, whilst admitting to writing a 'hooligan's-eye view' study, adds 'though I have never been a hooligan in the true sense of the word' (p. 190). However, he is being coy; the book is full of Ward-as-hooligan; all the same, his book remains a very important, informative (and good), if slightly sensational description of London hooligans and England fans travelling abroad. The only academic research which I consider complementary to mine are the recent (1989*a*, *b*, and 1991) Scottish studies by Richard Giulianotti. One other academic, O'Brien (unpublished thesis, 1986), has touched the fringes of the hooligans in a study which did not pretend to be a hooligan analysis, but is praiseworthy all the same.

So in total, what do we have? Marsh's thesis rests ultimately on the assumption that punches are pulled; Taylor's thesis falls unless the hooligans are fascist thugs; Robins's thesis suggests the fans are fascist fodder, dangerous unless led by the intelligentia, but are meanwhile led by psychopaths. All that Dunning *et al.* have to say of theoretical relevance is that the lower working class (LWC) is significantly implicated in hooligan behaviour, at least as providing role models, while the media and police attribute a military structure to the groups. They all agree that the hooligans personify everything that is wrong in our society.

I had, while reading the above accounts, sufficient experience of fans to suspect that many of the ideas presented as the results of research, or at least as consistent with research, really stemmed from the assumptions and stereotypes of the writers. Because of these doubts therefore, I believed it necessary to go back to look at 'the facts' in order to decide the nature of the phenomena about which theories needed to be constructed. I proposed, before proceeding to analysis of the reasons for hooligan violence, to try to discover, in relation to a particular group, who was violent and when—and equally important, who was not violent and when. Clearly, the phenomena to be explained ought to influence the theory—and we did not know if the violence was perpetrated always by the same or different people on different occasions. We did not know whether those charged and convicted were or were not those most guilty. We knew virtually nothing about these people in other contexts.

While this is the aim of the full research (see Armstrong and Harris 1991), the specific aim of this paper is to present the conditions of possibility which produced the end-product. This aspect of research has already been debated, but little has been seen to arise from it. As Bordieu (1984) says, researchers should question the basis of their authority and the positions from which they write what they do. Others have described the omission of details about the researcher and researched as '. . . one of the great silences in the midst of ethnographic description itself' (Pratt 1986, p. 42). These criticisms are valid. I believe, as Rabinow (1986, p. 253) has written, that the 'conditions of production of anthropology should be moved from the domain of gossip to that of knowledge'.

The purpose of my study was to look beyond mere appearances by taking Whyte's (1955) advice: 'The individual must be put back into his social setting and observed in his daily activities. In order to understand the spectacular event, it is necessary to see it in relation to the everyday pattern of life' (p. xvi). The research treated the football hooligans studied (that is, the Blades) as individuals who made their own choices within the constraints of the environment they shared. The hooligan and his activities are addressed but, at other times, the hooligan is workmate, boyfriend, brother, son, and neighbour. These relationships we knew nothing about, yet they involved basically what the fans did for the greater part of their time, when not confronting rival fans. The omission of all this presents an appalling lacunae.

While doing the study I did not feel I had to advocate any particular policy. Research was not established to look for a 'cure' for football hooliganism; it is not an illness to be cured. Besides, it is naïve to believe that something as complex as the human ability to be hostile is something curable. This raises also an ethical point of academic research; as Becker (1967) asked: 'Whose side are we on?' I did not consider it my job to work as a control agent of the State. On this point I agree with Polsky (1969) when he says that he has nothing against social workers, probation officers, policemen, or anyone else trying to stop people from breaking the law: 'If a man wants to make that sort of thing his life work, I have no objection; that is his privilege. I suggest merely that he not do so in the name of sociology, criminology, or any other social science' (p. 140). Other relevant advice to researchers came from Gill (1977, p. 196), who writes how research amongst deviants must also encompass the 'normality, dignity and integrity' of the research subjects. Further, he adds that the researcher, when returned to academe, should regard the subjects as looking over his shoulder. On this issue I will be at variance with the Leicester researchers who, acting as what Baritz (1965) would call 'servants of power' and funded by both the Football Trust and government departments, have taken on the role of government (and therefore policy) advisors. Their 1989 book claims that they are the 'experts' working to 'cure' hooliganism. The implications about their role as sociologists and the debate around the privatization of law and order has, to my knowledge, not been discussed.

It would seem for the Leicester researchers that the hooligans are implicity beyond what Fichter and Kolb (1953) would call their 'moral community'. As such, the consequences of research need not worry the sociologist. I disagree; I regard the Blade 'community' as consisting of individuals who have as much right to fair representation as anyone. It may be asked, then, what use is my study.

Whether I would contribute to a greater understanding of an important social phenomenon I always doubted, but I could offer some interesting descriptions. This is significant, because as Murdock (1972) noted, colossal ethnography was anthropology's main contribution to knowledge. Even this, I considered, was more useful than theory without evidence. While describing events I pursued a Ph.D. thesis which began with my wanting to 'do something about football hooliganism'. When asked what was my 'approach' or indeed my aim in my early years, I honestly had no good idea. I took comfort in Barley's (1986) words when he stated: 'After all, most research starts off with a vague apprehension of interest in a certain area of study and rare indeed is the man who knows what his thesis is about before he has written it' (p. 12). As a result I began without a focus, yet to counteract the vagueness I decided to record everything. As Barley (1986, p. 55) correctly observed: 'When in doubt collect facts'. An 'average' Saturday would result in thirty sides of notes hand-written on A4 paper. But the vagueness was an advantage because new opportunities arose over the years—areas which I had to exploit to the full alongside the original proposals. Without a doubt the new elements—the changes in hooligan manifestations, police charges and tactics, the 'Hillsborough Tragedy', and the pronouncements of various politicians took on more significance than many of the ideas I originally had.

Publicly the personal element of a research project has usually been totally submerged by claims that the main concern is to develop theory, yet here I was beginning a study on an area of which I knew a little, but sensed that there was a lot more to know. The origins of this research may be found in the words of Corrigan (1979), who wrote, 'people's work has an effect upon the way in which they choose a research problem; but the main set of reasons for choice is to be found in the biography of the researcher' (p. 94). This is not always so; for many the subject is the 'OK' thing to comment upon (witness the dozens of so-called 'hooligan' experts who were heard in the media during the 1988 European Championships and more recently the World Cup, 1990). For this study, though, it is an applicable statement; this was a subject I had grown up with, and took place in an environment with which I was familiar. So, for this study biography is synonymous with subjectivity; this acknowledged, I hoped it could be put to creative use.

Quite when the research began is difficult to say. My earliest memories of hooliganism go back to 1968, to the local recreation ground where, in between some of the greatest games of football ever played and some of the greatest goals ever scored, I, along with dozens of others, would sit around and talk to some of the 'older lads', daunting as they were at 14 and even 16 years of age, who would tell us about fights at football matches and what it was like to be a 'skinhead' or a 'suede-head' (the youth fashions at the time). Then, a year later when I first started attending matches at Bramall Lane, I was to see at close quarters the fights on the Kop. I was terrified and remained that way until around 1973 when, realizing I was not the target for these rivals, I thought that maybe I should not worry so much.

Throughout the 1970s, the era I consider to be the peak of football hooliganism, I, together with hundreds my age, would stand at the back of the Kop thinking I was extremely 'hard', chanting. In hindsight, I must have looked ridiculous wearing a scarf tied about the wrist or hanging from the waist, complete with Doc Marten boots bought by parents who did not understand the symbolic significance of what they considered 'sensible' footwear. As soon as the fights started, most of my age-group would run like hell, watch events from a safe distance, chant, then return when the fight was over, and afterwards talk about it at school on Monday. Football and violence were synonymous. Later in the 1970s, some of my age-group actually joined in (I continued to run away). For some the excitement lasted only for one match; others stayed around for years.

Even when this adolescent excitement had passed I continued to follow 'our team', and over the years got to know many lads who were also football hooligans. Thus my association with the supporters of Sheffield United goes back over twenty years. I ran on the pitch some ten years on, to congratulate my heroes, walked three miles in snow 4.30 one Boxing Day morning to join coaches travelling to a match in London, and still harbour a desire to play for United and personally humiliate Sheffield Wednesday in a Wembley Final in front of a world-wide audience. Through following the Blades to seventy-five out of ninety-two League grounds I saw England and

Wales, met hundreds of other fans, and had some of the saddest and most joyful times of my life. The team was everything, the camaraderie of the fans I have never been able to replace. Still Saturday brings one of the most anxious moments of the week: United's result first, followed by Wednesday's. A victory and defeat respectively makes my day.

In 1982, as part of an undergraduate dissertation, I combined my support for the club with research on the Blades. The research continued in 1983. Then, in early 1984 I began to immerse myself more in the personalities and events surrounding them; this continued until December 1990. From autumn 1988 I decided to reduce the previous level of intensive research based on and around the match-day, but continued to interview various individuals and tried to build up my understanding of personal backgrounds and the network of groups of mates that constituted the Blades, as well as attending matches. To help the writing-up process, for one period of four months in 1988/9 I did not attend a United match and spent my time in Holland and then London. My own reaction to this provided a kind of evidence as to fan motivation. As an unmarried postgraduate doing a thesis I found Saturdays empty; they needed occupying. I began by watching non-League football but found that was no substitute, I had to leave the whole scene alone. I began playing myself, but then got injured. Eventually I took a Saturday job; that cured my addiction somewhat but I still hung on the Radio 2 *Sports Report*, and I thought continually of the team and the lads. Saturdays will never be the same somehow.

Obviously, my own involvement had become particularly intense since 'the hooligans' had become not only 'mates' but the 'tribe' I was trying to analyse. I was involved, in a sense, even more than keen fans. I was also, of course, in a very different position from most of those, whether academic or not, who comment on 'hooligans'. Although I was never involved in football violence, studying hooligans involved me in none of the culture-shock experience by middle-class hooligan-watchers. After all, I was from the age-group of fans who did not know a football match without the possibility of a fight. Over the years I had seen many incidents at matches between fans, and football-related brawls in pubs and night-clubs between Blades and Owls. Moreover, I had walked the beat with the police during previous academic research so I had seen fights and violence in many other contexts, including fights and antisocial behaviour from students while at university. Violence understandably shocks and frightens, but you can get accustomed to seeing it. I began, because of my experiences, by being blasé about events around matches and, in the course of the research I sensed that I became more so. I was then 'at home' in the field. Because of this people may look down on the research, because as Barley (1990) noted of anthropology, one of its curious paradoxes is that to be classified as an 'expert' on a specific culture one has first to be completely ignorant of it, or what he calls 'a total foreigner' (p. 3). Yet, to have a-priori knowledge of a situation can lead to accusations of being a prior participant.

I was never a football hooligan by anybody's definition. Raised by a 'good' working-class family with parents who would like to have seen hooligans locked away for good, and preferably their son using his education to better purposes, my background is not far removed from many a Sheffield football hooligan. I grew up with hooligans, both Blades and Owls, and in the course of the study researched people I had been to school with and had known for years. Hence what I have done relates to the debate on the role of participant-observation (P.O.), and in this paper I have to confront my special position as someone of a similar culture to those under study, and one who, having some of the same advantages and disadvantages, was particularly well placed to become a participant in the phenomena observed, but instead chose Higher Education (an option a few football hooligans take, but not many), and later returned to study the events and people.

In the Field

The life of the anthropologist is full of incongruities: one day a seminar in academe, next day a mud hut in Africa or, in my case, a pub full of hooligans. Obviously I was to 'hang-out' with the Blades, go where they went and, to a considerable degree, do what they did. The presence of a researcher can be an enormous problem in itself, and how to behave in such a milieu certainly is. Quite simply, how does one conduct oneself when being a participant-observer with football hooligans? The previous research on football violence was of no help whatsoever. I was to be an observer, but as Punch (1979) has written: 'The complete observer role is a fiction, because he or she is always part of the situation and because distancing oneself may destroy precisely what one wishes to observe. Ineluctably, the researcher is drawn into some participation and must decide for himself where the border of legitimacy lies' (p. 6). From the beginning I decided to make myself and the nature of my research known, like Bulmer (1982, p. 219), believing that covert participation was a violation of the rights of the individuals being recorded. I did not 'infiltrate' therefore, and was not covert in my research. Had I taken this latter course I would, over time, have been found out, 'sussed', and possibly questioned or challenged as to my commitment to the Blades; or had I avoided that, I would have been the subject of ridicule and gossip as a member who went to matches and never got involved in confrontations, someone who thinks he's 'one of the boys' but isn't.

The Blades, like probably any social group which is the object of a social inquiry, found my position curious and at times difficult to comprehend. In the early part of the research a couple of the younger Blades, when I explained my position, thought it a wonderful excuse to 'steam into' people and then, if arrested, a great alibi as a way out of being charged. One of the older Blades, meeting me in a pub on Christmas Eve dinner-time, introduced me to his mate as 'a psychoanalyst' who was writing a book about the Blades. Others saw my role as completely humorous, cracking jokes about how I was a 'social worker' and how if they were arrested and put on probation, they could call and have a chat with me. Those who knew me well would describe me to more peripheral Blades as 'him whose doin t'book'. Blades and others aware of the study, having watched television and read popular daily newspapers, asked if my role was '. . . like that Desmond Morris?' It was difficult to reply yes or no to this.

Being open, then, gave me an honorary status as an acknowledged observer. This made it acceptable for me to move easily from one group to another at matches and on board coaches and, when in pubs, to join in many conversations with many groups. I also wanted to find out what their jobs were, their backgrounds, and to listen to words said in one context which could have a very different meaning in others. I was to learn how Blades changed their jobs, and how a job-title can often mean little with regard to the individual personality. Blades would suffer me going among several groups, realizing that I had a job to do, and would laugh as I 'popped up everywhere' asking questions. The fact that 'new faces' were always appearing meant that I had to be ever alert for new formations and networks and try to locate individuals I had never seen before. I tried to talk to newcomers, at times sacrificing time I could have used with Blades I had known a long time and whose company I would have enjoyed more. Had I not been open, such behaviour could have been seen as extremely insulting and ignorant.

While enjoying research I also valued full health, so that as a participant-observer when the 'action' came along the pressures on me were twofold. First, I was not to let Blades down—I decided to run away only if they did. Blades did not tell me to do this, it just had to be done. Conversely, if they 'stood' or chased rivals, so would I. Fortunately, the ephemeral nature of confrontations did not make for, or even allow, many crucial decisions. If I chased rivals I never caught one. When chased myself, no one caught me. On another level I did not want my presence to be one which encouraged further confrontation with rival fans in a 'stand-off'. So I adopted a policy that when there were encounters, I would stay as near to the middle of the group as possible. At the same time I would try to keep my hands in my pockets, but if rivals came towards me I would pull out my hands as a gesture of willingness to confront them. Over the years I had cause to make physical contact only twice. Both were rather feeble attempts at punching, and totally in character with my ability as a fighter. In turn, only once was I assaulted—this was nothing to do with a football match but was part of the Blade–Owl vendetta. A thick lip for Christmas 1985 was punishment for being caught in the wrong place—a night-club in the wrong company, that is, with a 'wanted man' Blade by three Owls. Such research is not for everybody. When bottles were thrown in pubs and forty rivals ran towards me and five Blades, I saw for the first time the advantages of armchair sociology.

Back Home

Being Sheffield-born and a United fan, this was never going to be the wondrous journey of a middle-class student researching into the exotic (and violent) working class. I sought to be detached, but I was able to bring to the research a degree of reflexivity. The task of a reseacher must always be to 'fit in' and act as naturally as possible.

This I found no problem in doing. I had what Bordieu (1984, p. 2) has called 'cultural competence' to participate with this gathering. It is, perhaps, 'not done' in academia to say so, but when researching with groups of people, the primary aim is to be both known and popular. When these two elements are combined, people talk to you. The researcher need not as a consequence 'go native' or achieve 'over-*rapport*'. The research subject knows that the researcher is different, recognizes that distinction, and reacts accordingly. The Blades knew the nature of the study and, I think, recognized its significance and realized what things would have interested me. When I missed something many would tell me: 'You'd have loved it . . .' or: 'It'd 'ave been reyt interesting for t'book'. At the same time I experienced emotions that had I not done such research I would never have known: being chased by a hundred rivals in a strange city; dodging bottles and glasses in pubs; the exhilaration of a successful 'stand' in the face of the 'enemy'; the chasing of numerically larger rivals; and the pride in 'posing', complete with police escort, in some city-centre 150 miles from home. Being 'there', though, could pose problems.

The most crucial element of the observations was the ability to locate myself near violence without participating in it. I needed to see what was happening, believing that if we want to understand violent behaviour we must be prepared to get close to incidents. As Coser (1956, p. 52) has stated, in studying conflict the researcher must be able to look at the 'exclusive values as divergent interests which the contenders pursue'. I felt it was important to know if some led the violence, if some were always or never violent, and whether perhaps it was a subject for boasts and lies. The most important quality, after the ability to locate oneself without imposing, is quite simply the ability to mix and mingle with a variety of people. As Whyte (1984) noted, 'a great deal of what is important to observe is unspoken' (p. 83). Perhaps like Parker (1974), my acceptance was due to a combination of similar character attributes: I too was 'amongst other things, boozy, suitably dressed and ungroomed, playing football well enough to survive and badly enough to be funny. "Knowing the score" about theft behaviour and sexual exploits' (p. 11). Being of similar age and appearance to many Blades, in Sheffield terms I 'looked the part', not that there was any risk of ostracism based on fashion. What to wear was not as important as what not to do when socializing in the pub and night-club. I knew how to drink, when and what to talk about, when to say the appropriate thing and, more importantly, when to say nothing. I could converse on the same level as those being observed, the banter was second nature. I could interact without calling attention to myself, thus remaining an unobtrusive part of the scene. If Blades did something which offended my personal morality I did not show disapproval but could, if disagreeing with actions, make statements implying my point of view or joke about events and, in a sense, 'laugh it off'—the typical way amongst the Blades; at other times, as Hobbs (1988) noted, judgement has to be suspended.

For the vast majority of the time I was simply part of the scenery or just one of the Blades, a situation which brought with it the problems of familiarity and detachment. As Whyte (1955) has written: 'Whenever life flowed so smoothly that I was taking it for granted, I had to try to get outside of my participating self and struggle again to explain the things that seemed obvious' (p. 357). Like many other researchers on other projects I enjoyed the company of those researched so much that at times I felt guilty that I was not being more academic in approach. At time I laughed so much I almost cried; I was more than once the worse for drink; and spent one match acting as one of the match sponsors after a slightly drunken confidence trick with Andy, who bluffed his way past the commissionaire and we thus enjoyed free stand tickets and buffet and bar. At times I enjoyed the company I was in endlessly; at other times I was very frightened, and wondered why I was doing such a study. As Leach (1961) truthfully stated, field-work is 'an extremely personal and traumatic kind of experience'. Research into football hooliganism became more than a job; for years it was almost a way of life.

Alongside these feelings came questions which could not be answered: how could I like lads who threw glasses and kicked and punched rivals, who (once) made and carried petrol bombs to throw at the Owls? How could I cope with them as, in one context, violent people, yet at other times offering to put me up at their homes and arguing for my credibility and reliability to those suspicious in my absence? How could I not be the expert defence witness for all the lads I worked alongside? Frequently I knew police evidence to be incorrect, at times pure fabrication, yet what could I do? The answer was to take notes in court or avoid the court-room. On one level this

aspect of the research proved the biggest dilemma: was I to become
the Blades' regular most-credible defence witness, or was I never to
help anyone so as to avoid this stigma. I chose the latter course, but
felt very guilty that I was not returning some help for all that they
had given me.

That the Blades accepted me despite this makes me grateful to
them; perhaps they respected my 'difference'. I did not actively join
in the fights; I did not spend much of my time when out with Blades
in saying how much I disliked individual Owls. I did not boast about
Owls whom I intended to punch. Like Whyte (1951, p. 304), I
found those researched did not expect me to be like them. The very
fact that I was doing such a study meant that I was different, and
they knew it and reflected this in various statements which ranged
from the serious: 'As an outsider what do you reckon to this Blade–
Owl thing?', to the more joking: 'He's like us . . . he just has more
"deepo's" [inner thought] than we do!' My role as I saw it was to 'be
there', watch, and listen carefully. If Blades considered I was one of
them, or only slightly different, that was fair enough by me. In
return I tried to be natural, remembering Polsky (1969) who, when
writing about criminals, suggested that in studying them sociologists
should neither spy nor become one of them. As Whyte (1984, p. 67)
has written, the researcher has to live with himself more than worry
about what other people think. I do not feel guilty about what I did.
But taking Polsky's statements further, it must be stressed that
within the Blades were such diverse groups and individuals that to
have tried to be One of Them as defined by any standard of
behaviour would have been futile, and would probably have resulted
in both alienating them and receiving hostility or contempt from
various factions. The task is to become accepted, while making it
clear that there is a distinction between oneself and those studied.
This has been better stated by Powdermaker (1966): 'The ethnographer must be intellectually poised between familiarity and
strangeness, while socially, he or she is poised between "stranger"
and "friend".' Following this advice, Freilich (1970, p. 100), called
himself a 'marginal native'. I saw myself in the same role, taking
comfort in the words of Agar (1980, p. 456), who wrote: 'to be
knowledgeable is to be capable of understanding what is going on on
the basis of minimal cues', and be sensitive enough to look beyond
words for what Geertz (1975) called the intentionality which
distinguishes the wink from the twitch. Not all researchers are

capable of this, and I suspect that some will accuse me of 'going native'. This is a problematic concept, with its anthropological origins and imperialistic overtones. I would argue that one can sympathize with the activities of those researched without becoming a practitioner of their aims and values. Also the term indicates that there are two worlds, research and reality, and that there is no overlap, obviously nonsense in this case.

Note-Pad and Pints

During six years of participant observation I was constantly involved in informal interviews with various individuals, and achieved around seventy semi-structured interviews with various Blades, all of whom I had known for at least two years. The aim was twofold: to try to locate individuals within the group networks that constituted the Blades; and to ask individuals about themselves and their backgrounds and, of course, attempt to ascertain motivation. This was the hardest and, at times, most embarrassing part of the research; some of the Blades whom I had known for years and even attended school with thought some of my questions 'daft'. One asked me why I questioned him about earlier happenings when I could answer them just as well, having been around as long as he had. I used note-pad and pen but found at times this inhibited conservation. When I put them away the conversation, (and the beer) flowed. I would then write the recollections into the early hours.

Unfortunately the week in 1987 when I began interviewing was the week when ten Chelsea fans stood trial at the Old Bailey, surrounded by massive media coverage about a 'brilliant undercover police infiltration' of their group—named appropriately, considering the later acquittal of the fans, 'Operation Own Goal'. The police operation had not really involved infiltration, but the media and police failed to see the inadequacies in their collective self-congratulations; this and further police activities posed problems. However, over the next year I continued interviewing Blades from different areas of South Yorkshire and met them wherever they chose. Some interviews were conducted in their homes, others in a café; the majority, however, were held in the evenings in a city-centre pub which had a relaxing atmosphere that allowed for private discussions and, incidentally, provided amusement for the two pub bouncers who knew what I was doing. On occasions when I was interviewing Blades in their local pubs, other drinkers (their mates) found the situation exploitable. A shout across the pub of 'Tell him I had six Chelsea fans in t'chip pan t'other night' remains in my memory.

The formal interviews I conducted proved a fascinating insight into personality clashes. Before being interviewed many asked who I had already spoken with; on hearing the different names many would single out individuals, saying: 'They'll tell you a load of crap' or suchlike. Every Blade warned me to be wary of what other people said, for each seemed to believe that if others were placed in the position of interviewee they would make nonsensical claims! For the most part I trusted the Blades' replies, although anything remotely controversial I checked (discreetly) with others. After seventy interviews I did not believe that any of them had 'sold a load of bullshit'. When Blades learned I had also spoken to a few Owls their attitude was always one of disdain. To a man, Blades told me the Owls were all total liars!

Informal occasions proved to provide for more interesting and significant ethnography than anything prearranged. As Whyte (1951, p. 510) has said, learning when in the field comes in flashes when we least expect it, and such flashes came variously in meetings with Blades while swimming, eating kebabs, sheltering from rain in the city-centre at 2.00 a.m., and attending engagement 'do's' and weddings. Other information on other hooligans came from my living for four years between three of London's rail terminals. Saturday mornings and evenings would see the movement of various northern groups of lads, sometimes pursued by or pursuing their London counterparts. My estate was a favourite haunt of many fans, providing many pubs and the odd fight. By hanging about I was able to talk with many different groups and learn a lot. Even shopping on Oxford Street in Central London one August Friday afternoon in 1990 saw my interest in shoes lost in pursuit of hooligans: why were a hundred lads sitting outside a pub outside of the football season? The answer was they were from Edinburgh, following Hibs to Millwall for a pre-season friendly. Two hours later I had a good idea of the hooligan scene in Scotland, details on how they had travelled and what they were intending to do. Only a work commitment that night prevented my taking up their invitation to go with them to the match.

At times I was to be found seeking information in the most

potentially fraught of situations. One Sunday morning, when standing in a park chatting with a Blade whilst watching a local-league match, I was joined by the then-Lord Mayor of Sheffield whom I had known since childhood. On his leaving I told the Blade of his local fame; the Blade told me he had recently burgled his house (the Blade was to begin a nine-month prison sentence two months later).

'Is he o'reyt?'

The personal relationships the researcher develops are far more important than explanations of intent. As Whyte (1955, p. 300) found: 'If I was alright, then my project was alright; if I was no good, then no amount of explanation could convince them that the book was a good idea.'

This issue is related to that of the role of 'gatekeepers' of the research. Were there people whom I had to know in order to penetrate deeper into the group and its various activities? If there were, I was not fully aware of their importance but throughout just fell upon the 'right' people. In the beginning it was important that I knew Blades and had Blade mates. When the research began in 1984 I sought out two individuals, Ray and Andy, and told them about the proposed study and that I needed their help. During the previous year I had noticed that these two seemed to know Blades everywhere and would entertain all by that mimicry and wit. Both were extremely talented in these fields, in fact they were two of the funniest lads I had (and still have) ever met. They in turn had seen me at matches over the years and, both there and in city-centre pubs, would exchange, in Sheffield terms, the friendly and familiar greetings 'How do' and 'O'reyt?' They proved invaluable in the first two years of the research; both enjoyed talking for hours about 'the scene' and the personalities involved, both Blades and Owls. Being of a similar age, we had a lot in common. I learned a lot from them, as I did from many other Blades; we spoke on many subjects. If I were short of money they helped me out and I did the same when the boot was on the other foot. Both agreed that I had made the right choice in them, as individuals who knew what was happening and as 'people to be seen with'.

The two were quite different personalities. Ray initially advised me on how to 'get in' with the core of the group. In September 1984, seeing me in a city-centre pub, he came over and said 'We're all gonna' Leeds in a couple o' weeks . . . four coaches, Pond Street, 10.00 o'clock, two hundred of us and we're gonna have 'em in their town centre. If you're serious about this study you'll be down there on one of 'em.' I often travelled on the same coach as Ray; he would then sit with me at matches and in pubs and point out Blades, giving me background information. Sometimes he would start conversations with Blades about incidents which he knew I wanted to know about, and afterwards would ask 'Did you get all that down then?' He also warned me about certain groups with whom I should 'take things slowly', and whom to be 'wary' of. During the 1985/6 season I wondered, at one point, whether Ray and I had a competition going, to see who had the latest information. On meeting he would say: 'Go on then', and we would then exchange details about the Blades which invariably corresponded. Ray finished his involvement with the Blades in the middle of 1986. He continued to attend matches though, and when I saw him he would ask me about the situation and the personalities, in effect an acknowledgement that I was 'in' and knew the score with the lads as much as he did.

Andy, although a great mate of Ray's, was very different in character. His extroverted character often had the whole pub or coach rolling about laughing at his impersonations, jokes, and impromptu singing. Opinionated and at times political in his discussions, he had a very serious side which manifested itself in his initial suspicion of me. Whereas Ray thought I was 'o'reyt' (alright), Andy thought I could be a 'copper's nark' and disliked the idea of studying people. When out drinking, away from the football crowd, he would often ask questions such as 'Are you studying us now?'—a difficult question to answer. I was picking up information, yet enjoying a social outing. At another time Andy commented: 'It's a bit spooky all this participant observation bit . . . we don't know how to 'tek yu.' There was no good explanation I could give. Later, after realizing that I was getting to know a lot of people, Andy made a very significant point, saying: 'It must be a big ego trip writing articles which all t'lads like to read. You love it as much as I do, you know, going to these pubs on a Saturday and everybody knowing you.' Ceasing his Blade involvement in 1986, Andy criticized me, accusing me of glorifying the subject and not addressing what he considered the correct issue, that is, the class system of Britain.

Declaring he was ashamed of his past involvement, he said he did not want to be in the end-product and he later accused me of 'using' him and all the Blades. In 1986, after an incident in Cambridge town-centre, I was asked loudly in the pub the following Saturday by a Blade if I was there. Before I could answer Andy heard and jumped in, saying: 'you can guarantee he was there, standing in a shop doorway with his notebook.' A recognition, perhaps, that as Humphreys (1970) has said, the role of voyeur 'is a role superbly suited for sociologists' (p. 28). Andy's accusation is valid; participant-observation will always mean the researchers 'using' their contacts. In return, it is hoped that the end-product will in some sense be my gift: to present the reality of the Blades in contrast to the uninformed opinions surrounding them. I hope this is compensation for my 'using' them.

I continued the research for another four years, and while the relationship with Ray remained the same, that with Andy suffered; however, other individuals took their places. There was never one particular informant; rather, there were many Blades I could ring up and meet at any time, who were part of the core and would always welcome a beer and a chat about 'It', or tell me who I 'ought to 'ave a word wi' '. In the later years five Blades, Taff, Nick, Gordon, Joss, and Jim, all 'core' members, became close confidants and argued my position with those suspicious of me when I was not present. My biggest regret of the study was not being able to have Ray and Andy as great mates. They were research subjects, and to this day I regret we could not surmount that barrier.

Perhaps alone amongst researchers on this subject, I do not mind admitting that some of my 'hooligan subjects' became and remain good and valued friends. Parker (1974) achieved similar familiarity with his 'boys' and I totally support his sentiments when he writes: 'To some, talking about friendship in relation to social research may seem misplaced. Perhaps to those who have attempted a depth-participant observation study such sentiments will seem less irrelevant. All I can say is that *this* study would not have survived without that reciprocity' (p. 16). The journalistic technique of 'Hit and Run' is not confined to the tabloids, but exists too in sociology departments of academe; defenders of it might call it 'objectivity'.

Hanging About

A Sheffield background was vital for taking part in the chat and gossip which took up a major part of the time when Blades met together. Since the late 1970s I had become familiar with the city-centre night-clubs and pub 'scene' and the personalities who frequented them. When I was out with Blades I could add my anecdotes and observations to the chat. This is important, as Marcus and Fisher (1976, p. 31) noted: 'Empathy can be a useful aid, but communication depends upon an exchange.' Such knowledge was particularly crucial when Blades got on their favourite subject, the Owls. I knew and had known many Owls for years, some personally, others by sight or name—hence listening to the gossip I knew who was being spoken about and the places where they were seen. Simply by 'hanging around' the city-centre, I was also able to recognize Blades away from the match and compare an individual's behaviour in different contexts: the hooligans around the match versus the same lads out with girl-friends buying Christmas presents, and later when they were watching the match with their toddlers on their knees. To enhance this aspect of the research, I trained with a football team consisting of Blades and spent winter Sunday mornings watching another similar team. Sheffield has an amazing information network based on 'the lads'. Frequently I had information about fights the previous night given to me while watching Sunday matches. Another time of note was one Christmas Day in the pub at lunch-time, as a Blade and Owl argued over which side had run away the previous lunch-time in the annual city-centre Blade–Owl 'set-to'. This was rather an unfestive subject and probably un-Christian, considering that all of us had just left 11.00 a.m. Mass.

From these arenas and from the city-centre pubs and night-clubs I made many contacts and picked up as much, if not more, information than I would on a match day. At times, with prior knowledge based on experience, I visited city-centre pubs with the specific intention of meeting groups of Blades. At other times I was with other mates from Sheffield who were not part of the football 'scene'. Only later in the research did I appreciate the value of the latter when rumours abounded about me as undercover policeman. At this point some non-football mates 'put a word in' about my legitimacy to Blades they knew either from work, playing football with them, or from living in the same neighbourhood. The references I received from them would, of course, be taken back, told to other Blades, and the suspicion would then end. How anyone from outside Sheffield, considerably older than myself or speaking with what would be considered, a 'posh' accent, would have managed I do not know. I think the research would have been impossible or, at best, superficial. While a few Blades might well have agreed to give interviews, these would not even have scratched the surface of events.

Because the culture, surroundings, and people researched were not alien or exotic to me, my work cannot be everyone's idea of a classical anthropological ethnography. It could be said that, being familiar with the scene and the participants, I may have been insensitive to some aspects of the research which might well have struck, perhaps shocked, a stranger or a complete outsider. This I have to accept as a possible weakness, yet I have been fastidious in recording the most violent incidents to show readers that I am not 'covering up' for anyone. All the same, I believe that while I have never been 'in' the hooligan element I had, in a sense, left the Blade scene that I knew years previously only to return somewhat changed, and with the ability to see things objectively. A year abroad in 1979/ 80 followed by three years at university in London opened new horizons. A combination of seeing things differently and the knowledge provided by a university education gave me a general disenchantment with accounts of football hooliganism, and convinced me that I should put my previous knowledge on this topic to better use. Like any social researcher, I had to distance myself in order to look at the events and people I was studying. For two years this was facilitated by my working and living outside of Sheffield. Over the years an average of three days a week were spent in the city, but living away allowed me to give the subject a sense of proportion and a chance to evaluate the material I was working with more objectively. Like Hobbs (1989, p. 15), I avoided going native by going academic.

One aspect of this involved a constant exercise in self-denial. Stolen goods were not uncommon and at times I was considered an ideal market. I was offered football boots, T-shirts, and wrist-watches. 'I've got a lovely watch for you Gary . . . just something you'd need in your line o' work . . . fifteen pounds.' It was a bargain. I refused all 'bargains' with a joke. Travelling to away matches on a coach I took the newspapers I always read, the *Guardian* or the *Independent*. None of the Blades laughed, none of them cared, a few had their own copies, others asked to read. I wore what clothes I felt the season required, choice was not made to gain acceptance, nor to achieve anonymity for covert participation (for more discussion on research and clothing, see Liebow 1967; Patrick 1973; Parker 1974; Hobbs 1989). However, a conscious decision to dress differently *was* made for a couple of 'big' matches when I knew that trouble was likely and I would probably be in the thick of it. This was more to keep the police at bay rather than rival fans, and it worked. Once, after a confrontation between rival fans, two mounted police galloped into the Blades, lashing out with large truncheons. Trapped against a wall I saw the officer raise his truncheon, only to stop short of hitting me. I sensed he found my sports jacket and the rolled-up copy of the *Guardian* not quite the 'stuff' that hooligans were made of, and probably thought me an innocent, liberal bystander caught up in events, and I was told to walk away. This could, however, work the other way. Before another match, after a fight outside a pub in a town-centre, twenty officers arrived and escorted the thirty Blades to the ground. A PC decided that I was 'shifty looking' wearing a sports jacket and a long trench coat. He warned me: 'If there's any trouble today, I'm holding you responsible and you're nicked.' The PC stayed on my shoulder, staring continuously at me. If I turned towards him he accused me of being the 'ringleader', threatening me with: 'Don't pillock me', and adding: 'I'll fucking pull you and hammer you.' I was allowed to enter the ground on condition I did not go into the visiting fans' enclosure. I had to conform and spent the whole match alone, still receiving occasional glances from the officer.

The Research Tools

The only research items I ever carried when with the Blades were a small note-pad and a small 'bookmaker's'-type pen, which could fit in the pocket of any garment. A camera was out of the question, and when interviewing only a note-pad and pen were used. A tape-recorder would inhibit some, while others were horrified by the idea of what could be seen as self-incrimination in the light of police activity at the time the interviews were conducted. Hence the most essential elements of this research, as in all research, is the researcher himself and his ability to be at the centre of events and see what is happening. To me this involved thinking ahead to what might possibly happen, and then deciding on a strategic position to listen and observe—the pub, the coach, the ground, or on the streets. For years I was a presence amongst the Blades and, throughout those years, I do not consider my presence affected a single incident nor any views held; mainly because I never saw it as my job to be a missionary against types of behaviour or to act as a moral example to others. In this field the method complemented that of Hobbs (1989), who explains: 'When contentious issues were being discussed, a compromise was reached and I often kept my mouth shut in favour of acquiring information that I considered to be more important than the sound of my own voice' (p. 11). The question that some will ask is, why did I take this stance? The answer is twofold: there was nothing to be gained from such a display of personal arrogance, and P.O. is pervaded by pragmatism.

In such a milieu personal values may have to be submerged. In effect, I had to agree with Hobbs (1988), who found that research: 'necessitated total flexibility on by behalf, and a willingness to abide by the ethics of the research culture and not the normal ethical constraints of sociological research. (p. 7). Or to quote Bruyn (1966), the participant-observer should be 'interested in people as they are, not as he thinks they ought to be according to some standard of his own'. At the same time I do not take the position that each field-worker should be his or her own moralist. There is more to dilemmas than just the individual psyche, and research is fraught with guilts.

Because I had been around for many years with the Blades my face was familiar. Most of the time when a confrontation was likely, I was considered part of the Blades and counted in when various individuals were assessing the relative strengths of the group, with comments such as: 'Come on, we've got a good twenty here, a few old lads, we can have a go.' I counted fifteen occasions when, in confrontations, Blades at my side said to me: 'Come on Gary, let's "steam" these over 'ere', or 'let's get together and run in'. One match day in a rival town-centre talking to two local girls, one of the Blades I was with, whom I had known for three years, said to them, 'I'm a hooligan', and then pointing to me said, 'and he used to be one'. Others would laugh about how they remembered me years earlier 'whacking kids' at matches. I had no knowledge of such incidents. Normally, however, there was no pressure on me either to 'steam' or thump anybody, mainly because there was no one with the authority to demand or enforce such behaviour. Besides, over the years perhaps 50 per cent of the Blades who travelled on the coaches never got round to assaulting anyone. Significantly, though, while sitting in a pub late at night after Blades had chased Owl's all around the city-centre after a benefit match between the teams, one of the core looked at me and said: 'You'd have been as sick as any of us here if t'Pigs had 'ave run t'Blades tonight.' He was correct. From this a reader may question my violent predilections, but why? Is it not obvious that any outlook one has, violent or pacific, will affect research?

There was certainly some ambiguity in my role. Because I was often out and about with the 'core' Blades confusion over my true role could arise; one would joke when I was talking to him: 'Are we talking Blade to Blade? Which head have you got on, your journalist's or your hooligan's?' Other Blades were quite curious as to why I had chosen them and not what they considered a 'big club' like West Ham, Chelsea or Leeds. Many showed great interest in the study and asked a lot of intelligent questions about my role, the aim of the research, and the end publication. They were derisive about newspaper accounts of hooliganism and, I sensed, pleased that someone was taking the trouble to study the phenomenon at close hand. In the course of the research I published two articles; these were widely passed round and read and, if nothing else, helped clarify my position as to what exactly I was up to. On the day of the first publication in May 1985, more than a hundred Blades were gathered together in a benefit night for a colleague who had died. Two copies of the article were passed round that evening. Many, having read it, expressed surprise that I was the author, telling me that they had seen me around and did not realize that I was doing the study. Two years later, while sitting in a pub, another Blade showed me this article and asked me if I had seen it. When I told him I wrote it he too was surprised, because he had known me for six months and had not realized. Blades were also my critics. Some criticized a second article, published in February 1986, because it 'made us look daft', and while some said that I should not write anything bad about the Blades, others criticized me for glorifying football violence, saying that it was through people like me and the media that football violence existed. One, a core member, was extremely perceptive and said: 'You can't win, no matter what you write. You try to be impartial and present the truth, but no matter what you do there'll always be someone who'll complain.'

When together the Blades liked nothing more than a laugh, and frequently I was the object of their humour. Some would laugh about how I 'popped up everywhere', not only on the streets but before and after matches and incidents, listening in on their conversations. Because of this, throughout the research there were endless comments from the Blades of: 'Do you want a quote from me?'; 'Have you got that down in your little book?' and: 'That's another chapter for you.' The strange thing was, they had never seen me write anything in a book. Assuming that I carried a book, when they needed paper and pencil for a card score or for writing addresses or telephone numbers, I would frequently be asked to supply them. They would then be returned with thanks.

The Copper's Nark

Throughout the course of the research opinions about me were not uniform within groups. I was neither sought after nor disliked by any one particular group; rather, opinions about me were dependent on the individual: within the same group some believed I was a police informer, or in Sheffield terms a 'coppers' nark', while at the same time mates of the same group would openly meet me and discuss in detail events both recent and from years before.

A few Blades over the years did, of course, resent my presence. A few made comments on my lack of activity when it came to trouble. For example, at a match one complained: 'You come with us, you never get into a feyt and all you do is write about it. You're just riding on our backs.' Fortunately at that point events overtook the situation: the teams came out on to the pitch and the subject was left alone. Thankfully, criticism about my lack of activity was not frequent. What was frequent and more serious, though, was the fear that I could be a police informer. The original rumour that I was one was spread by a former Blade in his early thirties and an acquaintance whom I had regularly met in London while an undergraduate. We would drink together and travel north at the weekends. In 1984 when he learned of my further research with the

Blades, for reasons known only to himself he decided to tell a few of his Blade friends that I was an informer. He persisted in this until 1986. Fortunately nobody really wanted his opinion, but the belief struck a chord with one of the well-known older Blades who, after allowing me to travel to away matches on his coach for a year, decided after reading the articles I wrote to ban me on suspicion of being a coppers' nark and, even worse, a Tory. In August 1985, after the first article, he said to me: 'It's people like you have made it impossible for all of us to have a drink and a day out—everywhere we go coppers are on to us. Also it's stuff like that which winds the young lads up.' More criticism from him came shortly after another article in February 1986, when, on seeing me at a match, he said: 'I don't know why you don't change your life-style. You've fucked it with us, you're not comin' on t'coach anymore, I don't know what you're telling them, "Johnny Law" on Monday. You're just a coppers' nark.' My arguments for the study did not make much impression, being summed up as: 'It's all middle-class crap. I hope you make a lot o'money out of it.' When I told other Blades what he had said they laughed, told me not to worry about it, and dropped the subject. The Blade also forgave me over time and would drink and chat with me.

Blades told me (as people in other walks of life had) that part of the problem was that I looked like a plain-clothes policeman. For this reason the suspicion that I was a police informer stayed with me throughout the research. It was not helped, of course, by the fact that in 1984–5 I was employed by a university and later by a polytechnic conducting studies on different aspects of policing, one in Derby the other in London. I decided not to keep this aspect of my life secret from Blades even if I did not wish to expand on precise details of my work. The first accusation came in November 1984 from Ray, after a local newspaper report stated that the police had detailed knowledge of the Blades' activities. At various other times throughout the next three years I continued to come under suspicion from a number of Blades. Significantly, though, none approached, confronted, or challenged me directly to prove my credentials, but always discussed the possibility with Blades they thought knew me well. These Blades would then tell me who feared me and why, and would give advice. In late 1986 Ray told me that two Blades, whom I had known for years, had asked about me before a match in a pub, and said: 'I told them you're a Sheffield lad who's knocked about wi' t'Blades for years, and knows he'd get killed if he "narked" on anyone.' He advised me to make sure that I explained myself and the research fully when speaking to people, and then added for confidence: 'I just fall about laughing when people say that', but told me that I had to remember that not everybody knew me as well as he did. Similar advice was given to me by one of the core members in 1987, who said that one youth I approached for an interview wasn't quite sure who I was. He said: 'I told him you're sound, but you have got to learn Gary that some lads you've got to take it slowly with and maybe you should come out wi' us a bit more, have a few more drinks, then approach him.' Duly reprimanded, I did as I was told and got an interview with the lad. My questions continued but became more subtle with strangers; at the same time, to those I knew well they became more straightforward.

There was a definite correlation between media publicity of police infiltration of football groups and the Blades' suspicion of me. Ironically, though, I was always amongst groups of Blades when news of the infiltrations and arrests resulting from them broke in the papers. In August 1987, I stood with seventy Blades on the sea-front on the south coast, waiting to go to a match nearby, while all read the headlines of the popular daily papers shouting that two Chelsea fans had been sentenced to ten years' imprisonment after a successful police undercover operation. I guessed that a few had suspicions about me as we stood in the sun.

In 1987 I was told that the question of whether I was an undercover policeman or not was debated by the core of the Blades on three separate occasions over a nine-month period, while they were out drinking on Friday nights when I wasn't there. Fortunately there were only two out of the approximately twenty-five present on each occasion who decided I was not to be trusted. Later one of these said to me, in effect voicing his suspicions in front of everybody else: 'You're the only one out of us who's sensible; all t'rest of us feyt.' The other said, referring to the possibility of the group having been infiltrated by an informer: 'It couldn't be one of us, we've known each other for a long time, we've been to school together.' Despite their suspicions, it did not stop them from talking to me or drinking with me throughout the rest of the research. While I was not there to defend myself in the debates, others were, and would mysteriously cite examples of me getting into fights in the past as proof that I couldn't really be a copper. Others considered the period of my involvement to be too long to be that of a police operation; after all, they had read in the papers that other operations had only lasted for between nine and eighteen months. Others could simply say they had known me for years and knew my mates away from football.

Problems still arose though. Withdrawal from the field made some suspicious about my absence. 'Leave t'door on a jar, set alarms for six, Armstrong's gone, "Dawn Raids" comin' ' was once said in jest, but I sensed there was an element of fear about it. Eventually two of the core hatched a plan to have me checked out. Both had given me interviews and had been forthcoming with details of numerous incidents. Six months later they went to elaborate lengths to check their suspicions that I was also writing for the *Sunday Times* under a false name of Bill Buford, citing an article in March 1987 and saying it was my style of writing. Knowing I had written for *New Society*, one rang the editor's secretary and, using a false name borrowed from a weekly football magazine, pretended to be a journalist who liked my work and wanted to contact me with a view to asking me to write for them. The secretary gave three addresses, none of which I lived at anymore. Later that month, on the occasion of a Blade's engagement party, the two asked the DJ to announce a message, which specified the name of the journalist who they believed I was, asking him to meet a Mr David Lipsey, (then editor of *New Society*), outside. The two, along with others, watched my reactions; perhaps fortunately for me I did not hear the request. Later in the night, after asking me to give various addresses where I had lived in London, the two told me of their plot and, along with five others, sat and had a debate about me. Though all the worse for alcohol, they decided I was not a policeman or journalist but, they asked, could I see how worried they were? Significant here is the fact that, when doing research, 'access' and 'information' is negotiated every time the researcher meets the subjects; it never remains in suspended animation.

All were wary and, in interviews, always specified I was not to use real names. Others were worried about what would happen if the police raided my flat and stole all the information. Later in the research Blades stayed with me in London, and others I was to show around the university. Months after I finished active research amongst the Blades, two core Blades told me that if it had not been for my presence they and, they believed, dozens of others would have been arrested and charged in a dawn raid by police. They said that what other Blades failed to see at the time, but not realized, was that my presence amongst them was probably the biggest deterrent to a police raid in the whole country, since I would have been a perfect defence witness—a fact which the higher echelons of the police must have been considering when, in 1988, Scotland Yard (Territorial Operations and Policy) made a discreet enquiry to a former academic employer as to whether they thought I would act as a defence witness at a trial of football hooligans.

One of the ironies of the research was that, in the course of it, I was never actually assaulted by a rival fan at or around a match. Apart from a solitary punch from an Owl, the only other punches I received came from the police. In total I received four thumps—two by the South Yorkshire police when I had been thrown on the floor and kicked by two others. Another time I received a punch in the face as a police officer ran past me; and once again by a mounted policeman outside the grounds of a match in West Yorkshire from whom I learned that the height of a toe-cap of a police boot when in stirrups was roughly equal to my neck! I was pushed by police dozens of times and called every expletive possible by various police forces. I was arrested on one occasion in March 1987, along with thirty other Blades on board the same coach. Initially told by the police that the charge was manslaughter (a youth was unconscious in hospital, and they probably genuinely feared he might be seriously hurt, although it turned out to be nothing of the kind) and, having been photographed, forced to give personal details, and interviewed, I, along with all the others, was released without charge. The police now knew of me and the research, and this was to have repercussions in Sheffield.

For the most part of the Sheffield police, once they knew of the study, left me alone. In part this was due to my supervisor explaining to the Assistant Chief Constable and two Chief Superintendents my activities at a special meeting held at their request in 1987. For the next three years various police officers gave me knowing stares when at matches in Sheffield; two, who were to follow the fans home and away for the next three seasons, went a step further and would occasionally stand nearby looking at me, making quiet comments to one another and any other officer with them. I sensed these words were not complimentary and had my suspicions confirmed when, as explained in the opening paragraph, one advised me on both the next step of the research and his general attitude to what I was doing. Disliked by police, suspected by some of the Blades, the researcher's life can indeed seem lonely!

Why Bother?

When all is said and done, what did the study show? The old argument in social anthropology is above whether it is ideographic or nomothetic. Sometimes, however, the researcher must wonder whether it is even ideographic; that is, can we even account for the behaviour of small groups we know intimately? By 'account' I mean, explain to others the reasons for behaviour that is apparently anomalous. One of the aims of the research was to try to seek motives. This was a massive problem, not least because the amount of motivation for individuals varied over time. This results in the problem of what is the correct way to understand motivation. From a theoretical viewpoint, constructing a model of what motivates people is actually impossible, because meaning only has value in its interpretation. So what fans do and the way they act is subect to interpretation; the way you as a researcher interpret depends upon your outlook, and this should never be forgotten.

It is as well to raise the limitations of the study. First, it is about the supporters of one club only and therefore cannot be presented as a general theory of football hooliganism. Secondly, it is a specific case-study with a specific research period of six years. In years to come the Blades will contain totally different faces; perhaps they will also have totally different standards of acceptable behaviour. But at the same time I believe that prolonged study with one group had its benefits, because research continued on 'quiet days' when rivals were not perceived as worthwhile opposition, as well as on 'big days' when hundreds would look for the confrontation. By seeing the quiet moments and the busy moments, any violence could be put into context. At the same time, continuing research outside the football season, I could address the question completely neglected by previous research—what do football hooligans do in the summer months when there are no match days and, more important, the rest of the week away from football matches? Perhaps the greatest asset of ethnography is the way in which the work can challenge those studies which use statistics as 'facts'. The study was able to examine both the level and frequency of violence, the extent of organization and leadership, the degree of racist and fascist involvement, and the backgrounds of the participants. Previous research, in most respects, will not be supported by it. The Blades were in no way influenced by 'outside' fascist groups, had no 'general' or hierarchical structure, and, unlike some sociologists, could differentiate amongst their ranks and could speak of 'rough' lads both in a football and non-football context. The composition of the 'core' hooligans was not the lower working class of Sheffield. The level of violence was also far lower than observers would have us believe. Blades recognize the diversity of their membership, even if the media, police, and researchers lump them together and label them. One Blade, a year older than me, well educated, successful in his business, and one of the main hooligans said: 'You've got a difficult job trying to make sense of all this. There's so many different groups and different views. All you can do is say this is how you saw it as an outsider and this is your interpretation.' He was right, that is all I can do, and at this point it is as well to state that I do not know why some men are more violent than others and I have no grand structural theory to explain hooliganism. My role was to investigate, try to interpret, and then ask how and why. What results in the analysis is a combination of me as an individual and me as an anthropologist acting with anthropological knowledge.

I am not a mirror of the Blades; I cannot claim to represent them. I recognize that I am what Parker (1974, p. 63) calls the 'third man'. I both reconstruct the action and interpret in my writing-up my version of events. There was a reality to be represented, but there was no set mode of representing the reality I saw. It must also be remembered, as Clifford and Marcus (1986) stated, that there is no such thing as a culture which is finite; someone else doing the same job could write about different aspects of the Blades. Individuals within the Blades might see matters differently, either because they were more involved or saw events from another perspective. Every ethnography, then, is incomplete; it is only a partial truth and is no more than a statement of the rules of the study of the discourse: work has always to be done. Meanwhile I can only aim through description to present myself as what Atkinson (1990, p. 27) would call a 'credible witness', remembering, as Humphreys (1970, p. 170) has said of ethnography, that it 'is always a matter of greater or lesser misrepresentation'.

I do not condone what the Blades did, hence I have no apologies for them. The aim was to show the facts (as I saw them); the intention is that the reader will find the accounts enlightening and thought-provoking. Perhaps then, when compared with the 90 per cent of time when their behaviour is considered 'normal' and socially acceptable, the Blades' violence and occasional antisocial behaviour can be put into its correct context. In a wider framework, one could look at and examine violence such as state-controlled torture, mass murder, inter-ethnic and religious violence, genocide, and war in a world-wide context, then look at football hooliganism and see that it is just a drop in the ocean. This is my point of view, in an area where there are thousands.

While analysis will draw in references to violence and antisocial behaviour cross-culturally, perhaps the greatest help to my research was my years spent working in factories, on building-sites, teaching, and doing various other occupations in Sheffield and London while financing both the Ph.D and years of study and, not least, being a student at university and living for three years in university halls of residence. Through a combination of all these experiences and the people I met on the way, I found that football hooligans were not so greatly different from many other people in other walks of life. Far from Williams's (1986) claim of their 'anti-intellectualism' Blades had a high regard for education (but not students). Many were curious about university and polytechnic, some had ambitions to study. They were not stupid, neither were they, to borrow from Giddens (1979, p. 71), 'cultural dopes'.

I do not expect the research will change attitudes towards the phenomenon in general and the hooligans in particular. One of the more fascinating aspects of the research was the reaction it provoked. I have met hundreds of people who knew what to do with 'Them': the ex-naval captain who refused point-blank to believe his Falkland heroes could be and were, at times, football hooligans, and the Italian literature lecturer who, five feet tall, middle aged and middle class, was convinced that she was a prime target for hooligans. For this reason neither she 'nor all my friends' ever travelled in London on a Saturday afternoon. Years of research could not convince them that the hooligans were not out to get them; I had obviously got it wrong. Academics often reacted with hostility or amusement. Well, wasn't it funny? Here was someone writing about hooligans; what did I have to do on Saturdays, get drunk and beat people up? Ho ho. Previous studies I had conducted on the police (see Chatterton 1987 and Edwards and Armstrong 1988) had never received this response; the researcher is 'good' and credible and the research similar if conducted on the forces of Good in society. Study the 'baddies' and you either become one too or at least compromise yourself.

The hostility I occasionally received was a symptom of the complexity of this issue. While every good-thinking citizen disliked 'Them' and 'It'—the hooligan and hooliganism—the fact that I had been given a grant to study the phenomenon was, to many people, a waste of public money. If I were a television war reporter than I would be doing a great job. That I was reporting on events which few people knew about did not make people think it worthwhile. I did not start events, yet everybody assumed that my job and duty was to stop them happening. When my response to questions on hooligans was not either retributive or totally condemnatory, people did not seem to understand. Rather like Pavlov's dog, the very mention of the term 'football hooligan' seemed to produce in many a dribble at the mouth.

A study of what Fielding (1982) would call an 'unloved' group whose collective activities invite total condemnation from all sections of society will raise controversial matters; perhaps the most significant one being the fact that I was in the company, and enjoyed the friendship, of a group of young men who were collectively abhorred by all; this will (and has) irritated people; arising out of this, judgement will be passed on the research and the researcher. This, though, is a by-product of the study; my main aim was to seek an 'understanding' of the fans and their behaviour, which is not necessarily to forgive but which may moderate condemnation. My task is to explain, not justify; or, to borrow from Kuper (1983, p. 204): 'the proof of our progress is that we can explain more.' For me, that justifies the research.

References

Abrams, M. (1982). *Historical Sociology* (Shepton Mallet: Open Books).

Agar, M. (1980). *Professional Stranger* (New York: Academic Press).

Allan, J. (1989). *Bloody Casuals: Diary of a Football Hooligan* (Aberdeen: Famedram).

Appleby, A. (1990). Independent Television News, 10.00 p.m., 13 March.

Appleby, A. (1991). Talk given to conference 'New Times for Football', Birkbeck College, 10 March 1991.

Armstrong, G. and Harris, R. (1991). 'Football Hooliganism: Theory and Evidence', *Sociological Review* (August).

—— Hobbs, D., and Maguire, M. (1991). 'The Professional Foul: Covert Policing in Britain the Case of Soccer', Paper given at Law and Society Annual Meeting, University of Amsterdam.

Atkinson, P. (1990). *The Ethnographic Imagination: Textual Constructions of Reality* (London: Routledge).

Baritz, L. (1965). *The Servants of Power* (New York: Wiley).

Barley, N. (1986). *The Innocent Anthropologist* (Harmondsworth: Penguin).

—— (1990). *This Native Land* (Harmondsworth: Penguin).

Becker, M. S. (1967). 'Whose Side Are We On?', 14 *Social Problems*, 239–47.

Bourdieu, P. (1977). *Outline of a Theory of Practice* (Cambridge: Cambridge University Press).

—— (1984). *Distinction: A Social Critique of the Judgement of Taste* (London: Routledge & Kegan Paul).

Bruyn, S. (1966). *The Human Perspective: The Methodology of Participant–Observation* (Englewood Cliffs, NJ: Prentice-Hall).

Bulmer, M. (1982) (ed.). *Social Research Ethics* (London: Macmillan).

Chatterton, M. (1987). 'Front Line Supervision in the British Police Service', in G. Gaskell and R. Benewick (eds.), *The Crowd in Contemporary Britain* (London: Sage).

Clifford, J. and Marcus, E. E. (1986) (eds.). *Writing Culture: The Poetics and Politics of Ethnography* (Berkeley: University of California Press).

Corrigan, P. (1979). *Schooling the Smash Street Kids* (London: Macmillan).

Coser, L. (1956). *The Function of Social Conflict* (New York: The Free Press).

Critcher, C. (1979). 'Football Since the War', in J. Clarke *et al.*, *Working Class Culture: Studies in History and Theory* (London: Hutchinson).

Douglas, M. (1970). *Natural Symbols* (London: Crescent Press).

Dunning, E. and Elias, N. (1986). *Quest for Excitement* (Oxford: Basil Blackwell).

Dunning, E., Williams, J., and Murphy, P. (1984). *Hooligans Abroad: The Behaviour and Control of English Fans in Continental Europe* (London: Routledge & Kegan Paul).

—— (1987). *The Social Roots of Football Hooliganism* (London: Routledge & Kegan Paul).

—— (1988) 'Soccer Crowd Disorder and the Press: Processes of Amplification and Deamplification in Historical Perspective' in *Theory, Culture and Society*, Vol. 5.

—— (1989). *Hooligans Abroad* (second edn. with new introduction).

—— (1990). *Football on Trial: Spectator Violence and Development in the Football World* (London: Routledge).

Edwards, S. and Armstrong, G. (1988). 'The Game and the Job: The Street Offences Squad', *The Police Journal* (June).

Evans-Pritchard, E. E. (1951). *Social Anthropology* (London: Routledge & Kegan Paul).

Fichter, J. H. and Kolb, W. L. (1953). 'Ethical Limitations on Sociological Reporting', 18 *American Sociological Review*, 544–50.

Fielding, N. (1981). *The National Front* (London: Routledge & Kegan Paul).

—— (1982). 'Observational Research on the National Front' (in Bulmer 1982).

Freilich, M. (1970) *Marginal Natives: Anthropologists at Work* (New York: Harper and Row).

Geertz, C. (1975). 'Thick Descriptions: Towards an Interpretive Theory of Culture', in *The Interpretation of Cultures* (London: Hutchinson).

Giddens, A. (1979). *Central Problems in Social Theory: Action, Structure and Contradiction in Social Analysis* (London: Macmillan).

Gill, O. (1977). *Luke Street: Housing Policy, Conflict and the Creation of the Delinquent Area* (London: Macmillan).

Giulianotti, R. (1989a). *A Critical Overview of British Sociological Investigations into Soccer Hooliganism in Scotland and Britain*, Working Papers on Football Violence No. 1 (University of Aberdeen, Dept. of Sociology).

—— (1989b). *A Participant–Observation Study of Aberdeen Fans at Home and Away*, Working Papers on Football Violence No. 2 (University of Aberdeen, Dept. of Sociology).

—— (1991) 'Scotland's Tartan Army in Italy: the Case for the Carnivalesque', *Sociological Review* vol. 39, no. 3, August, pp. 503–530.

Goffman, E. (1974). *Frame Analysis* (Harmondsworth: Penguin).

Harrington, J. A. (1968). *Soccer Hooligans* (Bristol: John Wright).

Hobbs, D. (1988). *Doing the Business: Entrepreneurship, the Working Class, and Detectives in the East End of London* (Oxford: Oxford University Press).

Home Affairs Committee (1991). *Policing Football Hooliganism* (London: HMSO).

Humphreys, L. (1970). *Tearoom Trade: Impersonal Sex in Public Places* (Chicago: Aldine).

Ingham, R. (1978) (ed.). *Football Hooliganism: The Wider Context* (London: Inter-Action Inprint).

Kuper, A. (1983). *Anthropology and Anthropologists: The Modern British School* (London: Routledge & Kegan Paul).

Leach, E. (1954). *Political Systems of Highland Burma* (London: Bell).

—— (1961). *Rethinking Anthropology*, LSE Monographs on Social Anthropology No. 22 (London).

Liebow, E. (1967). *Tally's Corner* (London: Routledge & Kegan Paul).

Malinowski, B. (1922). *Argonauts of the Western Pacific* (London: Routledge & Kegan Paul).

Marcus, C. and Fisher, M. (1976). *Anthropology, a Cultural Critique* (Chicago: University of Chicago Press).

Marsh, P. (1978*a*). *Aggro—The Illusion of Violence* (London: Dent).

—— (1978*b*). 'Life and Careers on the Soccer Terraces' (in Ingham 1978).

McCall, G. J. and Simmons, J. L. (1969) (eds.). *Issues in Participant-Observation: A Text and Reader* (Reading, Mass.: Addison-Wesley).

Murdock, G. P. (1972). 'Anthropology's Mythology', *Proceedings of the Royal Anthropological Institute* (1971), 17–24.

O'Brien, T. (1986). 'Football, Violence, and Working-Class Culture', unpublished Ph.D. Thesis, Dept. of Communication Studies, Lancashire Polytechnic.

Parker, H. J. (1974). *View From the Boys: A Sociology of Downtown Adolescents* (London: David & Charles).

Patrick, J. (1973). *A Glasgow Gang Observed* (London: Eyre Methuen).

Phillips, D. (1987). 'Football Fans and The Police', in T. O'Brien (ed.), *Proceedings of the European Conference on Football Violence, Preston, Lancs.* (School of Community Studies, Faculty of Social Studies, Lancashire Polytechnic).

Polsky, N. (1969). *Hustlers, Beats and Others* (Harmondsworth: Penguin).

Powdermaker, H. (1966). *Stranger and Friend: The Way of an Anthropologist* (New York: Norton).

Pratt, J. and Salter, M. (1984). 'A Fresh Look at Football Hooliganism', 3 *Leisure Studies*, 201–30.

Pratt, M. L. (1986). 'Fieldwork in Common Places' (in Clifford and Marcus 1986).

Pryce, K. (1979). *Endless Pressure: A Study of West Indian Lifestyles in Britain* (Harmondsworth: Penguin).

Punch, M. (1979). *Policing the Inner City* (London: Macmillan).

Rabinow, P. (1986). 'Representations are Social Facts: Modernity and Post-Modernity in Anthropology' (in Clifford and Marcus 1986).

Robins, D. (1984). *We Hate Humans* (Harmondsworth: Penguin).
—— and Cohen, P. (1978). *Knuckle Sandwich: Growing up in the Working Class City* (Harmondsworth: Penguin).
Taylor, I. (1971) 'Soccer Consciousness and Soccer Hooliganism', in S. Cohen (ed), *Images of Deviance*. (Harmondsworth: Penguin).
—— (1982). 'Soccer Hooliganism Revisited', in J. Hargreaves (ed.), *Sport, Culture and Ideology (London: Routledge & Kegan Paul)*.
Trivizas, E. (1980). 'Offences and Offenders in Football Crowd Disorders', 20 *British Journal of Criminology*, 276–88.
Turner, V. W. (1957). *Schism and Continuity in an African Society* (Manchester: Manchester University Press).
Vanderbrug, M. M. and Miejs, J. (1988). 'Dutch Supporters at the European Championships in Germany', unpublished paper (Dept. of Communication Studies, University of Amsterdam).
Van Limbergen et al. (1987). 'Research on the Societal and Psycho-Sociological Background of Football Hooliganism', Unpublished Summary (Catholic University of Leuven, Belgium).
Van Maanen, J. (1988). *Tales of the Field: On Writing Ethnography* (Chicago: University of Chicago Press).
Ward, C. (1989). *Steaming In: Journal of a Football Fan* (London: Simon and Schuster).
Whyte, W. F. (1951). 'Observational Field Methods', in M. Jahoda, M. Deutsch, and S. Cook (eds.), *Research Methods in Social Relations*, Vol. II (New York, Holt).
—— (1955). *Street Corner Society* (Chicago: University of Chicago Press).
—— (1984). *Learning From the Field: A Guide From Experience* (Beverly Hills, Calif.: Sage).
Williams, J. (1986). 'White Riots: The English Football Fan Abroad', in A. Tomlinson and G. Whannel (eds.), *Off The Ball* (London: Pluto Press).
Willis, P. (1977). *Leaning to Labour: How Working Class Kids Get Working Class Jobs* (Farnborough: Saxon House).

2

Peers, Careers, and Academic Fears: Writing as Field-Work

DICK HOBBS*

I have given my students several exercises to sharpen their perception as writers and to help them make their own enquiries into the nature of word and image as they manifest themselves along associated lines. The exercise that has elicited the greatest response and produced the most interesting results has been the Walk Exercise. Basically it consists in taking a walk with the continuity and perceptions you encounter. The original version of this exercise was taught me by an old Mafia Don in Columbus, Ohio: seeing everyone on the street before he sees you. Do this for a while in any neighbourhood, and you will soon meet other players who are doing the same thing. Generally speaking, if you see other people before they see you, they *won't* see you. I have even managed to get past a whole block of guides and shoeshine boys in Tangiers this way, thus earning my Moroccan monicker: 'El Hombre Invisible'. Another version of this exercise is simply to give no one a reason to look at you. Sooner or later, however, someone will see you. Try to guess why he saw you—what were you thinking when he saw your face?

William S. Burroughs

If field-workers are taught their craft, they are informed of a research process of some considerable rigidity. They must gain access, engage in field-work, and finally leave the field to carry out analysis. This final stage involves a return to the academic environment from whence they came. Numerous texts reinforce the notion that the ethnographic enterprise consists of blocks of segmented activity, and while variations on this process do exist, the basic premiss that one engages, disengages, and returns to base in

* Department of Sociology and Social Policy, University of Durham.

order to write is a consistent feature of books that explain how to (Hammersley and Atkinson 1983; Burgess 1984).

The codification of procedure (Mills 1959, p. 215) is a generally problematic, time-consuming exercise. It seeks to neatly dissect the research process, packaging its various components into self-contained, hermeneutically sealed units bonded with a common epistemology. This view is problematic in that it presents sociological work in such concrete terms that it ignores the context in which the product is constructed.

Ethnography is an academic vice, and academic life has hierarchies. As a way of making a living, academia remains sufficiently attractive to enough people to ensure that competition at the base of the slippery pole is intense. The rookie academic learns informally the process by which some purchase may be acquired to enable ascendancy. The rules of the game are not written down, but the context in which sociological work is produced is easily noted by anyone reading the political pages of a national newspaper. For, as part of higher education, sociology has suffered. Jobs are few and far between, promotion is difficult, and research funds are increasingly controlled by a diminishing number of all-powerful, pragmatically orientated institutions (see Ditton and Williams, 1981).

I shall draw extensively on a previous work (Hobbs 1988), and in particular its first chapter which purported to be a 'Biography of a Research Project'. I shall attempt to textualize the entire research project in terms of how, by moving through the academic system, the various texts that have emerged from this research have been affected by contact with a range of individuals. These individuals I shall refer to in terms of 'field relations'.

Not every academic, publisher, or student that I had contact with during this period will relish being lumped together with Harry the Fish, Nob, Punter, or Jump Up Merchant. But there are some stories to be told.

Ordinary People: Part One

Field Relations and Relations in the Field

The research consisted of an ethnography and chapters on history and theory, the focus being East London, the area's relationship with detectives, and the predominance of entrepreneurial culture amongst both the police and the policed. On commencing the research, I was keen to enter a field, that is, to be a *real* academic (p. 5) with a clipboard, a firm notion of what I was about, and a self-confidence that would no doubt emanate from my newly acquired status. However, this status did not put money in my pocket and I survived by eking out a living along with the rest of the populace of East London. The start of the research coincided with a wave of interest in both the East End and in the sub-criminal world of working-class London. Several television programmes on this latter theme retained massive audiences throughout the 1980s and early 1990s. The redevelopment of London's Dockland became a reality, and a major feature-film won wide critical acclaim for its portrayal of the meshing of politics, business, and organized crime, using the East End as a backdrop. It became apparent, therefore, that crime and policing in the East End might make an interesting study, and it was then that I started to become confused about sociologists' fetish for the field. I wrote about what I encountered and what I knew as a citizen of the East End. There were no 'Docs' or 'Tallys', no natives of such power, charisma, and insight as to afford access to a special world (Hammersley and Atkinson 1983, pp. 63–76). But there was a Jacko.

During a brief spell as a schoolteacher, I had taught Jacko's son. I taught him badly, but his parents took to me. I picked him for the school soccer team, and in-between the gore and the perverted aspirations of the spectators, Jacko and I found that we liked each other. At the time Jacko was a truck-driver, a large man who wore designer polo-shirts and a lot of gold jewellery. Our grandparents had been neighbours and we had much in common. When I started to organize a youth football team outside school, Jacko helped out. He bought an elderly van, painted it bright green, and we called it the team bus. His business, meanwhile, had collapsed and Jacko was stealing anything that was not nailed down. Although he was never violent to me, he did have a reputation for pub- and streetfighting and often carried weapons.

Within the context of this paper Jacko is important because, like any field relationship, the nature of ours changed and, as the work progressed, I re-evaluated data in the light of these changes. We went into business together, he took me to work, and he confided in me. But when I finished the study, and became, in Jacko's own words 'Dr Dick the Academic Prick', I became somewhat removed from Jacko's reality. In his eyes I had made it, and while he viewed my progress with some paternal pride, my cultural bolt was shot. Eventually we entered into a business deal together and he 'did a runner' owing me a considerable sum of money (see Goffman 1972, p. 154). Various articles and papers were written after this occurred, and were undoubtedly informed by this change in the nature of a vital field relationship. Yet these changes had taken place outside the sanctified confines of field-work. The study was over, the book in print, yet I was more in a cultural vacuum after 'leaving' the field than I had been before I 'entered'. If we subscribe to the assumption that 'experience underlies all understanding of social life' (Van Maanen 1988, p. 3), we must recognize that our experiential and interpretive faculties continue to function long after the gate to the field has been closed. Funding may be turned off but intellectual work keeps flowing.

   Similarly, informants in the field interacted with their perceived status of my research in a variety of ways. For instance, I reported in rather bellicose fashion that, due to the demands made upon me to indulge in long drinking sessions, the following morning would result in the dilemma of 'whether to write it up or bring it up' (Hobbs 1988, p. 16). This led to some problematic confrontations with individuals who were even more confused about what research actually constituted than myself. One particularly helpful informant, who lived nearby, observed me staggering home in the early hours and confronted me the next day with: 'I see you were doing some of that research last night them.' From then on he was uncooperative. Research and sociology were obviously excuses for getting drunk and on state money at that. For others, however, my willingness to drink beer made me safe, one of them, whereas my former neighbour thought I should be some how different, conforming to a different set of norms (Humphreys 1975, p. 25). This development of multi-faceted fronts as each field relationship evolved took its toll. Relatively few informants that I started off with were still there by the time the book was published. However, as the study progressed, a new group emerged who made a fresh set of role demands: academics.

The Pretext of Context

As a Ph.D. thesis and then academic publication, the study was subjected to a series of demands specific to the academic community.

One of these demands is to present papers at seminars and conferences, for it is in this way that you gain feedback and, most crucially, draw attention to the study. Speaking about the East End with an East End accent provided some insight into the vulnerability of ethnographic data. Subtle, and not so subtle, clues as to the authenticity of an account are dished out in helpings, not always proportionate to its validity. Descriptions of sexual encounters between 'inserters' and 'insertees' (Humphreys, 1975), the switch from wine to surgical spirit (Archard, 1979), or narcissistic displays on a nudist beach (Douglas, 1977) testify to the writer's proximity to the subject. If the writer appears a little singed around the edges by the flames of truth, then this adds a certain edge to the account.

The 'Icarus with dirty feet' (Boon 1982, p. 5) has been there, down those mean streets. He carries the dirt of toil under his finger-nails and is now weary and battle-scarred. By producing confessional tales, the dialectic between experience and interpretation (Van Maanen 1988, p. 93) is imbued with a certain vitality that underlines the authenticity of the entire account. As I began to present my work verbally to academic audiences, I started to realize that the crassest, starkest generalizations were greeted without criticism. I was apparently telling THE TRUTH. I was seldom questioned or interrogated on any issue, theoretical or methodological. I became an expert. Yet I had published nothing; those early verbal accounts owed little to the sophisticated, tactically aware game-plans of the written accounts described by Van Maanen (1988). They were naïve, loosely formulated, and theoretically vacuous, but people believed me, they considered that what I had to say about petty crime in East London was true, and I didn't know why. Other researchers, far more experienced and technically competent than myself, would be given a tough time, yet at this early stage what I had to say was accepted. Then I noticed that a male audience was less likely to question the feasiblity of a woman speaker presenting a paper on rape or domestic violence, and that white audiences appeared reluctant to interrogate black speakers on subjects such as police harassment or racism in schools. There was an added frisson of authenticity to their accounts that male and/or white liberal academics were not prepared to mess with.

As Rock has noted (1979, p. 70): 'The most authentic appreciation of the world is lodged in an immediate confrontation with it.' But the middle classes do not really want to be oppressed, working class, black, or poor; better to identify vicariously via a surrogate. For although: 'As knowledge becomes deracinated and available to reflective examination, so it incurs the risk of losing authenticity' (Rock 1979, p. 71), when this reflection is in the vernacular yet contains all the presentational orthodoxies of bourgeois discourse, then both curiosity and academic expectations can be sated.

Likewise, my own brand of banality was sealed with a London working-class accent, and while I stuck to East End crime as my topic, the account went unquestioned. It later became apparent that audiences assumed that, because of my accent, I had actually been involved in the crimes that I described. Indeed, a visiting American academic listened to a talk that I gave and then offered me money to buy some pornographic videos for the purpose of a study that he was conducting—the assumption being that, as I was involved in crime myself, the underworld was at my disposal. Although this was not strictly true, for a period of about six months I wallowed in this minor celebrity and did nothing to disabuse my audiences of the darkness of my soul. I was, however, promptly brought back to earth when I arrived to address a group of community-workers. The audience was composed entirely of socially committed, mature black men and women for whom my tales of pilfering from the docks or the similarities between citizens of the East End and detectives had no credibility, and even less relevance. I subsequently retired from live performance and spent the next two-and-a-half years inhabiting pubs, clubs, and libraries.

At this point nothing was written. I was involved in the process, but as yet no product had emerged (Agar 1990, p. 73), yet this period was important as I was learning how the text might be received, and as such could experiment with language and presentational styles in a variety of settings. This was, I argue, a crucial pre-textual period that was for me impossible to separate from 'fieldwork', and as I was writing throughout this period, it helped to formulate the work as a conventional text. As Van Maanen has noted (1988, p. 117): 'Fieldwork, at its core, is a long social process of coming to terms with a culture. And that includes the culture of the audience who inevitably will inform the shape, density, and ultimately the context of the text. 'Textualization' (Ricoeur 1973) is a process which, in the social-science sphere, is disproportionately influenced by the mores of bourgeois expectations. In the case of the very early stage of *Doing the Business*, the limits and possibilities of these expectations became apparent to me before I had made one written word public.

However, it is important to note that a variety of practices that might be called orthodox field-work were also taking place. Some grist was required for the textualization process, some donkey-work was taking place. For it should be stressed that, in exposing the construction of a text, I am not suggesting that, 'like the lady sawed in half it isn't done at all' (Geertz 1988, p. 2). Notes were taken, informants met, crimes committed, books read, and theories built. Yet, as the intellectual and career processes gained momentum, then academia, which housed my primary audience, made increased demands for written accounts. Speaking like a native was not sufficiently convincing to persuade my audience that I had been there, and as Geertz has noted (1988, p. 5) 'persuading us that this offstage miracle has occurred is where the writing comes in'.

I was, in effect, exploring two cultures: one working class, my native culture; the other academic, to which I aspired. If I didn't need a 'Doc' for the former, I did for the latter. In fact I needed several. My Ph.D. supervisor was the most important siphon of my work and guide to academia. It was already apparent to me that, at least in terms of oral presentation, even if I was expressing views contrary to those of my academic audience I was protected from criticism for, as Tom Wolfe explains, 'they don't dare say a word against him because he's hard core, and he has that ghetto patter. He's the one who must know' (Wolfe 1970).

However, I needed to learn to do the same thing in print. With my supervisor providing periodic jolts from an epistemological cattle-prod, I began to explore a variety of textual styles. These processes occurred simultaneously with field-work, and my supervisor, along with two other significant 'Docs', helped shape, restrain, encourage, and cajole the text, constantly reminding me of the academic context in which the research was being produced, and more importantly, the context in which it would be read. For

This is the world that produces [sociologists], that licenses them to do the kind of work they do, and within which the kind of work they do must find a place if it is to count as worth attention. In itself Being There is a postcard experience . . . It is Being Here, a scholar among scholars, that gets your sociology read, published, reviewed, cited, taught. (Geertz 1988, pp. 129–130)

Ordinary People: Part Two

Any time not spent in an academic setting was spent in East London, where I continued to live throughout this phase of the production process. 'My family, friends and neighbours were all potential sources of data. There was no social situation I encountered during the three years of this research that did not warrant some inductive analysis' (Hobbs 1988, p. 10). Informants, like other rational beings, have certain interests at heart that relate to their own aims, ambitions, and potentials. Within a working-class environment it was common for me, as someone with an education, to be regarded as a resource (Hobbs 1988, p. 4–5). This phenomenon has been documented elsewhere (Parker 1974; Klockars 1975; Barley 1986). Yet in all of these accounts the emphasis has been on the obviously instrumental use of the researcher, as a manipulator of 'the system'. My informants, however, particularly those who afforded me access to illegal activity, sought to stress levels of competence which in turn I was expected to reproduce in the text. Yet what I ultimately reproduced often stressed levels of ineptitude or incompetence sometimes of comic proportions. For instance, one man who had insisted to me for some time that he was an accomplished thief, robbed an office, emptying the safe of its contents. He then took me for a meal, explaining that he would pay the bill with the contents of the safe—luncheon vouchers. 'The waiter hovered, and my anticipation turned to consternation as I realised that the £15 bill was to be paid entirely in fifteen-pence vouchers' (Hobbs 1988, p. 9).

This passage was written up as an example of getting it wrong, yet was presented indigenously as an example of getting it right. On another occasion I was invited to spend some time on a caravan-site participating in an annual family vacation. This eventually involved several visits over a two-year period to the same holiday venue. 'The caravans are kept on a farm in Essex for fifty weeks of the year, their sole function being the forty-mile trek to Clacton for the last two weeks of August' (p. 229). The object of being invited was to show, with a great sense of pride, how traditional values were maintained. Yet I used the material to underline how traditional values are regurgitated at key moments to conform with the contemporary market-place. These and other occurrences were, in the various publications that followed, filleted of their expressed indigenous meaning and imbued with my own, which in turn had been shaped from other texts.

At various periods, working-class contacts that I had made in the field made attempts to influence the text as it evolved. The most common strategy was based upon my perceived incompetence within the culture. As a bad thief, a poor joke-teller, a non-driver, or a sufferer of hangovers, I obviously needed help. Usually from five to ten years older than myself, these individuals would tell me what to write about women, blacks, or money; and it was money, or my lack of it, that confirmed my sorry state of a human being. Yet these overt attempts at influencing the text only occurred when my role was overt; as a covert researcher and full member, attempts to influence me were driven by motives relating to the local economy.

Therefore, roles were created for me whereby I could be involved in legal and illegal entrepreneurial activities, and this would appear to conform with ethnographic orthodoxies relating to covert field-work (see Humphreys 1975, pp. 167–73; Adler 1985, p. 25; Bulmer 1982). Yet the relationship between the covert role and the text in the case of *Doing the Business* relates more to Lofland and Lofland's gritty realization that the academic world is not so remarkable as to pose a different set of ethical dilemmas from those of the non-academic (Lofland and Lofland 1984). So by adhering to the ethics of the citizens of the East End (Hobbs 1988, pp.7–8), there was a level of continuity of action from the pub or warehouse to the text. The worlds of petty crime, scams, and business were mutually exclusive, so as 'to make "Being There and Being Here" ' Geertz 1988) literally academic. Indeed, as I explain, I avoided going native by going academic (Hobbs 1988, ch. 1).

Variations in perceived competences, then, are crucial in defining field roles, and the reverberations of the researcher's varying tones of reflexivity will, ultimately, find their way into the resultant texts (Hammersley and Atkinson 1983). When I was cast in an incompetent role, informants would explicitly attempt to impose upon the text, and I would subsequently interpret those occurrences according to academically orientated frameworks. However, in covert roles, when my competences were unquestioned, the heat generated by shared action made for both denser description and textualization that informs academic orthodoxy as much as it is informed by it (Ricoeur 1973).

A Scholar, not a Gentleman

When my supervisor and I agreed that the thesis was ready, it was bound and presented for consideration as a doctorate. The ritual oral examination followed, and I emerged licensed to practice. I meanwhile obtained a three-year post as a contract researcher, but in a discipline far removed from my own; administrative criminology 'is marked by a decelerating rate of innovation, a drift towards normal science, and a new pragmatism which addresses above all else, the problems of victims, social control, the police women and ethnic minorities' (Rock 1988, p. 68). The sociology of 'nuts, sluts, and perverts' carried little weight in such an environment. It was last year's haircut during an era when both left and right of the political spectrum reached agreement on crucial areas of study all relating primarily to prospective social policy. Consquently, the general reaction to someone claiming that: 'Crime is but one option available to individuals operating within the maelstrom of market forces' (Hobbs 1988, p. 14), was something less than lukewarm. Such a view was a heresy against the prevailing orthodoxy; more importantly, such a view would taint the criminological enterprise with the brush of dilettanism, or the 1960s. What was called by one colleague 'petty, trivial, irrelevant ethnography' was not only apparently intellectually redundant by the mid-to-late 1980s, but interfered with the corporate imagery that perpetuated criminology. Rising crime and its high public profile had made criminology a serious business.

Furthermore, with funding for research increasingly controlled by a handful of agencies, everyone's snout was in the same communal trough. The viewpoint of policemen who bend the rules or the converging ideologies of petty criminals and small-time businessmen were regarded as irrelevant, as academic careers were forged in the fight against crime. Indeed, as these careers progressed, they could be seen to parallel the careers of key personnel in the gatekeeping control agencies. The resultant discourse was often disturbing for the way in which, for instance, at conferences policemen would discuss 'the importance of the decline in the infrastructure when discussing variations in regional crime rates', while academics would point out that 'the M.O. [*modus operandi*], remains a crucial indication in the profile for a good result'. Additionally, the harm done by crime and the need to muster governmental and community sentiment in order to deal with it led to a consensus on the focus of empirical research, and a shift from the aetiology of crime to critiques of crime control and the administration of related policy. Indeed, the most coherent of these critiques are grounded so firmly in the ethos of social administration that it is sometimes difficult to see how criminology can claim to be a separate discipline within the social sciences. However, it is difficult to top Foucault's famous critique (1980, pp. 47–8):

Have you ever read any criminology text? They are staggering . . . One has the impression that it is of such utility, is needed so urgently and rendered so vital for the working of the system, that it does not even need to seek a theoretical justification for itself, or even simply a coherent framework. It is entirely utilitarian.

My work was not only out of time but, due to its stress on some of the life-enhancing attributes inherent in committing crime, politically incoherent. Crime meant burglary, mugging, and sex offences; all produced victims and a symbiosis of policy and sentiment was created (Rock 1990). Victims were both vote-winners (see Gerald Kaufman's introduction to the *Islington Crime Survey*: Jones *et al.* 1986), and legitimate subjects for academic study. Furthermore, governmental interest in victims generated valuable research funding at a time when polytechnics and universities were being evaluated for the first time by their ability to attract moneys from outside academia.

Understandably, therefore, colleagues in the field of criminology were not overwhelmed by my work. However, initially, these antagonistic feelings were interpreted by me as a conflict of paradigms, the interpretative, ethnographic, sociological tradition clashing with the pragmatic, administrative, criminological one.

Publishers were no more enthusiastic about the manuscript. Eight academic publishers turned down the book, although one encouraged me to 'cut out all the academic verbiage and sell it on the strength of the funny stories'. My idea of the published text was of an academically formatted and marketed book, but in the vernacular of those that I researched—I couldn't get arrested for it. Finally an act of subterfuge led to a meeting with an editor who agreed to publish the book. Much of the Ph.D. was rewritten for publication and several new sections added. However, the desire to present an authentic account was tempered by my awareness of this new audience. Criminologists were informing the text as it was rewritten, and certain key elements of the thesis were apparently unacceptable within a modern criminological framework. These elements referred to my own involvement in crime, and more specifically my collusion with police officers to commit crime:

In one instance I decided to test the credibility of an officer by obtaining a quantity of goods for him. I realise now that half a dozen people were put at risk by this gesture, as the 'client' officer was fully aware he was buying stolen goods, and where and how they were acquired. However, I was involved in setting up the theft and the delivery, and was involved in both. Everyone was paid. I took field notes and all the participants are still carrying out their normal business today. (Hobbs 1986, p. 306)

In my attempt to perform an ethnographic ventriloquist act (Geertz 1988, p. 145) I was using two dummies, and the voices were getting mixed up. The above passage was excluded from the book. My 'vent act' now featured two voices of two cultures. I was performing ethnography by way of a text with a head in two cultures, and the heckling from one was beginning to drown out the story being told by the other. The original 'confessional tale' was being moulded into a 'realist tale' (Van Maanen 1988) by the demands made on the text by a newly significant audience.

As publication drew nearer, the few administrative criminologists that knew of the work made their objections crystal clear. Publication would damage my career, the career of close colleagues, and the reputation of my employing institution. Finally, I was told that I would never work again, for governmental funding agencies would reject me. While senior academics made useful suggestions regarding my formatting of the text, peers made their objections in terms of content. When that didn't work, moral turpitude was invoked in an effort to censure the manuscript. This latter tactic involved the exaggeration of my field role to the extent that one colleague asked me in hushed priestly tones if I had robbed a bank as part of my research.

I maintained contact with both police and non-police informants during this period, and this caused some consternation among colleagues as these contacts were regarded as potentially damaging to the integrity of the policing research that paid my salary. As Polsky has noted in his critique of criminological methods (1971, pp. 120–1), we know little of the working culture of criminals, and we need to study 'criminals *au naturel*, in the field, the study of such criminals as they normally go about their work and play, the study of "uncaught" criminals and the study of others who in the past have been caught but are not caught at the time you study them'. Nevertheless, for some criminologists at this crucial stage of both my career and the text, any contact with criminals was contaminating, while contact with senior police officers, prison staff, and civil servants presented no ethical problems. However, as Katz has indicated (1988, p. vii), 'A trip to the "other side" does not have to be a permanent change in spiritual address'.

Yet contact with the lower orders *in situ*, apart from being unfashionable, proffered ethical problems that were impossible to cope with within the institutional portals of administrative criminology. Such contact apparently posed a positive threat to the well-being of any research that I was involved in, and eventually a research site in London was turned down on the grounds that the information that I would acquire on police practice might, in a moment of alcoholically induced *bonhomie*, be relayed to one of my 'friends' in the East End, and that these friends might 'not be gentlemen'.

Criminology is a 'blurred genre', its practitioners coming from a range of social-science subjects. Diverse strains of psychology, anthropology, law, geography, history, sociology, politics, and social administration can be traced in texts which, when exposed to their influences at any length, are both 'nervous and nervous making' (Geertz 1983, p. 24) in their insistence on a form of analysis that has become increasingly devoid of interpretive links between structure, culture, and power (see Cohen 1981; Rock 1988).

As a consequence of criminology's symbiotic relationship with the ideologies, structures, and arguments of both key government departments and control agencies, disputes and conflicts are relatively rare, as Rock has noted (1988, p. 63): 'It is about the margins that skirmishes are now being fought.' It is perhaps naïve to expect otherwise, for as he has noted in his incisive commentary on the state of British criminology (1988, p. 67):

British criminologists know one another, they educate one another, they sometimes marry one another, they read each other's works and they gossip about each other. Criminologists must meet repeatedly in conferences, committees, seminars, pressure groups and in boards of examiners and editors . . . They form a social world.

Meanwhile, mischievous non-criminologists who were definitely not gentlemen developed the habit of telephoning my workplace when I was not there, leaving messages such as 'Big D' phoned, meet in the usual place', or 'the money's in the usual place'. However, my spirits were lifted somewhat by a well-known criminologist who asked me to acquire some stolen goods for a DIY project that he/she had undertaken.

Minding the Media

As publication day emerged, overt criticisms and attempts to alter or stifle publication ceased. A sharp-eyed editor, however, showed imaginative foresight in locating 'fucking arab' (p. 153) and 'fucking Bibles' (p. 162) as possibly initiating some complaint.

Yet once the possibility of a theological backlash was acknowledged, the process of physically producing the text went smoothly. Publication day brought a flurry of media enquiries and a number of terrifying engagements on both local and national radio. The most prestigious of these involved me sitting around a table at 9 a.m. with a famous actress, a playwright, a theatre critic, and a convicted terrorist who had written a book. The ensuing breakfast fare for the chattering classes was hosted by a formidable media matriarch who clearly terrified the backroom staff with an efficiency and profession-alism that belied both the time of day and the fee paid to her 'guests'. The treatment of me (and therefore my text) during this and all subsequent media encounters has significantly shaped and textured publications that have since emerged from the same database. I was treated as light entertainment, my accent was always commented on, and before going on air, detailed biographical snippets were fed to the host or hostess. I was selling a book. A big-circulation newspaper took photographs of me sitting on a dustbin, and published one accompanied by four cartoons depicting 'characters' featured in the book.

A film company wanted to adapt the book, threatening to make me rich until a screenwriter was flown in from 'L.A.' to announce that we needed 'a spade, some violence, and someone to fuck someone's wife' in order to make the film commercial. A media personality wearing next month's designer suit interviewed me for a radio programme and then used the material for a magazine article, with no acknowledgement to his source. A particularly sordid tabloid newspaper enquired about the serialization rights to the book, and an equally sordid Sunday newspaper enquired as to whether I had any photographs of the crimes featured in the book. A publisher wanted me to accompany an ex-Vietnam war photographer who had left a portion of his brain in some unspecified part of South-East Asia 'to take pictures of crimes as they happen'. Then, thankfully, it stopped.

My foray into the world of the media had reaped less than £150, bed and breakfast in a Mayfair hotel, a short trip in a limousine driven by the uniformed chauffeur and a conversation with a victim of the 1960s, now working as a middle-of-the-road DJ who, after each on-air explanation by myself about the uniqueness of East End culture, asked me (four times in all) how many children were in my family.

I was left with a series of new impressions of what I had believed was to be the final text. These impressions were largely shaped by unread interpretations of the text (Geertz 1988) that related to the 'readers' perceptives of my story-telling performances. These perceptions were welded firmly to a notion of the world that I had researched as being interesting, funny, and dangerous. The first supplementary text to emerge was written during the period of intense peer criticism; consequently it is a rather dry, firmly focused piece, gorged with sociological jargon and emphasizing police culture in a manner which suggests that I invented the term (Hobbs 1989*a*). The piece written during my 'showbiz' phase is light and journalistic, using field-notes which emphasize the funny and dangerous (Hobbs 1989*b*).

Ordinary People: Part Three

Respondent validation is a convention much favoured but little used by sociologists, who regard it as a crucial test of the validity of their accounts (see Hammersley and Atkinson 1983, pp. 195–8). I was certainly keen to use this technique and was encouraged to do so by a significant number of my peers. I felt that encouraging comment on the main text might enable me to hone the data to some finer point. Other writers working in the same ethnographic/interactionist tradition have used this tactic with varying degrees of success. For instance, Erikson (1981) gave space in his book for a reply from his respondents, a reply that was largely critical. The response to

Patrick's (1973) study was death threats; Bittner found himself educating his police respondents (1967, p. 101); while Willis's (1978) study prompted the following response: 'Well I started to read it. I started at the very beginning, y'know I was gonna read as much as I could, then I just packed it in just started readin' the parts about us and then little bits in the middle' (p. 195). This was typical of my experience. East Londoners are not used to anyone taking notice of their words, their actions, their lives. Consequently, when they identified themselves, their friends, or their relatives in print, they were extremely pleased. Some people actually bought copies of the book because they were in it, and one man stole a copy from his local library for the same reason. Nobody commented on anything other than their tenuous celebrity; they were like North American Indians seeing their reflections in a mirror for the first time. If this appears patronising, it should be remembered that my respondents were not *au fait* with sociological language nor, for that matter, were they used to reading books of any sort. There is no reason why they should be, they were too busy doing their business, and their language is consequently dominated by the commercial discourse of the contemporary London working class, not by sociology, its language, or the *raison d'être* of acadmic enquiry. Sociology is no more of a cultural melting-pot than any other political activity and to expect otherwise is a liberal misreading of the relationship between academics and the subjects of their studies. I was not in the business of action research, nor of selling a vocabulary to my respondents (see Bittner 1967).

On occasions the two worlds have merged. Individuals have recognized structures and concepts as well as personalities and episodes, but their comments have been supportive, reinforcing rather than challenging the text. Furthermore, because of the problem of my use of academic language, when East Enders disagreed with some aspect of my analysis, their points were made in ways which were not readily translated into a coherent, constructive critique. For instance, a close relative commented: 'It's interesting, yeah, but I wish you wouldn't swear so much. And you make us out to be all bleeding villains.' After presenting a lecture on the book's findings, I was approached by a member of the public who quietly and authoritatively explained

'It's all bollocks, no offence mind, but it's bollocks. You make us all like fucking wallies, they must be them dopey ones who fuck up everything, but us no. Like me, I'm a face, East End face. I own two houses. I'm her landlord, yeah, the student she pays me rent. I could pull up 250k if I had to. I'm a face. No offence, but all these people in this book they must be fucking backward. I know a good champagne, Bollinger I always drink. I'm not the only one, there's lots like me, all my mates we're all like it, all got a few bob. The Pakis they come in, all this about capitalism and the docks, we moved out 'cos the Pakis. That's why we all vote for Maggie, fucking Labour won't let you buy your Council house. We got money all of us.'

D.H. 'Have you read the final section in the chapter on entrepreneurship?'

'No, I just had a look at some of her notes, all these silly fucking stories so I thought I'd come and front you with it.'

But why should he read the book? Time is money and he was able to function extremely efficiently without having to confront spurious concepts written in an alien language. As Blum has noted (1971, p. 131): 'Sociology exists because sociologists have managed to negotiate a set of practices for creating and acting upon external worlds.'

There is, therefore, no reason why burglars, plumbers, warehouse-men, barmaids, policemen, or criminologists should understand us. Sometimes they will, but when they do not it doesn't mean we are bad people. Academic careers are made, not laid, and it is from the vantage-point of an academic teaching-post that this text has been produced. With no pressure to bend to the wind of the market-place or the whims of fashion it has been possible to write this critical piece. More time has been spent analysing and writing than I ever spent in the field, and consequently Robert Parks's famous instructions to his students to get their hands dirty seems somewhat romantic and ultimately misleading. The text is influenced at every stage of its production up to and beyond publication by the rules specific to the intellectual, political, and economic milieu within which the writer performs. As assembly-line production determined the shape, price, and quality of modern automobiles, so the socio-economies of academic institutions, the point-of-research production, will shape, textualize, the talks, papers, articles, and books that are produced.

Field-work is much more than 'an observational approach involving a relationship between the researcher and those who are researched' (Burgess 1984, p. 5). As Turner has noted (1990, p. 13): 'the field can be conceived of as a space—better an attitude—which far from being neutral or not is itself the product of disciplinary technologies.' Educational policy, academic salaries, research funds, and career structures all affect the various cultural performances of the ethnographer. Rehearsals, matinees, opening nights, from first jottings to their various, published texts, there is no free lunch and 'no neutral money' (Gubrium and Silverman 1989, p. 2). In this respect Jacko, Nob, and the rest are no more or less implicated by the various ensuing texts than are Professor Anon and Dr Elsewhere.

This over-indulgent sociology of ethnography will hopefully serve as the last text derived from *Doing the Business*, and I have only been able to write it as the original text has put me a couple of feet up the greasy pole. Jacko and the rest are still down there, but it now requires a special effort—dare I say, a descent—to observe them. However, while we review each other's books, listen to each other talk, and quote each other's work, we are in the process of creating something as interesting and exclusive, if not as spectacular, as East End culture. Field-work is a crucial part of this process, but not *the* most crucial. The 'dialectic between experience and interpretation' (Van Maanen 1988, p. 93) starts before field-work and goes beyond publication, and as a consequence the status of field-work as a self-contained milieu requires some revision. Such a revision would have to lend primacy to the social context in which research is produced, for currently, as Barley has pointed out, field-work has a cult status that serves to stymie theoretical concerns, thus promoting the activity to the status of an eccentric interlude (Barley 1986, pp. 7–13). Machismo, as well as a veil of eccentricity, is responsible for the cult of field-work, as some of the grime of 'real' life is brought back to the office, and it is Robert Parks's famous evangelical exhortation that has led researchers Philip Marlowe-like down the darker mean streets. Fleeting acquaintance with robbers, mental patients, factory workers, policemen, and so on often shapes the master status of academics as they grow paunchy on their six months or a year spent in the recesses of what is often referred to as 'real life'. Those they leave behind on the streets, who experience 'real life' every day of the existence, find heroic status eluding them in the daily grind of survival, while the ethnographer, who was nearly arrested, almost beaten up, and didn't quite go crazy, builds a career on a brief youthful flirtation with the terrible immediacy of life amongst the lower orders.

Out

As Giddens has noted, 'to study the production of the text is at the same time in a definite sense to study the production of its author' (1979, p. 43). As an analysis of discourse, *Doing the Business* is as indicative of the enacted environment of sociology in the 1980s as it is of East End culture. The reflexive monitoring of a text at every stage of its production, and of subsequent texts, needs to be performed sympathetically in non-censorious fashion. Going into the field can be a good deal less dirty, dangerous, and traumatic than the world one finds oneself immersed in at other, taken-for-granted stages of the research process. It is within these seemingly polite portals of academe, publishing, and the media that 'the author constitutes him or herself through the text, via the very process of production of that text' (Giddens 1979, p. 44). Studying cops and robbers *in situ* is interesting and changed the way that I looked at the world. The process of producing the various texts changed the way that the world looked at me.

On a bus to the university, the passengers are the usual mid-morning clientele, kids playing truant, shift-workers, shoppers, and pensioners using their off-peak travel permits. Conversation is polite and low-volume as we stop to pick up passengers near a park in which a travelling fair has pitched. The hum of mundane gentility is ferociously butchered by a blast of tuneless profanity as three men in their early twenties board the bus. Each is drinking from a can of strong lager and they sit on the bench seat at the back of the bus where I am the only other occupant. They are nearly drunk, loud, rude, and sing football songs with broad London accents. They are apparently from East London: 'I'm for ever blowing bubbles—you fucking wankers!' 'You gonna get your fucking heads kicked in!' 'We all fight for the claret and blue, West Ham, West Ham, West Ham!'

Despite the violence of this intrusion, I am glad to hear familiar accents and I feel myself smiling benignly as the other passengers stare ahead, suffering silently in the hope that their reticence is not punished by being singled out for special abuse. Eventually the drunks turn to me as the only person on the bus willing to make eye-contact. I feel unperturbed by their long consideration of my appearance, for I surely am one of them. I have lived worked, and drunk with them, talked and researched their backgrounds, and eventually written about them. I know them and I am confident that they will know me. Eventually, a youth with a pockmarked nose and a home-made tattoo of a crucifix on his neck smiles and leans towards me: 'You a probation officer?—You fucking look like one.' I rang the bell and the bus ground to a halt. It was time to get off.

References

Adler, P. A. (1985). *Wheeling and Dealing* (New York: Columbia University Press).

Archard, P. (1979). *Vagrancy, Alcoholism & Social Control* (London: Macmillan).

Barley, N. (1986). *The Innocent Anthropologist* (Harmondsworth: Penguin).

Bittner, E. (1967). 'The Police on Skid Row', 32 *American Sociological Review*.

Blum, A. (1971). 'The Corpus of Knowledge as a Normative Order', in M. F. D. Young (ed.), *Knowledge and Control*, (London: Collier-Macmillan).

Boon, S. A. (1982). *Other Tribes, Other Scribes* (Cambridge: Cambridge University Press).

Bulmer, M. (1982). (ed.), *Social Research Ethics* (London: Macmillan).

Burgess, R. (1984). *In the Field* (London: Allen & Unwin).

Cohen, S. (1981). 'Footprints in the Sand', in M. Fitzgerald *et al.*, *Crime and Society* (London: Routledge).

Ditton, J. and Williams, R. (1981). *The Fundable vs. the Doable* (Glasgow, University of Glasgow).

Douglas, J. (1977). *The Nude Beach* (Beverly Hills, Calif.: Sage).

Erikson, R. (1981). *Making Crime* (Toronto: Butterworth).

Foucault, M. (1980). 'Prison Talk', in C. Gordon (ed.), *Power/Knowledge: Selected Interviews and other Writings, Michel Foucault 1972–77* (Brighton: Harvester Press).

Geertz, C. (1983). *Local Knowledge* (New York: Basic Books).

—— (1988). *Works and Lives* (Cambridge: Polity).

Giddens, A. (1979). *Central Problems in Social Theory* (London: Macmillan).

Goffman, E. (1972). *Interaction Ritual* (Harmondsworth: Penguin).

Gubrium, J. and Silverman, D. (1989). *The Politics of Field Research* (London: Sage).

Hammersley, M. and Atkinson, P. (1983). *Ethnography Principles in Practice* (London: Tavistock).

Hobbs, D. (1986). 'Doing The Business' (Unpublished Ph.D. thesis, University of Surrey).

—— (1988). *Doing the Business* (Oxford: Oxford University Press).

—— (1989a) 'Policing in the Vernacular', in D. Downes, *Crime and the City* (London: Macmillan).

—— (1989b) 'A Bit of Business', *Social Studies Review* (November).

Humphreys, L. (1975). *Tea-Room Trade* (Chicago: Aldine).

Jones, T., McLean, B., and Young, J. (1986). *The Islington Crime Survey* (Aldershot: Gower).

Katz, J. (1988). *Seductions of Crime* (New York: Basic Books).

Klockers, C. (1975). *The Professional Fence* (London: Tavistock).

Lofland, J. and Lofland, L. (1984). *Analyzing Social Settings* (Belmont, Cal. Wadsworth).

Mills, C. W. (1959). *The Sociological Imagination* (Oxford: Oxford University Press).

Parker, H. (1974). *View from the Boys* (London: David & Charles).

Patrick, J. (1973). *A Glasgow Gang Observed* (London: Eyre Methuen).

Polsky, N. (1971). *Hustlers, Beats and Others* (Harmondsworth: Penguin).

Ricoeur, P. (1973). 'The Model of the Text', 5 *New Literary History*, 91–120.

Rock, P. (1979). *The Making of Symbolic Interactionism* (London: Macmillan).

—— (1988). 'The Present State of Criminology in Britain', 28:2 *British Journal of Criminology*.

—— (1990). *Helping Victims of Crime* (Oxford: Oxford University Press).

Turner, R. (1989). 'Deconstructing The Field' (in Gubrium and Silverman 1989).

Van Maanen, J. (1988). *Tales from the Field* (Chicago: University of Chicago Press).

Willis, P. (1978). *Learning to Labour* (London: Saxon House).

Wolfe, T. (1970). *Radical Chic and Mau-Mauing the Flack-Catchers* (New York: Farrar Straus & Giroux).

PART II
Politics

3

Feelings Matter: Inverting the Hidden Equation

TIM MAY*

Before starting the research on the changing nature of the probation service I had completed a postgraduate course in social-research methods. During this time my, as yet, unarticulated concerns about the 'detached' and 'sterile' nature of methodological writings, design, training, and procedures were reinforced. Attention to the detail of methodological procedure was encouraged and is increasingly so in postgraduate training. Forays into the theoretical justification for these procedures were not. In fact, they were frequently dismissed as mere 'philosophical speculation'.

Although not explicitly encouraged, I did begin the translation of what was a suspicion into a more systematic philosophical and theoretical understanding. The result is a belief that there are no easy answers to methodological problems, and that if I ever thought that I had learnt everything there was to know, I would have become either arrogant, conceited, or blinkered; to say nothing of the fact that the excitement of study would have long since departed from my work.

In going through this process of reflection I was examining the shortcomings of the discipline. The first stage had me thinking that it was simply my own inadequacies. I then realized that what I was being offered was a partial version of the discipline itself but, I hasten to add, this does not mean that I ceased to make frequent glances into the mirror of inadequacy. In this process, I still managed to hold on to a strong belief in the contribution which sociology has and can make to our understanding of social life (it is

* Department of Applied Social Science, University of Plymouth. I would like to thank David Rea, Delyth Rennie, Mel Landells, Louise Ackers, and Dee Cook for their comments on a draft of this chapter. Thanks also to Lyn for that 'sphere of sanity' in which to work.

not my first career and a radically different one from my previous work). This does not mean thinking it has any easy answers, because, quite simply, social life itself is complicated.

Up to this point this account may not seem so different from others. However, the reactions to such concerns, if they occur at all, take different forms. One of these has a profound influence on the collection and writing of research in general and on ethnographic research in particular. It is the form which this belief takes and the ways in which it affects the final product that I wish to examine first. Following this discussion, I will then turn to the process of my research to show how the arguments presented below are essential to ethnographic production.

The Mode of Academic Production

There is a tendency, to which many succumb, to dichotomize issues in social life. This happens in relation to different approaches to research: for example, the quantitative/qualitative divide. It also happens in relation to the construction of professional disciplines and their pursuit of something called 'scientific rigour'. A particular idea of what is scientific affects the production of ethnography.

Discomfort accompanies reflection on the discipline and the part one plays in it. For many within sociology and allied disciplines, the above account may appear to indicate an abandonment of scientific practices due to its implicit critique of the 'technical' aspects of the discipline. My point is that the inadequacies which I intend to raise stem not from the discipline itself, but from certain versions of it which are reproduced by successive generations of sociologists, albeit in disguised and subtle forms. It is in this academic context that ethnography is defined and reproduced. Thus, in the process of continuing reflection, how did I begin to examine this context and its effect on my product?

If we are discussing scientific rigour and professional practice as a foundation of the discipline, then the first question must be asked: 'whose rigour and whose discipline?' While reflection never ends, and with it an accompanying existential unease, I have not abandoned rigour. Instead, I ask about the ways in which rigour is defined, and by whom. Let me take an example to illustrate this. It is a way of viewing the social world which I consider produces a limited understanding of social life in general, but which frequently underpins approaches to field-work in particular. It is what I will refer to as 'the hidden equation'.

The Hidden Equation

Debates about what are 'true' data are never ending. Positivism has a conception of the social world which renders, for adherents, an answer in how to seek it. On the other hand, ethnography is said to practise a different form of research which pursues truth in other directions. Yet they often share a conception of truth, based upon 'scientism', which I wish to invert. They offer a certain type of technical answer to a term which is not only philosophically, but also politically contested.

The classic example of this contest is to be found in relation to the concept of rationality in philosophical thought. Its political translation takes subtle forms. One result is the construction of a discourse which forms a foundation upon which to base the pursuit of truth. However, this has several problems which ultimately lead to the production of partial accounts. First, the nature of this discourse is rendered highly problematic by its fundamental politics of exclusion. As Genevieve Lloyd notes: 'our ideas of Reason have historically incorporated an exclusion of the feminine, and . . . femininity itself has been partly constituted through such processes of exclusion' (quoted in Whitford 1988, p. 110). Second, from this discourse we base our ideas of scientific rigour upon reason and reason upon truth. Knowledge is not without its correlative power-base, as Michel Foucault (1980) has rightly pointed out. However, whilst power may or may not be capillary, Foucault's analysis, as writers have noted, is rendered problematic when applied to the power men have over women (see Fraser 1989). Social practices around this discourse then result in a crude dichotomy. Thus, and this is the third point, we speak of 'reasonable men' and 'unreasonable women': the former proclaiming a monopoly on truth through their ability to reason. Reason (read truth) may then be contrasted with feeling (read untruth).

Apart from the above being a limited version of claims to the truth, it is also not a dichotomy borne out by my personal experiences of the actions of women and men. Furthermore, while the methods in which this discourse operates affects men and women in different ways, it is still the case that if a man takes an oppositional stand to it, it can equally affect their work. This, as I shall document below, happened in the production of my own work.

The aim of this discussion and the essence of my argument—which I shall illustrate by an account of my field-work experiences—is that ethnography and methodology in general suffer from the same limitations. As a result, a myth is perpetuated whereby personal feelings (read as 'inaccurate' or 'untrue') during ethnographic research are typically viewed as impediments to good practice and analysis. In turn, this belief is reproduced and sustained by the types of power relations which operate in academic life. At its peak, the resulting discourse is antithetical to good ethnographic practice. It is a discourse of objectification, not only in relation to the subjects of the research, but also of the researchers themselves.

This discussion is important because it is usually forgotten that, having departed from the field 'out there', there is another 'field' to enter 'in here'—academic life. Its ways of operating are also structured. 'Subjects' of research are displaced into 'objects' by the adoption of the above partial version of the practice of the method itself. This is compounded by a neglected understanding of the process of 'writing-up', which the current vogue in textual analyses of ethnographic accounts would do well to capture.

Despite this neglect, some theorists have turned their attention to the academic field. Perhaps, given what I have argued concerning limited conceptions of truth, it is not just a coincidence that these writers are often, but not exclusively, theorizing from a feminist base.[1] As Dorothy Smith writes:

The traditional methods of sociology objectify the social process, eliminating from its representation the presence of subjects as active in bringing a concerted social world into being. The relations of people's real lives have been conceived as formal conceptual relations between factors or variables, expressing properties of social objects. These objects themselves have been elaborated as the constructs of sociological discourse embedded in its texts. (1988, p. 152)

Ethnography is supposed to be about the study of people, their interactions and environment. However, in this language of objecti-

---

[1] By alluding to 'feminism' I am simply saying that some aspects of feminist thought have had a considerable influence upon my thinking, and am not forgetting its aim of bringing women's voices into the public arena. As Sandra Harding notes: 'The issue here is not so much one of the right to claim a label as it is of the prerequisites for producing less partial and distorted descriptions, explanations, and understandings' (1987, p. 12).

fication, it can easily move away from this aim. What is required is an alternative approach which is both appreciative of the researchers' experiences (and this includes their feelings) and those of the people they are studying. Such an approach does not imply, as Smith notes (1988, p. 153), either a sole concern with the experiences of women, or just an account of the subjectivity of the researcher. It would then be problematic for *me* to include it as part of my argument. In addition, I would fall into another dichotomy of women (read truth) and men (read untruth), which would not be consistent with my arguments. Furthermore, this does not mean an exclusive concern with qualitative work (see Pugh 1990).

Of course, it is possible to retreat from the above considerations: for example, by taking refuge in 'scientism'. It is attractive in that it offers, as Gouldner (1971) has argued, both an ideological gloss and a social-psychological pay-off for the adherent—no more crises of confidence! That said, to reject it and look for alternatives, while remaining confident of one's discipline and accepting its limitations, is a difficult process.

One way to avoid falling into the trap of scientism, and with a pay-off for self-esteem, is to keep checking oneself against the tendency to see social science as second-best to natural science. Feelings, hopes, desires, beliefs, and failures during field-work are normally to be 'bracketed' in an environment where a limited concept of a scientific agenda is set. They can then be viewed as 'personal' and hence 'irrelevant'. In contrast, I would argue that this is not only a partial, but also a less productive mode of conducting research and understanding social life. However, in moving away from scientism the agenda changes, and in looking for alternatives we should recognize that:

It may well be almost impossibly difficult for social scientists to remain objective and not to allow their hopes and fears to colour their beliefs; but there is a world of difference between setting out to do something very difficult, and setting out to do something which makes no sense. It is the argument of this book that social science is difficult. (Ryan 1970, p. 240)

Yes, social science is difficult. Nevertheless, to respond to that by bracketing certain aspects of research work is not the answer. On the other hand there is the retreat to natural scientific methods, or the power of academia muffles the sound of dissenting voices. The first uses objectivity as its justification, while in the face of the second consideration retreat may become a practical individual solution to seemingly intractable institutional practices which are often, but *not* exclusively, perpetuated by men.

Experiences Within the Academic Mode of Production

Methodological debates conducted along these lines have a pernicious effect on apprentices to the social sciences in both the academic and research 'fields'. For me, this continued after my postgraduate course in my experiences as a researcher.

In researching the probation service I triangulated the research, using interviews, documents, an extensive self-completion question-naire, and observation (see May 1991). Despite triangulation, I insisted on the centrality of the observational data in understanding the dynamics and day-to-day pressures of work in the organization. At the same time, the work was registered for a Ph.D., the process of which is increasingly seen as a technical exercise for the budding apprentice. Once again, in relation to what is 'technical', an outlet for that discourse is created. Out goes the idea of 'producing new knowledge', and in comes methodological training, which is increasingly of a quantitative kind.

This alignment of the 'technical' with quantitative methods caused me particular problems because I wished to challenge the assumptions upon which the discourse I have referred to is based. As a result, and in reaction to my wish to emphasize the ethnographic aspects of my work, no time was lost in aligning the ideas of the 'new style Ph.D.' with the 'rigour' of quantitative methodology compared to 'soft' qualitative methods. If that failed to convince me—and it did—it was substantiated by veiled references to 'failure'.

I had experienced a version of that discourse in the academic field. I kept to my line of argument and was successful, but only after the work was examined by an established academic who validated my methodological approach; thereby invoking another power-base to counter the one I had clashed with.

At the same time, problems in the production of ethnography are not helped by the nature of the work itself. It is about the communication of experiences within analytic frameworks. The movement from the field 'out there' to the academic field 'in here' can have a cost, particularly if the latter is not conducive to such ways of working. As Paul Rock notes, ethnographers are directed 'into the world of experience' (1979, p. 76), but their experiences can so easily be negated by academia. We move from the context in which field-work takes place, to writing-up, as if the latter were the neutral absorber of the former. However, this is highly problematic because we move between areas of social life where authenticity is culturally defined (see Dick Hobbs's chapter in this volume). In addition, the control which can be exercised over the analysis of the data varies with its method of collection. A table, coding frame, or questionnaire are more easily checked than field-notes, which are so dependant upon what Bruyn (1966) calls 'subjective adequacy'. In this sense, if sponsors, other academics, and supervisors are not sympathetic to the aims and ideas of ethnography, it is not so easy for them to maintain control over the research process. The nature of control then alters between qualitative and quantitative work within the academic mode of production.

An absence of discussions on the context in which research work is conducted is not assisted by textbooks which do not contain references to the power relations in which research is collected, analysed, and disseminated. Perhaps it is the 'second-best' idea of social science which prevents this reflexivity. However, there are signs of change. Sociologists of science have rightly shown how the natural sciences are not immune from such considerations (see Gilbert and Mulkay 1984), and those willing to be reflexive about their work increasingly include people from other disciplines (see Steier 1991). Also, there are those who have turned their attention to the 'academic mode of production' (see Stanley 1990*a*, Introduction).

Despite the above exceptions, objectivity is frequently used as a disguise for an inability or unwillingness to be reflexive and engaged in research. As Martyn Hammersley and Paul Atkinson note, an abandonment of positivism and naturalism can lead to a reflexivity which at least admits that data cannot be collected untainted by the hands of the researcher. This leads to a different approach which I attempted to implement during my field-work: 'Rather than engaging in futile attempts to eliminate the effects of the researcher, we should set about understanding them' (Hammersley and Atkinson 1983, p. 17). Indeed, many manuals on 'how to do ethnography' and ethnographic accounts marginalize the researcher in order that a certain language of objectivity is maintained. Reflexivity, on the other hand, 'recognizes that texts do not simply and transparently report an independent order of reality' (Atkinson 1990, p. 7). What is central is not just understanding the effects *of* the researcher, but the effects *on* the researcher, as well as on those researched. Given attempts to marginalize such considerations, it seems reasonable to be suspicious of the seeming 'logic and chronology implied by the format of scientific papers' (Silverman 1985, p. 4), which disseminate results as if the collection of data was an unproblematic and irrelevant phase of the research. The 'real' accounts of the research process apparently require separate volumes such as this one (also see Bell and Newby 1977; Roberts 1990; Bell and Roberts 1984; Bryman 1988).

This all results in an impoverishment of the final product. In terms of my own work on the probation service, both Perrow (1978) and Bryman (1988, Introduction) have noted that the difficulties of negotiating access to an organization are frequently dismissed as methodological and/or theoretical inconveniences. This, as I have argued, is symptomatic of the partial version of the discipline that is frequently offered. In negotiating access and in other stages of the research we should take feelings seriously and not assume that true data result when we are absorbed in and accepted by the organization.

Taking Feelings Seriously: Inverting the Hidden Equation

My purpose is to show that not only is an understanding of the effects of researchers on observational work important, but also the effects on the researchers themselves. In so doing, the 'truth equation', which I have argued lies behind much academic discourse on research, must be inverted. We must move away from the simple idea expressed in the equation *feelings = weakness*. This is required for the intellectual and personal reasons that I have, albeit briefly, charted above. An understanding of the feelings evoked during field-work (and I include the academic field) should be seen as a source of strength, not weakness. This requires an honesty which is personally uncomfortable, but which produces higher-quality research. In this path of honesty let me start by saying that I can, to some extent, free myself of that pervasive and insidious discourse by invoking another power-base—I now have a full-time job.

There still remain limitations to the account which I will present to the reader, but surely an awareness of these is preferable to a dismissive attitude to their existence? Some of those limitations I can do little about: for example, there will be differences between my experiences during field-work and those of other researchers—I am both male and white. Nevertheless, to admit to my own hopes, experiences, and fears during field-work was (and is) personally uncomfortable, as I shall document.

What are now considered 'barriers' to research and the way in which they are overcome, if at all, is a topic of the research process. Not simply because they are interesting in themselves, but because they are important for the research process as a whole. As such, it is assumed that properly conducted and analysed observational work involves a full fusion of personal experience and intellectual commitment. The attempt is then to gain understanding rooted in the participant's and observer's personal experiences. The result seeks to redress the ways in which academic norms, as Smith (1988) puts it, 'suspend the subjectivity of the thinker'.

Of course, barriers to research will vary, but what I am advocating is a more honest approach by admitting their existence as a condition of understanding. I do not set myself up as having the 'answers'. However, for those who have similar concerns, I want to make what is frequently and wrongly termed 'failure' in field-work 'out there', not simply an understandable phenomenon, but to invert it so it becomes a topic which is essential to the research process itself. Overcoming feelings of personal inadequacy and moving into the realm of sociological reflection does and has yielded valuable insights into areas of study (see Hammersley and Atkinson 1983, p. 166). In my case, this area was a criminal-justice-system organization, the people who worked in it, and the daily pressures they experienced in their work.

While I have mentioned that it is fruitful to consider such instances as topics, they are also resources. I do not, therefore, regard myself as an ethnomethodologist, but I am influenced sufficiently by this tradition to see the place it has in ethnography. Frequently, as Liz Stanley (1990*b*) has noted, ethnomethodology has been marginalized within debates on ethnographic method and analysis. However, the tradition is not entirely blameless, as conversational analysts are often scathing of ethnographic research.

It follows from what I have advocated that the validity of the research and this account of it has not been based on the avoidance of the pronoun 'I'. This is because the collection of data relies on the researcher as *the* instrument in data collection (see Brown 1984). As I have suggested, a reflexivity is required in the research process in the pursuit of rigorous and systematic study. Feelings are not, then, bracketed in the language of objectivity, nor are they intended as 'infallible guides'; particularly given the possibility that they are simply mistaken. Instead, I take them as 'starting points to better understanding' (Griffiths 1988, pp. 146–7) which, when combined with a certain research training, I hope add to the quality of the end-result.

The following account, therefore, attempts not to bracket feelings, but to recognize and utilize them. Not only is the bracketing of feelings an impossible position to adopt, it is also not a desirable one—if the aim of research is to enhance understanding. Thus, it is hoped that this small contribution adds to the opening-up and exposure of partial approaches to field-work in particular, and methodology in general. Buried somewhere in many accounts of field-work, sometimes deep, is advice to the apprentice ethnographer. You can almost hear it now: 'I went through it and it did me no harm'. Or an alternative version: 'Its all down to experience!' Yes, it is all down to experience. It is *how* that experience is considered and reflected upon which is at issue. We cannot escape the social world which we study; we are part of it: 'This is not a matter of methodological commitment, it is an existential fact' (Hammersley and Atkinson, 1983, pp. 14–15).

Negotiation and Organizational Arenas

Moving In

'Who are you doing it for?' 'Why are you doing it?' These were the questions which greeted me two days after beginning the research. A disconcerting start, which was not helped by the fact that my partner and I had moved from one side of the country to the other for the purposes of undertaking this study, and I was on a temporary contract.

These comments were voiced after the Treen Probation Service's 'Research and Information Committee' had adjourned. Having already given approval for the research to be undertaken, they had just considered my research timetable. I was then questioned by two members of the service. They asked about my motives, methods, plans, and how I would disseminate the results of the research. This was not the most auspicious start to a three-year study on

'Professional Autonomy and Decision-Making!' Nevertheless, like a dutiful researcher, I went away and recorded this initial encounter in detail. Formally, the minutes of the meeting simply recorded: 'For the next six months or so Mr May would be engaged in background reading and in "getting to know" the Treen Service through informal meetings with colleagues.'

At first glance, this disjuncture between my experiences and the formal recording of the meeting does not seem a good beginning to accessing an organization. However, I gained some solace from the beliefs I have mentioned regarding the research process. Also, my experiences after this event, and reflecting upon it, have taught me not to approach such incidents with feelings of personal inadequacy, but instead to see them as part of a 'normal' process. Indeed, does this account of an incident only two days after starting field-work imply some personal inadequacy? Perhaps I should have immediately become part of the organizational culture (if one existed), in order to reduce that illusive thing, 'reactivity', in the pursuit of objective knowledge? Yet we do not expect this when entering an unfamiliar social scene in everyday life. In such instances we often feel uncomfortable and provoke a reaction of some sort. So why is it still often regarded as problematic in field research?

I was thus thrown in at the 'deep end' as the result of being asked a series of questions which were forcefully put and difficult to answer at the time. Retrospectively, I felt I could have replied in two ways. First, I could simply have said: 'I dont know at this stage'. Or second I could have drawn upon an existing stock of knowledge concerning my beliefs about the importance of research to an organization. People reading this may reply that the first option is the honest reply and the second not so honest. Nevertheless, I learnt from this episode. I did not dwell for too long on viewing this as my own failure. My reply was that I would not have any easy answers, and anyway, this was a question of organizational democracy. Plus, my task was to look at the organization from a particular vantage-point—as an 'outsider' who wished to learn. I also made the general point that I considered the confidentiality of the information received from individuals was fundamentally important.

I did (and do) believe in what I said. In the process of reflexivity I had learnt, so early on in the research, that suspicion was an understandable reaction because of the changes in the organization that were being implemented by management, the Home Office, and government. My credibility as an impartial researcher was, therefore, to be a central issue during the research for my level of entry was senior management, and not to have positively acted in the light of this initial suspicion would have meant, by default, carrying an organizational suspicion of management with me. This, then, told me something about the nature of power and decision-making in the organization. As Bruyn has noted: 'The participant observer who studies a complex social organization must be aware of the fact that clearance at one level of the organization does not insure clearance at another level. It is very important that the researcher takes into account the levels of power and decision-making extant in the group (1966, p. 204). Later on I learnt that the two people who questioned me had a vested interest in the changes taking place within the organization and, as such, in any research associated with this.

I moved from feelings of personal discomfort towards an understanding of reactions. I am not suggesting that I became immune to my own feelings; I did not, as I shall mention later. Reflections on this incident, however, told me a great deal about the organization. The so-called curse of 'reactivity' in observation was inverted to provide me instead with food for thought.

In the process of gaining entry a circular from the 'Chief' was sent to staff concerning the research. This circular carried details of the history of the research proposal, my appointment, background, and age. It was circulated to all staff except ancillaries, secretaries, and volunteers. The circular included the topics which my study would cover despite the fact that I had not fully defined the research questions. It noted how I was to: 'map out the differences between professional and administrative work; relationships with clients and how service goals are delineated and achieved'. It also stressed that I would 'be independent of Probation Service management and the confidentiality of all staff will be maintained during the period of study'.

As a result of this circular and that initial meeting, my role during the early stages of the research necessitated that I did not over-identify with probation management. Reactions to me were based on organizational politics, and I was to remain both sensitive to and aware of this. Indeed, organizational politics was a subject which became the topic of my study. In the process, this did not mean, to use Becker's (1967) phrase, the 'taking of sides'. Instead, I alluded to the importance of having the freedom to make decisions about the direction and content of the research, and was always cautious about adopting the role of 'expert'.

In the practice of negotiation, the academic field which had worked against me also worked to my advantage. I could move between the demands of the organizations and those of the academic institution. Like Dick Hobbs, I avoided ' "going native" by "going academic" ' (1988, p. 15). This movement involved turning a writing-up disadvantage into a field-relations advantage. Indeed, after I had finished the research the 'Chief' noted how I had not been 'institutionalized' by the service. I was able to avoid this by always returning to academia to 'write-up' my field-notes and reflect upon my experiences. I was also teaching during the research period, which served as a justification for my departures.

Having mentioned my beliefs about the research process, the onus was then on me to put these into practice. The doctrine of 'informed consent' was followed, whereby researchers should be at 'pains to explain fully the objects and implications of their research to individual subjects' (BSA 1989, p. 4). This involved a series of formal and informal meetings with staff of the service. I was then able to fuse ethical concerns regarding consent with political ones on suspicion about the purposes of the research. All the probation teams in the service's area were visited over a period of five months. During team meetings I spoke about the aims of the research and gave all present a one-page summary of its outline.[2] At the end I wrote: 'Bearing in mind what has already been stressed about confidentiality, may I take this opportunity of asking for your full co-operation in this research. The probation service has been, and still is, undergoing considerable changes. Research of this nature will help to further understand these changes, the rationale behind their conception and, importantly, the effects on working practices.' This sharing of information enabled me to break down

[2] I was asked, during initial meetings, if I intended to produce a set of policy proposals at the end of the research. I believe the issues here are twofold. First, my work was not action research in the sense of being a combination of knowledge and research which is then explicitly designed to achieve change. This is due, as noted, to the political nature of the research. Secondly, my research had policy implications rather than policy suggestions. These require collective decision-making, which may involve the researcher, given the study and its conclusions. To avoid any appropriation of my findings to achieve ends which they do not endorse, I sent a copy of the conclusions to all teams. Beyond this, I have been given the opportunity to address members of the service and, unless invited to take part in policy discussions, it is difficult to imagine that I can do any more than to remain sensitive to the political dimensions of my work.

any barriers of suspicion which may have existed as a result of the level of entry into the organization. It also gave me an opportunity to see team members and make initial enquiries about the type of work they undertake and any concerns they had about the direction of the service and its effects on their practice. I was then able to explain that I was not assuming the role of expert, but simply sought an understanding of 'everyday work' within the service.

I had agreed to report on the progress of the research, and attended the Treen Service's Research and Information Committee several times and produced two interim descriptive reports. I deliberately chose them to be descriptive as the research was only half-completed. In this process, I also discovered that there existed within the service (and still does) a predisposition to regard quantitative data as providing 'hard facts' upon which to base decisions (a parallel in organizations to the academic discourse I have charted). Politically, therefore, I did not consider it expedient to release any analytic data until the research was completed. The management agreed with this arrangement and were also pleased to receive feedback at the half-way stage of the research; to which, I should add, the service was entitled.[3]

After contacting one team, I was granted permission to attend their team meeting. Quoting from my notebook, I later recorded the following: 'George, at first, was unclear as to what purpose my visit was going to have. I therefore found it necessary to say that my first period in this research was familiarising myself with the "set-up" of the Service, attending team meetings and simply observing the "everyday" business of what goes on.' After two hours with the team, I had made only brief notes which I then fully recorded within an hour of leaving. Some of my initial reflections and those of the team in question are worth repeating:

It was clear at the time that the issues which were being discussed were of a sensitive and difficult nature . . . these need more exploration, but there is little doubt that as a first impression I have learnt a great deal on this occasion . . . they hoped I would return in order to explore more of these issues and engage in 'constructive dialogue'. In that sense this reciprocal relationship could be beneficial and also adds a dimension to the research which makes it constructive and pleasurable to be engaged in.

[3] I asked that these papers should be generally available to members of teams through the Senior Probation Officer. They were informed of its circulation and I reminded individuals of its existence during my time 'in the field'.

In addition, I became involved in chairing a working party on the role of volunteers in one of the teams. This provided the beginnings of an insight into the workings of the probation service—albeit at team- as opposed to organizational level. Because of the size of the probation area and the degree of communication between its parts, together with the role I was adopting, this did not appear to compromise my standing as an impartial researcher. However, it was not until much later in the research that I returned to this unit, just in case this work had prejudiced my role. On the other hand, the suggestion that I chair a working party on the reorganization of a team who had difficulties in terms of their structure and function would have been prejudical. Fortunately the suggestion did not come to fruition, thanks partly to my own unease, but mainly to that of the area assistant-chief probation officer.

Despite a guarded approach to entry into the organization, it would be foolish to pretend a resulting infallibility. Retrospectively, my over-identification with the team involved in these 'consultancy processes' would have prejudiced my research because of the suspicion with which some probation personnel viewed its role and motives.

This period of familiarization—attending team meetings, a probation committee meeting, and interviewing staff at different levels of the organization—was supplemented by further reading and understanding of the history of probation and the contemporary issues, both organizationally and in terms of practice, which it faced. This combination informed subsequent decisions regarding the methodology of the research. This is not to say that the data already gathered was not used. On the contrary, as I have suggested, it was invaluable in the reflexive process of data collection.

The question of reflexivity was important at this early stage. To some practitioners, observation relies on the notion of the individual being an 'empty vessel' into which information is poured, only later to be rendered intelligible within a conceptual framework. However, this 'theory out of facts' method has its problems, for it is 'only theory which can constitute them as facts in the first place' (Stedman-Jones 1967, p. 42). At the same time, the qualitative researcher seeks a description of the context of action, which means that 'such contextual understandings and empathetic objectives are unlikely to be achieved without direct, firsthand, and more or less intimate knowledge of a research setting' (Van Maanen 1979, p. 520).

Given the above relation between theory and facts, I had armed myself with the belief in reflexivity and continued the research by meeting different people within the organization and asking them about their roles and beliefs about probation and the direction of the service. These were informal meetings which arose when the opportunity was presented. For instance, I spoke to one senior probation officer, who introduced me to another, and so on . . . Similarly, the opportunity of a day spent visiting clients in prison arose, and I accepted the offer. However, I also made 'conscious' rather than just 'opportunistic' choices to attend meetings. In particular, I wished to go to a probation committee meeting (it meets three or sometimes four times a year), and after seeking permission from the chair of the committee, attended one two months after starting the research.

I have mentioned the ideals of honesty, reflexivity, and attachment to feelings. However, these are tempered by practical considerations. As Buchanan *et al.* (1988) suggest, organizational researchers should be 'opportunistic' in their field-work. I was fortunate, for as these authors note, if the possible and the desirable clash, the former will always win through. Furthermore access can, quite simply, be prevented. That said, I know of only one occasion when it was suggested that I did not visit a team. This was a prison-based team undergoing some changes. The senior was on sick leave, so it was felt that I should wait for his return. In talking to team members during a later visit, I was able to discover the reasons for this decision, which stemmed from intra-team conflict.

In approaching negotiation into the organization in this way, I do not pretend that this approach would be effective in all organizations. Nevertheless, not only was I able to combine political and ethical considerations, as suggested above, but also theoretical ones. Moving from feelings of personal inadequacy in the original meeting towards a negotiated entry into all organizational levels and arenas, told me much about the workings of the organization. In these initial stages, questions requiring answers were raised. However, there was no end to the process of negotiation which led to a green light, after which 'true' data could be collected untainted by my presence. It is the case that any person affects a social scene in one way or another.

One of the theoretical questions raised in these initial stages concerned information flow through the organization. Although the probation service organization had a relatively 'flat' hierarchy, in discussing the aims and information-needs of the research with teams, I was able to ascertain that there was an 'information gap' between the front line of the organization and the management. People's experiences were of vast amounts of paperwork with apparently no purpose in terms of how they defined the realities of their work. In the face of such information, I then had to question why such a disjuncture existed. Furthermore, in moving through different teams with different specialisms and experiencing a suspicion and clash of values over changes in the organization, the functionalist framework of the only previous study on the organization (Boswell 1982) had to be questioned.

The degree of change in the organizational environment led to a desire to discuss the reasons for this among the organizational members that I met. Interviews were then more of a dialogue, which was not problematic but beneficial. In a situation subject to constant change and a clash of values, people were more likely to be aware of the political issues. I found that at several levels, but in different contexts, people both acted on and were acted upon by organizational, interactional, and environmental constraints. In such instances negotiation provided me with the opportunity to begin to understand the organizational environment, a condition of which 'is getting to know what actors already know, and have to know, go to "go on" in the daily activities of social life' (Giddens 1984, p. 284). Furthermore, in being subjected to the different probation-team specialisms (prison work, community service, resettlement, courts, divorce, welfare, and so on) and what was often a politically charged atmosphere in relation to policy changes, I had no trouble in 'fighting familiarity', often seen as an impediment to observational methods. Feelings ran high and demanded understanding, not marginalization.

Between Familiarity and Geographical Dispersal

The demands of participant observation are said to require intensive periods with relatively small groups of people in order fully to understand the social milieu which they inhabit. One limitation of this form of research is in relation to the study of large organizations (see Hammersley and Atkinson 1983, p. 237). For this reason, the research was triangulated. However, given that the Treen Service is geographically dispersed, for the purposes of the observation it was important, given the limits on time, to focus on particular settings and 'people's strategies' (Lofland 1971) within those settings.

I was the only person undertaking the research and I had a fixed time in which to complete it. At team meetings when I was explaining the research it was assumed, on several occasions, that I was working with others on the project.[4] This worked to my advantage to the extent that I alone was responsible for the work, which meant, when asked direct questions, I could clarify any misunderstanding and ensure confidentiality without referring to other members of a research team.

Due to this geographical spread, the observation had to be selective for both practical and theoretical reasons. The ethnographic method requires a 'subjective adequacy' (Bruyn 1966, pp. 180–5) which involves, among other factors, spending time in social settings for the purposes of enhancing understanding. Following initial investigations and the results of the questionnaire, I therefore chose to concentrate on specific areas, thus broadly paralleling the method of 'theoretical sampling' which Glaser and Strauss (1967) suggest. These were: a rural team; two urban teams; three day centres; a probation hostel; a civil work team; prison teams; and meetings at different levels of the organization, including major policy meetings. I also went into courts with officers, enabling me to see them work in different settings. In the courts there was a ceremonial and sometimes imposing ambience (one officer told me that he said to clients who felt inhibited by this to 'imagine the judge with no clothes on'!) In interacting with clients and with colleagues there was a variance between formality and informality, which through interviews I learnt was dependent upon the 'operational philosophy' (Strauss *et al.* 1964) of the officer, as well as the context of the setting. This allowed me to witness the 'doing' of probation work in different environments. The advantage is to see displays of organizational action in changing forums; as Goffman observes (1969; p. 129): 'there tends to be one informal or backstage language of behaviour, and another language of behaviour for occasions when a performance is being presented. The backstage language consists

---

[4] On several occasions I was asked how long I had to spend on the project. There was full understanding on the part of those who asked when I explained that I was employed for three years, and therefore had a material as well as a personal and an intellectual incentive to finish the research.

of reciprocal first-naming, co-operative decision-making, profanity
. . . The frontstage behaviour language can be taken as the absence
(and in some sense the opposite) of this.'

Organizational Arenas and Role Performance

I have spoken about sharing information and the importance of
gaining trust (rendering explicit a tacit feature of social intercourse),
but have said little about what my role became during the research.
The honest and, at the same time, ambiguous answer is that it varied
according to the social setting. Because of the diversity of the work
which I had decided to examine, an opportunity was afforded to
experience a variety of actions which left me constantly exposed to
stimuli in the reflexive process. At the same time, it meant that
moving in and out of different settings took its toll on my stamina!
Again and again I slipped into reflecting on my personal inadequacies,
but again and again I fought this predisposition in order to enter the
realm of sociological, political, and ethical reflection. A few
examples may serve to illustrate my point.

I had already visited one team which I had decided to spend some
time in, and so was known to most of its members. When I arrived to
undertake the observation, I knew I could not simply move in and
out of the team since, apart from anything else, it was a long way
from home and work. So, in order to justify my being there, I
decided that I was going to spend as much time as possible observing
during my time with the team. The senior of the team, whom I had
spoken to on several occasions, introduced me to a few team
members over coffee and asked me about the research. This gave me
an opportunity to re-emphasize confidentiality and explain my
purpose in being there. Having already asked what I wanted to do,
he then took me to the local court and introduced me to the officer
on court duty.

The formality of the court proceedings provided an opportunity
which was continually to assist me throughout the research. In such
settings a strategic rationality of action affords the researcher an
ability to undertake study. As long as you 'fit in' and record your
feelings about what it is to fit in, then the agenda of the setting works
to your advantage. People have to get on with their work, and as long
as you are no bother, you can observe this with the minimum of
disruption to the setting. However, the achievement of this does not
necessarily entail the adoption of a passive role; you may have to

'join in', which means the method of note-taking has to change as you become part of the setting. During my period with this team, at one moment I found myself sitting in an office writing up notes; at another, being part of an alcohol study-group, expected to participate fully; and at another, being asked my opinion about particular events and clients.

Due to the diversity of tasks which I was examining, the presence of these 'organizational arenas' meant that I had to become adept at judging the context. However, while the strategic rationality of action and formality in these settings afforded an opportunity to fit in, it also meant that I had to pay attention to the normative context of action in order to become part of the setting. In the case of court observation, I needed only to fit in, since the court did not recognize me as part of the formal proceedings.

Not Getting it Wrong, but Invoking a 'Right'

On one occasion, however, I was launched into the social scene. This was because the rules of the setting were more open to negotiation and somebody invoked the right to expect my full participation, not just my participant observation. I was undertaking observational work in a prison, whose reputation provides it with an aura of being a high security institution. While not a maximum-security prison, this reputation is manifest in its working culture.

My experiences within prison settings were varied (see May 1991, Chap. 6). However, on this occasion I was visiting the prison's segregation wing with a probation officer. We entered the wing, whose inmates' recreation often included picking up the 'shit parcels' thrown from the cells of other wings. After meeting the wing officers, we entered a room which contained a large table set for dinner. One of the few concessions to everyday life allowed to the prisoners was occasionally to sit in here and watch a football match on the television. The probation officer then returned after having seen the client and asked his permission for me to be present. Another inmate entered the room and removed the knives and forks. The officer asked: 'Why are you taking those?' 'Well luv,' came the reply, 'you don't want him to stick one in you . . . do you?'

We sat waiting for the client. I felt uncomfortable. I had been in a variety of settings, but not in a scene like this. I had fitted in and mixed in, and staff had found me 'no problem'. This was different. I had learnt that the person we were going to see was not only having to deal with life in the segregation wing, with its stripping of an individual's 'normal economy of action' (Goffman 1968), but also with his sexual orientation. He was married and had children, but was also beginning an affair with a man on the 'outside'. He was to provide a mirror for my own attitudes and sexuality. Here was a man who had consented to my listening to very personal issues, and this made me feel both privileged and uncomfortable.

He came in and sat down. We exchanged those half-nods with temporary eye-contact which men tend to reserve for each other. It was a sign of simple acknowledgement of presence, which is usually enacted in public settings (plenty of examples in pubs). I formed the spacial triangle around the table and the officer asked how he was? He was not, understandably, very happy. They talked, and the officer suggested he try various techniques of self-analysis. The conversation continued with revelations of a personal nature, leaving me feeling I was exploiting the social scene. I could take refuge in being the apex of the triangle and being in, but not of, the interaction. His refuge 'inside' was to take pride in his body. He 'worked out' and had been a good amateur boxer.

I was then wrenched from the relatively security of this uneasy social distance. He suddenly turned to me and said: 'Why are you sitting with your arms folded? Do you always do that?' I had been debunked. He had been in an institution where all bodily movements are provided with meaning for the purpose of self-analysis. Foucault's (1977) techniques of gaze and interiorization do have their institutional outlets. He told me that folding my arms was a defensive mechanism on my part. Immediately, and self-consciously, I dropped my arms to one side. In fact, my posture probably was induced by this social scene.

Having established co-presence, he then looked at me and asked if I was a boxer: 'you look like one'. Then, and rightly, he inverted the roles. I was the only other man in the room and he wanted my opinion on his deep concerns. I looked towards the probation officer. Was I about to ruin months of counselling? She smiled and nodded. However, my mind was already half-made up. My belief was simple: he had granted permission for me to be there, so he had a right to my participation. We talked. Afterwards, we exchanged smiles, shook hands, and he left the room. Together with his deep personal problems, he returned to a place which would only magnify them. Me? I could walk away. I was fortunate. I now carry a memory of this afternoon which I hope I will never forget, while Ann Oakley's comment on interviewing still rings in my ears: there can be 'no intimacy without reciprocity' (1990, p. 49).

The above account aligns feelings with ethics. This may offend those who hold to a deontological, reason-based morality. I would argue that feelings are not simply worth examining on some utilitarian calculation for the purposes of study; they are important in field relations, which are simply a reflection or extension of human relations. In this sense, the taken-for-granted nature of human interaction must be rendered problematic in order to understand the dynamics of field-work. Research is both shaped by and shapes social life. It is, as Anthony Giddens (1976) attempts to state in his formulation of the 'double-hermeneutic', not simply a neutral recording product. This also means that people within the study have a right to claim your participation.

Obviously, I did not take notes in the above setting! Nor did I when sitting in a small room with a divorce-court welfare officer who was attempting conciliation with two people who had once been close to each other and who now argued over access to and custody of their children. In such circumstances no sensitive person sits there taking notes. Nor did I when I was invited to attend a day-centre group, where people are supposed to be talking about their past, their reasons for offending, and personal details. In such a group your participation is expected—you are not just in the group, but also of it. If you are there to understand, they too have a right to your understanding and participation (to say nothing of the fact that group-work would not function well without it!)

At other times my role was, by comparison, non-problematic. Meetings, at which I spent a great deal of time, always had an agenda and the conversation was focused around this. Also, taking notes simply replicated what the other members of the team or committee were doing. I became a familiar figure. As one member of probation management put it, 'people are used to you now'. Still, blending in was important. It was not without its theoretical significance that I found myself at one chief officers' meeting and felt 'naked' without a pile of papers in front of me. Looking in my bag I found academic articles and field-notes and placed these on the table! In courts, as I have suggested, note-taking was also not much of a problem, except when we suddenly had to leave to go down to the cells if an offender was remanded or received an unexpected custodial sentence. On another occasion, the usher asked me to 'step outside' just to check my bag due to bomb threats. There were also times when I ceased note-taking: a day out motorcycling with the 'banger group' and playing cricket for the probation service, for instance.

Feelings, Organizational Arenas, and Theory Generation

The last examples I wish to examine again start from feelings of unease. Out of this comes a double bonus since feelings are not only personally understandable, but theoretically and ethically important. One example comes from my experiences within a team which included in its specialisms a day centre, where a court either orders clients to attend or they do so voluntarily.

Day centres are busy places where staff are constantly reacting to the daily demands of the clients. On my second day in this team, I sat in the coffee room writing-up notes. The doors to the offices which surrounded it were closed. Some officers were out visiting, while others were writing reports or seeing clients. I sat writing notes from the previous days observations and felt reluctant to knock on people's doors in case I disturbed a 'session'. However, the day centre was always a place I could go. If it was busy, I could fit in because I helped the staff who were in such demand. Thus, it became an easy option. Rather than disturb people I went to the day centre because it was accessible.

Because of the centre's accessibility I began reflecting on my own inadequacies. Why didn't I knock on someone's door and interview them—ask if I could spend a day with them? After a couple of days I did just this and spent time with officers in court and meeting clients. However, rather than dwelling for too long on my own failure, I began asking myself why it was that it was relatively easy to go into the day centre. Furthermore, why it was that some officers appeared reluctant to go in there? Seeing the issue in a movement from the personal to theoretical actually generated ideas on the types of power relations which operated in these settings.

In day centres staff often practice group-work, and there is a debate within social work on the efficacy of this method. However, because the work is more visible and participatory, it also meant that it was less easy to control than a one-to-one session with a client. Indeed, clients would question officers in the corridor or within groups. They would use their friends to support them in an argument with staff and, on one occasion, use the group to undermine the credibility of an officer.

My accessibility was afforded by this visibility of the day centre. This arose due to the nature of the interactional power which had an effect on the working practices within this setting. Further, because of this increasing accessibility to the demands of clients, some officers tended to avoid it. In a few cases, despite the car-park being next to the centre and it being possible to walk through to the main building, they walked around the building to another entrance. Thus, I moved from reflections on my inability to negotiate entry towards an understanding of organizational arenas and power relations.

The tensions I picked up as I moved through different parts of the organization found their outlets in meetings. This included attacks on the nature of the research the management were conducting (not mine, I should add), and I was told by officers during some of these meetings that I should study this aspect of the organization.

It was in these forums that people were temporarily relieved from the pressures of day-to-day work in courts and with clients. In such instances they would react to major policy proposals with some anger. Thus, it often felt as if the meetings with colleagues were taking place in a different organization to that where the work with clients was done. Rather than see this as a problem, it became a topic of interest. The result was that I wrestled with the reasons for this disjuncture in experiences. My understanding was heightened by seeing these instances in conjunction with senior-management meetings where vast amounts of paperwork were circulated. The organization operated at several levels. They appeared distinct. One would affect the other, but only indirectly (changes over time may well alter this relationship). As a result, I saw the organization moving from an historcal, client-based, 'problem-solving' one at the front-line, to a 'performance organization' at the management level and this was an agenda set by environmental factors such as a 'law and order' government (see May 1991, ch. 7).

Summary—No One is Perfect!

Because feelings can so easily be dismissed in the discourse I described at the beginning of this chapter, a great deal of understanding can be lost. The process of negotiation and getting on within field-work will involve the feelings I have described: of personal inadequacy in uncomfortable situations, and the need to make ethical choices. Yet while acknowledged, these are often approached in a limited way. Furthermore, while experiences will vary, this is not a reason to be dismissive of their presence. Of course my research did not match up to all the expectations this reading makes of it, and before finishing I should add some caveats to save misunderstanding.

It would be foolish to suppose that my personal attributes led to all successes in negotiating entry. Negotiation is a two-way process: 'Members of organizations become adept at judging the personalities of those with whom they work closely, and the same applies to researchers with whom they come into contact' (Bulmer 1988, p. 153). To this extent there can be no doubt that the 'openness', not only of the probation personnel I spent time with, but of probation management, was pivotal. I even approached the 'chief' requesting to see a Home Office Inspectors' Report on the management of the service. There was some initial reluctance, but I pointed out that I had had access to confidential information about other processes and people, and not to have such access would mean my research was 'incomplete'. Having read the document I could understand the sensitive nature of my request. With just one or two exceptions, it is a tribute to the members of the Treen Probation Service that I was permitted to undertake the research in the manner I have described above.

There is also the political dimension to contend with in a changing organization. I have said that this worked to my advantage. In times of change the people who are the subjects of the research are likely to be reflective. Similarly, the constant movement between organizational arenas prevents a dullness of reflexivity in the researcher. It can also leave a feeling of confusion. Such movement exposes you to constant change in the environment and your social self. This disadvantage can be alleviated by staying 'in touch' with your feelings and having a supportive environment in which to work. This, as I hope I have shown, is both ethically, politically, and theoretically important.

I have made much of feminist theory in this essay and I am sure there are sound feminist challenges to be made in relation to the final product of my work. However, a commitment to change in the light of experience and reflection is, presumably, something which should be encouraged. My experiences are those of a man influenced by feminism. To some this can mean they are immediately invalidated. For me, this would simply supplant the falsehood of denying feelings with another one of a different complexion. This is not to blunt or deny the importance of women seeking equality with men on their own terms.

Recently, the probation service invited me to hold a half-day seminar on the implications of my research. I avoided the 'expert' status. Lasting and meaningful change does not simply come from above. It was a successful morning and the same issues I identified continue. There is hope for change. Research must never be parasitic—it should be available for contemplation, sometimes even as a guide to action, but the researcher should be prepared to engage in dialogue over the research. If feelings are bracketed it can fulfil none of these aims successfully: they are fundamental on a personal, political, and intellectual plane. A fusion of these aspects of the research process may or may not be possible; the attempt, however, is desirable.

References

Atkinson, P. (1990). *The Ethnographic Imagination: Textual Constructions of Reality* (London: Routledge).

Becker, H. (1967). 'Whose Side Are We On?' 14 *Social Problems*, 239–47.

Bell, C. and Newby, H. (1977) (eds.). *Doing Sociological Research* (London: Allen & Unwin).

Bell, C. and Roberts, H. (1984) (eds.). *Social Researching: Politics, Problems, Practice* (London: Routledge & Kegan Paul).

Boswell, G. (1982). 'Goals in the Probation and After-Care Service', Unpublished Ph.D. thesis, Liverpool University.

British Sociological Association (1989). 'Code of Practice, Part 2: The Interests of the Subjects', *Network* (Jan. 1989).

Buchanan, D., Boddy, D., and McCalman, J. (1988). 'Getting In, Getting Out and Getting Back' (in Bryman 1988).

Bulmer, M. (1988). 'Some Reflection upon Research in Organizations' (in Bryman 1988).

Brown, G. W. (1984). 'Accounts, Meaning and Causality' (in Gilbert and Abell 1984).

Bruyn, S. (1966). *The Human Perspective in Sociology* (Englewood Cliffs, NJ: Prentice-Hall).

Bryman, A. (1988) (ed.). *Doing Research in Organizations* (London: Routledge).

Foucault, M. (1977). *Discipline and Punish: The Birth of the Prison* (London: Allen Lane).

—— (1980). *Power/Knowledge, Selected Interviews and Other Writings 1972–1977*, ed. by C. Gordon (Brighton: Harvester Press).

Fraser, N. (1989). *Unruly Practices: Power, Discourse and Gender in Contemporary Social Theory* (Oxford: Polity Press).

Giddens, A. (1976). *New Rules of Sociological Method: A Positive Critique of Interpretative Sociologies* (London: Hutchinson).

—— (1984). *The Constitution of Society: Outline of the Theory of Structuration* (Oxford: Polity Press).

Gilbert, G. N. and Abell, P. (1984) (eds.). *Accounts and Action: Surrey Conferences on Sociological Theory and Method (1)* (Aldershot: Gower).

Gilbert, G. N. and Mulkay, M. (1984). *Opening Pandora's Box: A Sociological Analysis of Scientists' Discourse* (Cambridge: Cambridge University Press).

Glaser, B. and Strauss, A. (1967). *The Discovery of Grounded Theory* (Chicago: Aldine Publishing).

Goffman, E. (1968). *Asylums: Essays on the Social Situation of Mental Patients and Other Inmates* (Harmondsworth: Penguin).

—— (1969). *The Presentation of Self in Everyday Life* (London: Allen Lane).

Gouldner, A. (1971). *The Coming Crisis of Western Sociology* (London: Heinemann).

Griffiths, M. (1988). 'Feminism, Feelings and Philosophy' (in Griffiths and Whitford 1990).

—— and Whitford, M. (1990) (eds.). *Feminist Perspectives in Philosophy* (London: Macmillan).

Harding, S. (1987) (ed.). *Feminism and Methodology* (Milton Keynes: Open University Press).

Hammersley, M. and Atkinson, P. (1983). *Ethnography: Principles in Practice* (London: Tavistock).

Hobbs, D. (1988). *Doing the Business: Entrepreneurship, the Working Class, and Detectives in the East-End of London* (Oxford: Oxford University Press).

Lofland, J. (1971). *Analyzing Social Settings: A Guide to Qualitative Observation and Analysis* (Belmont, Calif. Wadsworth).

May, T. (1991). *Probation: Politics, Policy and Practice* (Milton Keynes: Open University Press).

Oakley, A. (1990). 'Interviewing Women: A Contradiction in Terms' (in Roberts 1990).

Perrow, C. (1978). 'Demystifying Organizations' (in Sarri and Hasenfeld 1978).

Pugh, A. (1990). 'My Statistics and Feminism—A True Story' (in Stanley 1990a).

Roberts, H. (1990) (ed.). *Doing Feminist Research* (London: Routledge).

Rock, P. (1979). *The Making of Symbolic Interactionism* (London: Macmillan).

Ryan, A. (1970). *The Philosophy of the Social Sciences* (London: Macmillan).

Sarri, R. and Hasenfeld, Y. (1978) (eds.). *The Management of Human Services* (New York: Columbia University Press).

Silverman, D. (1985). *Qualitative Methodology and Sociology* (Aldershot: Gower).

Smith, D. (1988). *The Everyday World as Problematic: A Feminist Sociology* (Milton Keynes: Open University Press).

Stanley, L. (1990a) (ed.). *Feminist Praxis: Research, Theory and Epistemology in Feminist Sociology* (London: Routledge).

—— (1990b). 'Doing Ethnography, Writing Ethnography: A Comment on Hammersley', 24 (4) *Sociology*, 617–27.

Stedman-Jones, G. (1967). 'The Pathology of English History', 46 *New Left Review*.

Steier, F. (1991) (ed.). *Research and Reflexivity* (London: Sage).

Strauss, A., Schatzman, L., Bucher, R., Ehrlich, D., and Sabshin, M. (1964). *Psychiatric Institutions and Ideologies* (New York: Free Press).

Van Maanen, J. (1979). 'Reclaiming Qualitative Methods for Organizational Research', 24 *Administrative Science Quarterly*, 520–6.

Whitford, M. (1988). 'Luce Irigaray's Critique of Rationality' (in Griffiths and Whitford 1990).

4

Taking Sides: Partisan Research in the 1984–1985 Miners' Strike

PENNY GREEN*

Introduction

The 1984/5 Miners' Strike was perhaps the most courageously fought, and most fiercely opposed industrial dispute in British history. Not since the 1926 General Strike, when the miners' leader, A. J. Cook, told strikers: 'You have been fighting the legions of hell', had workers been confronted by such a mobilization of state power. In 1984 the men and women of the British coalfields faced a highly co-ordinated, brutal, and massively resourced state assault designed to defeat their struggle to save pit jobs. Paramilitary policing of once-quiet villages, a media campaign unprecedented in its vilification of working-class struggle, and a welfare strategy designed to starve miners back to work—these were the key components in the state's campaign against the miners.

As a criminologist and a socialist I was concerned from the outset with the policing of the dispute and the way in which it was politically interpreted by the mining community. It was, however, only after being in Nottinghamshire for some time that I realized the significance of other agencies of social control, both in the policing of the strike and in terms of the way the mining community perceived the forces organized against them. I was thus concerned not only with the police but also with the law itself, the mass media, government, the National Coal Board, the DHSS, and (more contentiously) with the trade-union bureaucracy. My aim was to document the experiences of the mining community in relation to

* Faculty of Law, University of Southampton. This chapter is based on the field-work appendix to my book, *The Enemy Without: Policing and Class Consciousness in the Miners' Strike* (Milton Keynes: Open University Press, 1990). My thanks to the Open University Press for allowing me to reprint sections of it.

each of these agencies and to analyse the impact that those experiences had on the class consciousness of the community.

Conducting research in the midst of a strike, however, entails particular pressures, strains, and considerations which do not ordinarily pertain to the research situation. A strike is not a predictable event with an established course, time limits, and pre-defined protagonists. Instead, it is subject to the ever-changing balance of class forces and as such is capable of drastic and unpredictable turns. The researcher of industrial conflict must, therefore, be constantly reflexive, attuned, and quick to respond to changing research possibilities.

It is the object of this chapter to document and analyse the methodology that was employed in studying the experiences, perceptions, and consciousness of the Ollerton mining community in relation to the policing of the 1984/5 strike. The first section deals with the research setting and the pragmatics of the research methodology, while the second is more concerned with the contentious issues of partisanship and praxis, both of which have a direct bearing on the project.

Field-work

The Setting

The Nottinghamshire village of Ollerton was the first mining community to experience the form and force of the policing which was to characterize the twelve-month-long strike. The bitter divisions within Nottinghamshire, between striking and working miners, made the county critical to the government's strike-breaking strategy. The fact that this policing was transferred to other coalfields and mining communities as the strike progressed could not initially have been foretold. In the early months of the strike, then, Nottinghamshire as a whole presented immediate and exciting research possibilities for a study on industrial conflict, policing, and consciousness.

Ollerton is a village of 10,910 inhabitants, lying in the North Nottinghamshire coalfield. A 'model' village, it was built solely to service Ollerton Colliery, sunk in 1924, and remains today primarily a pit village. In close proximity to three major Nottinghamshire collieries, Ollerton, Thoresby, and Bevercotes, the village is totally dependent upon the fortunes of the mining industry. The only employment diversity offered to the village inhabitants (and mainly to women) was provided by two small factories producing hosiery and children's wear. Unemployment in the immediate region (the 'Mansfield Travel to Work Area') was 14.1 per cent in May 1986, while the county rate was 13.4 per cent.[1] The majority of miners living in Ollerton work either at Ollerton Colliery, which before the strike had 1,050 NUM members, or Bevercotes Colliery, with 1,300 NUM members.[2]

In the early weeks of the strike Ollerton (the village) sustained over 50 per cent of its miners on strike, but by late May, following Justice Megarry's declaration of the strike as unofficial, that percentage had dwindled to between 20 per cent and 25 per cent, where it was to remain until the 'drift back to work' following the Christmas 1984 break.

I was introduced to members of the Ollerton/Bevercotes Strike Committee by Mike Simons, a friend and journalist on *Socialist Worker* who had been reporting on the strike in Nottinghamshire. This connection gave me a sympathetic reception into the striking community, and I received such a hospitable response from the Strike Committee to my research proposal that not to have taken advantage of the goodwill offered would have meant the abandonment of a unique research opportunity.

For most of my stay in Ollerton I lodged with the family of a striking miner, and the personal relationships I was to build up over the following five-and-a-half months ensured a never-ending source of research material, advice, inspiration, and enthusiastic support.

The Interviews

If I was to study miners' perceptions in a systematic way, an interview seemed the most appropriate method. The general expectation in March and April of 1984 was that the strike would be relatively short-lived, so it was important to get into the field as quickly as possible.

---

[1] Ollerton/Boughton Village Plan: written statement (Newark and Sherwood District Council), and personal communication with the council, June 1985.
[2] Personal communication, Notts. area NUM offices, July 1984. It was very difficult to obtain accurate figures from either the NCB or the NUM. The figures cited correspond to Strike Committee records and other accounts of the strike (Coulter *et al.* 1984; Callinicos and Simons 1985).

A semi-structured interview schedule was designed to gather both uniform and varied qualitative data. It combined semi-structured and open-ended questions—designed to elicit perceptions, experiences, and attitudes with a standardized 'fact-sheet' for the collection of biographical data. The semi-structured approach lent itself as the most appropriate method for several reasons. The first relates to the nature of the subject under study. Consciousness is a complex and fluid notion, particularly in the context of a strike where new experiences and ideas can be generated raidly. It cannot, therefore, be usefully ascertained by a series of forced-choice answers designed for static conditions. A semi-structured interview allows the respondent to develop and qualify his or her ideas in the interview setting, and in addition allows for the introduction of contradictions which in themselves can provide valuable insights into consciousness (see for instance Nichols and Armstrong 1976, p. 150).

Another important reason for employing the semi-structured method concerns the sensitive nature of the topic and the assistance this method offers in establishing a good rapport. The open-ended nature of the questions allowed respondents to discuss issues tangential to the question in hand, and these diversions proved to be both relaxing and informative. Questions were initially informed by my own knowledge of the strike, the historical policing of industrial conflict, and of the mining industry (derived largely from the media, journalist contacts, and labour histories).

The original schedule was piloted in the Yorkshire coalfield in the third week of March 1984 on a random sample of ten striking miners from Markham Main, Manvers, and Armthorpe collieries. As a result of these pilot interviews, the schedule was significantly adapted (and continued to be so in minor ways throughout the duration of my study) as it responded to the immediate concerns of the sample.

In any interview there is a dialectic in operation, and many researchers have found that each new piece of information they discover inevitably affects their own ideas or encourages the asking of different and more pertinent questions, and may even take the research in a direction quite different from that originally intended (Newby 1977, p. 119; Corrigan 1979, p. 7: Burgess 1982, p. 16). The men and women of Ollerton's striking community educated me on local mining issues, the history of their union, and on local terminology, and in their responses guided me to the issues which had originally not been included in the schedule. As a result, my interviews became much more comprehensive and relevant, providing for a much richer assessment of perceptions and beliefs.

In all, 101 members of the Ollerton mining community were interviewed: fifty-one picketing strikers, ten non-picketing strikers, fifteen women active in strike support, and twenty-five working miners, five of whom had spent at least three months on strike prior to returning to work. The schedule was essentially the same for each group, with adaptations tailored to elicit the specific nature of each group's experience and perceptions. Methodologically, the interview was the backbone of my research. It allowed for both concise and more-detailed qualitative responses, and respondents were encouraged to elaborate on their experiences wherever possible.

Interviews with striking miners were held in the office of the Strike Committee, which was attached to the Ollerton/Bevercotes Miners' Welfare. The Strike Committee very generously allocated me an interview room (albeit the children's washroom!) and enthusiastically encouraged miners visiting the office to be interviewed. Interviews lasted for between one-and-a-half and two hours, and were tape-recorded with the permission of the respondents. Confidentiality was assured, although for most striking miners and their wives this was not a personal concern. (Only twice was I asked to briefly turn off the tape-recorder while particularly sensitive information was passed on to me).

Interviews in a centre of strike organization and activity have their problems, however. We were often interrupted, and on many occasions I was required to change location mid-interview when the room was required for more urgent needs. These disruptions were not, however, unduly problematic, and the flexibility of the method employed ensured that the interview was readily conducted elsewhere. Often this meant sitting on the grass outside the Welfare.

Interviewing women (in each case related to striking miners and themselves active in the strike) was logistically more difficult. On the whole, more of their time was consumed by the strike and strictly dictated by the hours of the soup kitchen. An excerpt from my research diary reveals my own disquiet at the interruptions I inevitably caused: 'the women are only at the Welfare [soup kitchen] until 2 p.m. and are frantically busy for most of that time. I feel very much as though I'm imposing on them when they are so busy and have better things to do.' Recognizing the importance and value of your own research project here is clearly of fundamental importance. It is easy to be deterred in such conditions if the researcher is neither committed to the work she is undertaking nor considers it of significant intellectual value. Documenting the experiences and perceptions of women active in the strike was crucial to my analysis. In order to cause the least possible disruption I made appointments or attempted interviews in the quieter periods. I found women to be generally more reticent in expounding their views, as several reported they were only just beginning to 'sort out their ideas' on many issues that they had previously not confronted. Visiting Olerton towards the end of the strike I found this reticence generally gone, replaced by a new sense of confidence.

Non-picketing strikers were difficult to identify because they remained at home, rarely visiting either the Welfare or the Strike Office. The Strike Committee kept no record of active and non-active strikers (a sign of the general weakness of the rank-and-file organization), and I found pickets generally unaware of who and how many were on strike but not involved in picketing or other strike-support activities. These men, when I did locate them, were generally interviewed in their own homes.

The nature of the topic under research was of immediate and absolute interest to the striking sample, particularly in view of the mass media's representation of events. The very fact that I was seeking information about the strike from them—that I was particularly concerned with their experiences and their perceptions—was very important in gaining me both credibility and easy access to the striking community.

While the twenty-five working miners interviewed did not provide the central focus of this study, their experiences and perceptions were interesting in their own right as well as providing a valuable contrast by which the consciousness of the striking community could be better understood. The five working miners who had experience of being on strike in the current dispute are discussed separately throughout the study. Their perceptions most closely parallel those of the picketing strikers, and to include their attitudes with the other twenty working miners would have confused the picture. They themselves distanced their position from miners who had worked from the beginning of the strike. As one explained: 'there's no way I would ever feel like a scab because we had thirteen weeks out and some haven't even tried it.'

Interviewing working miners proved a very difficult and sensitive exercise. Tensions within the village were running high and working miners proved very reluctant to discuss their views. Whereas I had received a 100 per cent response-rate from the striking community, only 30 per cent of working miners approached consented to being interviewed. I was generally met with suspicion and sometimes with open hostility. Much of the suspicion related to my being a university student—most working miners had heard of university collections for striking miners and were therefore on guard with me.

Locating working miners willing to be interviewed was a major problem. An entry from my research diary for 3 July 1984 demonstrates some of the difficulties I experienced:

Tuesday morning—Phoned Ollerton Colliery's Administration officer who put me through to the union's new working-miner president Ernie Valence. He was *very* reticent to assist me and said that in the 'current climate' I'd be lucky to get anyone to agree to an interview. He said he could only help if he went to his members and there wasn't another meeting for a fortnight and even then he couldn't guarantee anything. I think its time to door-knock. This business is a real strain. I feel that if I talk to the newly elected union men (and they are essentially the only potential respondents who have been suggested by the few working miners interviewed) they may well advise their working members not to speak to me. Atmosphere certainly hostile.

Interestingly, when I was most despondent about the prospect it was striking miners who urged me to interview those working. They offered me the names of friends and acquaintances, but only rarely did those contacts elicit a positive response.

Eventually, as a desperate strategy of last resort, I did decide to door-knock. In this way I could approach the prospective respondent from the perspective of an 'outsider' concerned with the views of the 'mining community', rather than specifically with striking or working miners. Particular care was taken in this respect to allay the suspicions and hostility which often met my enquiries. None the less, it was a dispiriting and arduous experience. Several doors were banged in my face, and some men shouted at me for daring even to approach them. These instances were fortunately isolated ones, and most declined politely with a characteristic 'not bothered, love'. Persistence, though, won me an interview with Ernie Valence, the new Branch President, following which I was able to convince several working miners to be interviewed, since I had already interviewed their president. (He was elected in the June 1984 elections, when all but one of the new branch officials were working miners.)

There was (compared with striking miners and leading working miners) far less desire on the part of rank-and-file working miners to explain their position and recount their experiences of the strike. This was similarly evident in their negative reactions to requests for interviews by the media. Unlike rank-and-file striking miners, rank-and-file workers were not consumed by a passionate urgency to 'tell their story'. After all 'their' story was being splashed across newspapers and television screens on a daily basis. The individualized nature of the working miner's experience, compared with the collectivity of the striking miner, may in part have contributed to this apparant lack of confidence. But the evident discomfort they felt about 'scabbing' in a strike to defend pit jobs, which I perceived in many working miners, was also a probable underlying reason for their reticence.

The Participant Observation

Living in Ollerton over a period of five-and-a-half months afforded me many similar experiences to those of the people I was interviewing. In this respect my status as participant observer provided both corroboration of the accounts and perceptions documented in the study, and a greater understanding of those perceptions.

I spent a great deal of time between interviews talking with strikers and their wives in the Strike Committee office, in the Miner's Welfare, and in the soup kitchen. I also attended local NUM branch meetings, Ollerton Women's Action Group meetings, stood on routine picket-lines at Ollerton and Bevercotes pits, joined mass pickets of other Nottinghamshire pits and power-stations, and marched with the miners on rallies and demonstrations in Ollerton, Mansfield, and London. Despite my protestations the Strike Committee arranged a 'minder' for me whenever I attended mass pickets. Aside from any protection this amiable paternalism might have provided, it afforded me even closer relationships with striking miners. In addition to the authenticity these experiences contributed to my research, they also gave me 'street credibility', which was particularly important considering the crucial nature of the strike to the lives of all those I interviewed. This credibility also afforded me insights into privileged information not readily available to the casual observer, and ensured that my continued presence within the striking community was a welcome one.

The research was further supplemented by interviews with ten lawyers who were involved in representing striking miners, and by discussions throughout the strike with other researchers and journalists in the field. I also maintained close contact with the co-ordinators of the Ollerton Legal Centre who held up-to-date information on the arrests, detentions, bail conditions, and court proceedings of Ollerton striking miners. In addition I attended several court proceedings involving Ollerton miners arrested on picket lines. Several attempts were made to interview Nottinghamshire Clerks of Court but with little success. The one interview I was granted, with the Worksop Clerk of the Court, was largely fruitless because he was unwilling to issue any comment on legal procedure pertaining to the strike.

A newspaper file—combining national dailies, regional newspapers, the socialist press, and the NUM's *The Miner*—was maintained throughout the strike, and television news-coverage and strike documentaries were similarly noted. This data provided a running commentary on the strike as well as providing an important primary source for an examination of the ideological policing of the dispute. I also kept a research diary noting all important events relating to the strike in Ollerton and my own experiences of field-work.

Partisanship

It is the task of every academic who sympathetically investigates those censured as 'criminal' to justify and qualify his or her work with regard to the possibility of bias and distortion. This is even more necessary when the subject of research is politically controversial, as was the Miner's Strike. I remember long and heated arguments in the Institute of Criminology's coffee room (on my occasional and grudging reappearances in Cambridge)—how, my colleagues claimed, could my research be objective when there I was collecting money from them for the miners?

There is certainly a case for examining the effect of a partisan researcher on the research situation. Does it, for instance, encourage or obscure certain responses that another political position might not have done? In cautioning interviewers on the dangers involved in leading questions, Paul Thompson (1978, p. 170) made an important qualification: 'There are some strong exceptions to this. If you know somebody has very strong views especially from a minority standpoint it may be essential to show a basic sympathy with them to get started at all. I cannot claim to be objective or detached from the subject-matter of my research—as a socialist my personal and academic endeavours are inextricably linked with struggles for a fundamentally new and egalitarian society. Socialist researchers are reminded by Marx that: 'The philosophers have only interpreted the world in various ways; the point is to change it' (the eleventh 'Thesis on Feuerbach'). My concern to understand the consciousness of Nottinghamshire striking miners was, therefore, political as well as sociological—class-consciousness being fundamental to bringing about such change.

Howard Becker has argued that by lending credence to the ideas and perceptions of the criminalized (which Becker suggests is an inevitable outcome of taking their perspective seriously), the social scientist is left open to accusations of bias. If, however, non-deviant (or bourgeois) definitions are employed, accusations of bias are far less likely to arise (Becker 1967, p. 240). Becker accounts for this distinction by proposing the existence of a 'hierarchy of credibility' whereby the powerful both represent and enforce official morality. Thus, when the perspectives of the powerless are reported, the accusation of bias is more or less inevitable (p. 241).

The striking community was certainly at the bottom of the 'hierarchy of credibility' in terms of media representation, and my work is an attempt to elevate its credibility in academic research. But how adequate to our task of understanding society with a view to changing it is Becker's own 'insider' methodology? Taylor and Walton (1971) have characterized Becker's approach as 'camera sociology', because 'the limitations and problems of sociological analysis become transformed into the mere technical problems of the negatives' (p. 368). The camera analogy is apt, for Becker is interested only in the immediate perspectives of those he is studying and not with the historical or material conditions which have fashioned those perspectives. In consequence, Becker fails to offer a total picture or a structural location for the perceptions which he is intent on 'describing'. As Taylor and Walton suggest, Becker's approach of accurately representing only the perspective of those under study excludes a causal explanation of the behaviour (or censure) described. The other important criticism of Becker's work relates to the 'truth' and objective condition of the sample population. It is not possible, as Becker suggests, objectively to investigate society from within one particular value-framework. As Taylor and Walton cogently argue, this approach 'denies that actors' definitions are refracted through prisms of truth and falsehood' (p. 368). Here the problems of the interactionist perspective emerge as a barrier to scientific investigation—deviance emerges 'out of the matrix of analysed society' (Gouldner 1968, p. 106).

While my approach was partisan, 'camera sociology' was not the method employed in the study. The policing of the Miners' Strike and the striking community's perceptions of it were situated within their historical, political, and economic contexts. In addition, the views of striking miners, while remaining the focus of study, were not examined outside the context of the perceptions of other groups within the mining community. Picketing strikers were contrasted with non-picketing strikers, women, and working miners.

The experiences and perceptions of the police, judiciary, government ministers, Coal-Board management, media representatives, and trade-union officials were generally excluded, for several reasons. Apart from the significant problems of access and limitations of time, the agencies of the state were not the central object of concern. While detailed information on these agencies would certainly be of value, expression of their role in the strike and their perceptions of it received constant media publicity. The central aim of my research was to document and analyse a striking community's perceptions of the policing of the strike, and from those perceptions to derive certain conclusions on the nature of the consciousness that had emerged in the community as a result.

On the question of the possibility of neutral vision, there are several points to consider now. The 'Hawthorne effect' refers to the influence of the researcher upon the research situation. It arises from liberal social science's singular concern with the static description of existing social relationships. Taylor, Walton, and Young have cogently argued that the social-research situation is never static and can as such never be captured. Liberal sociology's concern to avoid influencing or disrupting the research situation, they suggest, arises from the contention that the researcher has no 'right to change a situation which other social forces in the community (or the group) under study would never deny themselves' (1975), p. 24). The point is that this abrogation is illusory, because the work of liberal researchers (particularly in the field of criminology) is frequently acted on politically by agencies of control over which the researcher has no power.

Partisanship, for Marxists, means more than describing 'subordinate' subjects sympathetically. It means praxis, uniting social research with theoretical practice. Like Taylor, Walton, and Young, I would argue that radical research 'has to develop methodologies for the realisation of societies its own critique would necessitate' (1975, p. 24). In important respects, then, controlling for the 'Hawthorne effect' is diversionary because, first, research settings are in a constant state of flux, and secondary, socialists are primarily concerned to understand the world *in order to change it*. Taylor, Walton, and Young argue, however, that the transformation of left-wing research into political practice must occur in the actual *process* of research (p. 24). This may be a noble prescription, but it is one made without an analysis of the contradictions and complications which inevitably arise when research is simultaneously combined with political activity. These problems were very clear in my own research—interviewing working miners in a small village where I had recently been attending picket lines was not unproblematic. The demands of research do conflict with the demands of political practice, and both can suffer as a result of combining the two with equal ardour. The researcher must be aware that the relationship between theory and practice is sometimes a complicated one. In the context of my own study, it was apparent that my research would suffer considerably if I was not primarily a researcher while I was in Ollerton.

It would have been both naive on my part and insulting to those I interviewed if I had ignored my own experiences of the policing of mass picketing when conducting the interviews. My own experiences and theoretical position could not be divorced from the research. As Glaser and Strauss have argued, the researcher should not (and I would add *cannot*) approach reality as a *tabula rasa* (1970, p. 3). Considering the perceptions of the striking community in relation to the mass media (see Green 1990, Chap. 8) and the refusal of many in the community to be interviewed by either press or television, I would suggest that my political sympathies facilitated research, because striking miners and their wives were able to report their experiences and opinions freely in an atmosphere of trust. My interviews were not conducted in an academic or political vacuum, and both the interviews and data analysis would have suffered considerably if this fact had not been acknowledged.

Interviewing working miners raised this general question more acutely, and interviews were sometimes uncomfortable as a result. Working miners were, to my knowledge, unaware of my partisanship. Several questioned me as to where my sympathies lay, but were generally placated by my explanation of interest in the whole community and the effects of policing the strike upon it. It is, none the less, admitted that working miners, particularly those in leading positions, may have kept back certain information on the basis of suspicions they held, but it also seems likely that such information would have been withheld from any outsider.

The fact that I was both female and Australian may also have influenced the research situation. Initially it aroused curiosity in the community, and as such facilitated rapport. Many respondents were interested in Australia and in my opinions about Britain, so that interviews could begin with my being the respondent. My status as an Australian female was not always so warmly received by working miners, as several confused me with Peggy Khan—Arthur Scargill's American research assistant—and were thus immediately set on guard.

Overall, I would assess my influence on the nature and type of response given as minimal. The evident desire of strikers to tell their story, often regardless of the particular question in hand, demonstrated the force of those experiences and the opinions held. I found the same themes emerging throughout an interview, and in all but one or two cases the reliability and integrity of the respondent could be ascertained by the internal consistency of the responses given.

No research is free from bias. The important question in controlling for it is the researcher's recognition of her own position and opinions, and how they might influence the research situation.

Limitations and Points of Caution

While I have been concerned to qualify those specific and political aspects of my research which might have distorted my conclusions, there are other contextual limitations which should also be accounted for.

First, my research was conducted in Nottinghamshire, an area both 'moderate' and divided, in comparison with other major British coalfields. In this respect one should proceed cautiously in generalizing from the perceptions and consciousness of the Ollerton striking community, which was both small and isolated.

Another limitation, which is probably unavoidable given the pressures of responding to a dynamic research situation, relates to the interview schedule. Having approached my field-work before commencing my study of class-consciousness (which formed the theoretical analysis of the work), I recognize through hindsight that several questions specifically concerning class-imagery and class-consciousness would have benefited the study. None the less, the interviews did allow for a comprehensive analysis of the relationship between miners' changing consciousness and the policing of the dispute.

Finally, it is difficult to assess the relationship between contemporaneous statements made in interviews and longer-term attitudes (see Green 1990, ch. 9, for a discussion of this relationship). A study concerned primarily with change and a dynamic concept like class-consciousness, therefore, demands some form of follow-up investigation. There are several reasons why I did not conduct one. Following the end of the strike and during the course of my doctoral research I returned to Ollerton on several occasions. These visits demonstrated to me that the memory of the dispute and its policing was still fresh in the minds of the ex-striking community. With several hundred miners sacked nationally, almost eighty in prison, an NUM campaign for their reinstatement and release, and the continued victimization of militants in the pit, that memory was forcefully sustained. The dispute and its policing was, therefore, still too 'alive' to render any particularly interesting or valid comparative data within the temporal limitations of my study. In addition, the mining community's memory of my interviews was similarly fresh. To ask the same or similar questions within a relatively short period would not, I believe, have yielded new information.

Seven years on, it is now time to reassess the Ollerton community's relationship and attitudes toward the agencies of state control that so transformed their thinking in 1984.

The Politics of Analysis

In terms of the way in which the data was analysed one might ask why the focus of this investigation was on the consciousness of the striking community rather than specifically on the consciousness of individuals within that community, and why the analysis was primarily concerned with the class experience of that consciousness.

To answer these questions we must first return to the major question addressed by study—the extent to which the policing of the Miners' Strike might affect the political consciousness of those policed. It was a study of one striking community's response to being targeted and criminalized by a state-co-ordinated strike-breaking intervention. It was not an ethnographic study of the kind presented by Dennis *et al.* (1956), examining all aspects—cultural, social, political, and industrial—of community life. It was the study of one community's response, in terms of political consciousness, to a dramatic and repressive event. In this context it should be pointed out that studies of mining communities demonstrate a homogeneity of educational, cultural, and political experience amongst the inhabitants (Dennis *et al.* 1956; Bulmer 1975; Allen 1981; Pitt 1973). The policing of the strike was a new variable—a dramatic experience which impinged on the life of the striking community. In qualitative terms it was both immediate and measurable. By assessing the community's pre-strike attitudes through interview-questions relating to previous experience of and attitudes to the policing agencies, and by comparing these with the strike-produced views, it was possible to examine the nature and extent of the impact that the policing had on political consciousness.

I focused on the class experience of the strike and its policing for important theoretical reasons. One of the key factors characterizing the policing of the strike was its overtly political nature (Green 1990; Callinicos and Simons 1985; Fine and Millar 1985; Scraton and Thomas 1985). Because it was political policing, I was particularly interested in how striking miners and their wives—the target of this political policing—interpreted the political component of their criminalization. From a socialist perspective the most important aspect of political consciousness is its class component (see Green 1990, ch. 9). I was therefore interested in assessing whether or not the experience of political policing, in the context of an industrial dispute, was able to engender class-conscious analyses both of the agencies involved in that policing and more widely of society generally.

While it was individuals I interviewed, my focus of analysis was not on the ontological development of political consciousness within the individual but on general movements of consciousness within the striking community. I focused my analysis on the consciousness of the striking community and the few significant groups into which the community was divided by the strike, for two important theoretical reasons.

First, the policing of the strike was fundamentally directed against specific working-class communities and not against criminal individuals within those communities (Blake 1985; Christian 1985; Scraton and Thomas 1985; Gordon 1985). Striking miners and their wives interpreted it first and foremost as an attack against their striking community (Green 1990). If they were arrested, refused DHSS benefits, misrepresented by the mass media, or threatened with eviction by the NCB, there was no tendency for members of the striking community to interpret these events personally—instead, they were perceived as strategic assaults on Nottinghamshire striking miners—as political and not personal. Because the policing was directed against the striking community, the major component of the response to the policing came from the community itself through the NUM, the strike committee, and the Women's Action Group. It did not, on the whole, come from individually determined and initiated responses (although, of course, to a certain extent this did occur). Overwhelmingly, on picket lines, at demonstrations, at rallies, and through the day-to-day policing of the village during the strike, experiences of and responses to the policing assumed a uniformity for the striking community.

As has already been mentioned, the strike divided the Ollerton mining community into at least four groups—picketing strikers, non-picketing strikers, women active in the strike, and working miners—which, for the purpose of this study, provided valuable comparative categories of analysis. The members of each group, by the nature of their role in the strike, had different levels of experience with the agencies of policing and therefore presented the possibility of varying levels of police consciousness. Like Lane and Roberts (1971), I was interested in examining the perceptions of the major groups within the mining community so as to provide an 'overall pattern' of experience and perceptions relating to the policing of the strike, and thereby to contrast different experiences with corresponding differences in consciousness.

The study could have focused on selected individuals as, for instance, Nichols and Armstrong did in their study of Chemco foremen; but this approach, as those authors conceded, meant that the most widespread modes of thought were not established (1976, p. 151). My focus on the striking community, criminalized in the process of industrial conflict, was designed to establish the widespread effects of repressive policing on the political consciousness of the policed.

The second reason for analysing the collective consciousness of the striking community lies in what class-consciousness theoretically describes. From a Marxist perspective class-consciousness describes 'the appropriate and rational reactions imputed to a particular position in the process of production' (Lukács 1971, 51). In other words, it describes the state of readiness—in mind and practice—by which the working class can achieve self-liberation through revolutionary change. According to Lukács: 'The historically significant actions of the class as a whole are determined in the last resort by this consciousness and not by the thought of the individual' (1971; p. 51). It follows, therefore, that the class, or significant sections of the class, should become the most important subjects of analysis in a study of class-consciousness. Rather than examining the characteristics, inconsistencies, and contradictions within the individual, these same variations are taken to hold more meaning when applied within the wider class framework.

While the approach adopted here derives much from Lukács, it nevertheless represents a significant departure from his work in that I do not (following Buraway 1979; Hyman 1973; Lane and Roberts 1971; Nichols and Armstrong 1976; Blauner 1964; Kornblum 1974; and others) dismiss, as Lukács does, 'the historical manifestations of *popular consciousness*' (Boggs 1976, p. 68). On the contrary, popular consciousness can and should be empirically studied for the insights it can provide into consciousness and change.

There are further but supplementary reasons for not exploring the consciousness of the individual, and they relate to the limitations imposed by the strike itself and to the time and financial resources available to the researcher. An empirical study which focused primarily on individuals and the ontological factors (political, social, psychological, and educational) which shaped their ability to interpret the policing of the strike would have required a far greater penetration into the personal lives and histories of those individuals. While it is acknowledged that this approach would have yielded valuable information concerning individual ideologies and the shaping of consciousness at the social-psychological level, it would have required far more time, and in consequence greater financial resources, than were available to the research student.

In addition, the dramatic circumstances surrounding the strike and the full-time commitment to the strike by the majority of those interviewed meant that an in-depth study of individuals was less viable than a more general study focusing on the wider community. At the time the research was carried out active strikers and their wives were preoccupied with the emotional, ideological, and practical demands of the strike, and finding the time for one- or two-hour interviews directly about the policing of the strike was often very difficult. In such circumstances, finding the time for more lengthy and personal interviews, less specifically related to the strike and conducted away from the convenience of the strike centre, would have been increasingly problematic and would, I suspect, in addition to the increased time required, have imposed strains on the community's ready willingness to participate in the research.

Conclusion

Research is a political exercise—what we choose to investigate is determined by the way in which we perceive the world—that is, by what and who we see as important, unjust, or repressive: the way in which we conduct that investigation is determined by research methodologies, themselves constructed according to the dictates of competing ideologies and of course the way in which we analyse the data gathered is in large part determined by our expectations of the research, by our acceptance or rejection of the *status quo*.

As a Marxist, my starting-point is that class struggle is the motor of history, that only the working class is capable of emancipating itself, and that this emancipation is predicated on class-consciousness. Researching the relationship between policing and class-consciousness in an historic strike may provide important insights into the circumstances by which class struggle can lead to class-consciousness—it may also reveal those powerful obstacles (for example, the trade-union bureaucracy) that limit any such potential development.

In the case of the Miners' Strike, holding strong political opinions and being firmly partisan only served to assist the research process. Although it sometimes made for uncomfortable interviews with working miners, this was more than compensated for by the freedom, trust, and opportunities which being partisan provided within the striking community.

References

Allen, V. L. (1981). *The Militancy of British Miners* (Shipley: Moor Press).

Becker, H. (1967). 'Whose side are we on?'; 14 (3) *Social Problems*, 239–47.

Blake, N. (1985). 'Picketing, Justice and the Law', (Fine and Millar 1985).

Blauner, R. (1964). *Alienation and Freedom: The Factory Worker and his Industry* (Chicago: University of Chicago Press).

Boggs, C. (1976). *Gramsci's Marxism* (London: Pluto Press).

Bulmer, M. (1975). (ed.), *Working Class Images of Society* (London: Routledge & Kegan Paul).

Burawoy, M. (1979). *Manufacturing Consent: Changes in the Labour Process under Monopoly Capitalism* (Chicago: University of Chicago Press).

Burgess, R. (ed.). *Field Research: A Sourcebook and Field Manual* (London: George Allen Unwin).

Callinicos, A. and Simons, M. (1985). *The Great Strike* (London: Socialist Workers Party).

Christian, L. (1985). 'Restriction without Conviction: The Role of the Courts in Legitimising Police Control in Nottinghamshire (in Fine and Millar 1985).

Corrigan, P. (1979). *Schooling the Smash Street Kids* (London: Macmillan).

Coulter, J., Miller, S., and Walker, M. (1984). *State of Siege* (London: Canary Press).

Dennis, N., Henriques, F., and Slaughter, C. (1956). *Coal is my Life* (2nd edn, 1969., London: Tavistock).

Fine, B. and Millar, R. (1985). *Policing the Miners' Strike*. (Lawrence & Wishart and the Cobden Trust).

Glaser, B. and Strauss, A. (1970). 'Discovery of Substantive Theory: A Basic Strategy Underlying Qualitative Research', in W. Filstead (ed.), *Qualitative Methodology—First Hand Involvement with the Social World* (Chicago: Markham Publishing).

Gordon, P. (1985). 'If they come in the morning . . . The Police, the Miners and Black people (in Fine and Millar 1985).

Gouldner, A. (1968). 'The Sociologist as Partisan: Sociology and the Welfare State', *American Sociologist* 103–16.

Green, P. (1990). *The Enemy Without: Policing and Class Consciousness in the Miners' Strike* (Milton Keynes: Open University Press).

Hyman, R. (1973). 'Industrial Conflict and the Political Economy: Trends of the Sixties and Prospects for the Seventies', in R. Miliband and J. Saville (eds.), *Socialist Register* (London: Merlin).

—— (1975). *Industrial Relations—A Marxist Introduction* (London: Macmillan).

Kornblum, W. (1974). *Blue Collar Community* (Chicago: University of Chicago Press).

Lane, T. and Roberts, K. (1971). *Strike at Pilkingtons* (London: Collins/ Fontana).

Lukács, G. (1971). *History and Class Consciousness: Studies in Marxist Dialectics* (London: Merlin).

Newby, H. (1977). 'Reflections on the Study of Suffolk Farm Workers', in C. Bell and H. Newby (eds.), *Doing Sociological Research* (London: George Allen and Unwin).

Nichols, T. and Armstrong, P. (1976). *Workers Divided* (Glasgow: Fontana).

People of Thurcroft (1986). *Thurcroft: A Village and the Miners' Strike—An Oral History* (Nottingham: Spokesman).

Pitt, M. (1973). *The World on Our Backs* (London: Lawrence & Wishart).

Samuel, R., Bloomfield, B., and Boanas, G. (1986). *The Enemy Within: Pit Villages and the Miners' Stike of 1984–85* (London: Routledge & Kegan Paul).

Scraton, P., and Thomas, P. (1985). (eds.), 'The State versus the People: Lessons from the Coal Dispute', 12(3) *Journal of Law and Society*.

Seifert, R. and Urwin, J. (1988). *Struggle Without End: the 1984/5 Miners' Strike in North Staffordshire* (Newcastle: Penrhos).

Taylor, I., Walton, P., and Young, J. (1975). (eds.), *Critical Criminology* (London: Routledge & Kegan Paul).

Taylor, L. and Walton, P. (1971). 'Industrial Sabotage: Motives and Meanings', in S. Cohen, (ed.), *Images of Deviance* (Harmondsworth: Penguin).

Thompson, P. (1978). *The Voice of the Past: An Oral History* (Oxford: Oxford University Press).

Walker, M. (1985). 'Miners in Prison: Workers in Prison: Political Prisoners' (in Scraton and Thomas 1985).

PART III

Ethics

5

Some Ethical Considerations on Field-Work with the Police

CLIVE NORRIS*

In the context of ethnography the debate about the ethics of social research has focused predominately on the issue of the morality of covert participant observation (Bulmer, 1982). In this chapter, by contrast, I want to consider some of the ethical implications of overt field-research, since it is this methodology which is more typical of the ethnographic enterprise. In particular, I want to consider, in the context of my own research on police culture, some of the dilemmas posed when the researcher is faced with direct evidence of misconduct by those he or she is researching.

A cursory examination of the literature of the sociology of work suggests that occupational deviancy is an everyday factor of working life (Ditton 1977; Mars 1982; Clarke 1990). Within the sociology of policing such deviancy is well documented (Cain 1971 and 1979; Shearing 1981; Punch 1985; Rubinstein 1973; Smith and Gray 1983), and it would, therefore, be naïve for the ethnographer to believe that he or she can escape contact with morally ambiguous situations. In essence, the police-researcher is presented with exactly the same problems which face those studying other deviant or criminal groups (Klockars 1975; Humphreys 1970; Patrick, 1973; Rainwater and Pittman 1967). Of course, they are given an added poignancy by the police's role as guardian of law and order, and by the implications such deviance may have for the delivery of justice.

For ethnographers, then, a number of subsidiary questions arise as to what they should do when their field-work (inevitably) reveals

* Department of Social Policy and Professional Studies, University of Hull. The research on which the chapter is based was supported by two Economic and Social Research Council (ESCR) (formerly Social Science Research Council) studentships, award numbers S82117305 and G00428325065.

misconduct. To what extent does the researcher become personally involved with deviant activities? To what extent is one implicated by mere presence, and does one's presence condone such activities? At what point does the researcher feel that their subjects' rights to anonymity and confidentiality is overridden by other claims?

Although there is now a growing body of observational studies on the police, there are few accounts which describe how the studies were conducted and, in particular, how the ethical problems of the field-work were managed. Some studies do not discuss the issue at all (Rubinstein 1973; Reuss-Ianni 1983; Manning 1977 and 1980), while others mention it merely to note its absence (Banton 1964; Punch 1979). Banton, for instance, writes: 'I have not been able to study what happens in situations where policemen are subject to strain and provocation and can say little about the sorts of incidents that attract newspaper publicity' (1964, p. xii).

Those who do write about the problem and the personal distress undergone by the researcher do not necessarily say how they resolved ethical dilemmas (Westley 1970; Chatterton 1978; Van Maanen 1974 and 1978). Hence, Van Maanen notes: 'There were, for example, moments during my study when disgust does not begin to describe what the police made me feel as I saw people thrown through windows, kicked to the ground and dogs put on them, or terrified beyond belief by a gun placed to their heads' (1981, p. 491). A few researchers, however, actually discuss both the cases and the reasoning behind their decisions (Ericson 1981 and 1982; Smith and Gray 1983; Holdaway 1983; Punch 1989).

There are three reasons why such information is important. First, without it, it is impossible to judge to what degree authors are practising self-censorship. For instance, has key data been 'lost', perhaps not written up due to the fear of subpoena or the feelings of betrayal it caused?

Secondly, unless one knows the constraints under which the researchers were operating and the degree of penetration they had gained within the organization, it is difficult to assess the reliability of their findings. For instance, if we have a field-work account which documents neither police use of violence nor how the field-work was carried out, it is impossible to decide whether the researcher has been duped and systematically excluded from various settings or whether no misconduct took place.

Thirdly, in the absence of honest accounts as to how the field-work was conducted, the novice researcher is continually faced with the problem of having to 're-invent the wheel'. As Van Maanen has rightly suggested, 'the best advice I could offer to a researcher just entering a police system would be precisely the same were he a recruit: simply keep quite and to himself virtually everything he hears and sees during his early days in the field' (Van Maanen 1978, p. 341). Yet there comes a point when the early days have passed and, if one is doing one's job well, the backstage is accessible. The researcher may then become party to events which raise serious moral dilemmas.

In addressing these issues, I do not want to fall into the trap of offering moral prescription as the codes of professional conduct have a tendency to do (BSA 1982; ASA 1971). As Bronfenbrenner has remarked: 'The only safe way to avoid violating principles of professional ethics is to refrain from doing social research altogether' (1952, p. 453). Rather, I am broadly supportive of Punch's position, which recognizes the situational complexity of field-work practice and suggests that to address the ethical dilemmas, 'we should rely on commonsense . . . academic convention and peer control through discussion' as these approaches, unlike formal codes, are 'more likely to promote understanding of the issues and compliance with them' (Punch 1986, p. 83). However, for Punch codes are not wholly redundant since they may be useful in alerting the researcher to the potential pitfalls and problems that he or she is likely to encounter.

Nevertheless, there are problems with this position. Common sense is a remarkably elusive concept and, as I have stated, academics are by no means in agreement on the key issues; and, given the nature of such research—often conducted by lone graduate students—peer control is likely to be remote and after the event.

However, Punch is right when he argues that 'ideally, every field-worker should be his or her own moralist' (1986, p. 73). Consequently, as Holdaway has observed, 'in the end it is the individual researcher who will make the decision, accepting the risks involved . . . they will have to live with the decision—and continue to do so' (Holdaway, 1983, p. 79). The strength of Punch's situationalist approach is that it is not prescriptive. It recognizes that the practice of field-work inevitably involves what Klockars has called 'the problem of Dirty Hands' (1979, p. 265) and suggests that moral sensitivity and maturity can only occur through debate, dialogue, and reflection. Therefore, the important issue is how field-workers can become more aware and sensitive to the moral and ethical dimensions of their enterprise.

The prerequisite of such sensitivity is honest accounts of the practice of field-work which can be used to focus debate and encourage critical reflection. What follows is, therefore, an account of how I constructed an observer-as-participant role in a police setting, which then goes on to focus on three particular issues which bear most heavily on ethical decision-making. These can be discussed under three headings: informed consent; the invasion of privacy; and trust and deceit. I then want to consider one specific incident which raises the central dilemmas a field-worker might face. Finally, I want to consider the choices available to the field-worker and the consequences of particular courses of action.

The Construction of a Research Role

The aim of my research was both to describe and elucidate the practice of policing from the perspective of the street-level officer. Accordingly, my attention was drawn to the occupational culture of the lower ranks, the shared values and norms that surround their work, and the formal and informal work practices which, together, constitute the patrol officer's work-world. Two types of data were viewed as salient. First, incidents of naturally occurring inter-officer talk which, in comparison with accounts generated for the researcher's benefit, say far more about the shared value-system of police officers. Second, detailed descriptions of how officers handled 'live' incidents. An observer-as-participant role was chosen as the only practical research methodology which would provide the necessary data for such an analysis.

For example, I went out on routine patrol, both on foot and in cars; I sat in the station office and made tea for the shift; I helped chase suspects and, at times, arrest them, counselled the distraught, and administered first-aid to attempted suicide victims. I have felt a sense of relief when we have slipped out of the cold into a warm tea-hole, and shared the fear, humour, and boredom that are part of the everyday lives of police officers.

Yet the participant-as-observer role also tends to obscure the variations inherent in the role. Gold (1958) has pointed out that 'participant observation' is a master term which covers a continuum from complete participant to complete observer. Unlike participant observation of other social or occupational groups, there are legal limits defining the extent to which one can become a complete participant in the police organization. As Van Maanen has noted, this has led to most research on the police being carried out from the position of the 'fan' (Van Maanen 1979, p. 344, and Fig. 5.1).

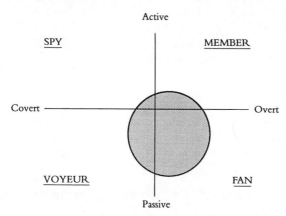

FIGURE 5.1 Pure Types of Participant-Observer Role
(adapted from Van Maanen 1978, p. 344)

As I have illustrated on Van Maanen's typology, my predominant research role was also that of the 'fan'. But there is always movement between roles. When I deliberately placed myself in a position to overhear private conversations between officers I felt like a 'voyeur'; when I excused myself to the toilet, hurriedly to scribble down notes, I felt like the 'spy'; but when I was attending incidents on the street, passively listening and watching, I was the 'fan'. However, when I was left guarding a prisoner, introduced as a fellow police officer, or helped in the arrest of a violent and disturbed drug-user, I was, to all intents and purposes, cast in the role of a police officer. As Van Maanen points out, short of wearing a sign 'there is no way for the field-worker to be sure that his research role in the organization is in fact the role that the others are responding to' (1978, p. 346).

The Ethics of the Research Role

In Table 5.1 I show how the research role that I constructed undermined many standard ethical considerations. It is to an

TABLE 5.1. *The degree to which the research complied or contravened with standard ethical considerations*

	Police	Public
Was the principle of informed consent adhered to?	Theoretically: yes Practically: no	Generally: no Sometimes: yes
Was the research subjects' right to privacy under-mined?	Generally: no Sometimes: yes	Generally: yes
Were the research subjects deceived by the researcher?	Generally: no Sometimes: yes	Generally: yes

examination of how and to what extent I broke the rules that I now wish to turn.

Informed Consent

Adherence to the principle of informed consent implies that two major conditions are met: first, that the research subjects are made aware of and understand the nature and purposes of the research; second, that, from a position of knowledge, they can freely give their consent to participating in the research. The explanations which one constructs for one's research are always conditional upon the audience which one is addressing. This is especially true when carrying out an ethnographic study where one has only a vague sense of what one is looking for. I, like others, constructed an account of my work which was serviceable, as the following extract from my field-work illustrates:

This has become my standard explanatory patter. 'Well, what I'm trying to do is to develop collections of different incidents such as "street stops", "domestics", "fights" etc. Then, at some point, I'll have to sit down and analyse them.'

This often elicits the question 'Do you write it all up then?'

'Yes, I tend to spend about as long writing as I do in the field.' I stress how arduous this is and that my tutor wants to see all my field notes which means that they've got to be good to keep him happy.

Then I talk about the analysis and say, 'Perhaps I'll break them down into just incident types or, it may be more interesting, say, to develop collections of "hostility", "resistance" etc., regardless of what the incidents are. In this way one can start to see the patterns which are emerging.'

Such accounts are not untrue, but they are veiled. They construct the research role so as to make it understandable and acceptable to the researched. When pressed, the veil becomes more transparent. For instance, early on in the research a young sergeant joined the table in the canteen where I was having dinner.

. . . I felt that I was being interrogated and set up to make a wrong footing so I could be felled — which nearly happened with the next question.

'What are you going to do if, in your opinion, you see the excessive use of force?'

'Well, I'll cross that bridge when I come to it but I'd be interested in explaining why it happened.'

At this point Mark came in, 'You were at the pub fight the other night — and a couple of people got hit — did you think that was an excessive use of force?'

I could have done without this side quip (I did think the use of force had been excessive). Rather than answer directly, I talked about how gory it had been when we had first arrived and said that one of the things that struck me was how arbitrary the arrests had been. 'If you gave a bit of lip you were liable to be nicked and roughly handled.' At this point, much to my relief, the sergeant got called away and the conversation broke off.

This was how I explained the nature of my research to the officers with whom I had to work closely. I would also constantly reiterate that nothing I saw or heard would be reported back to senior officers or colleagues, and that I granted everyone anonymity. In addition to this, I tried to give officers a chance to refuse working with me. For example, when I first introduced myself to the reliefs I would state publicly: 'If any officer does not want me to accompany them that's fine. They just have to say. I don't want to accompany anybody who doesn't want me along and if you want me to stay out of a particular incident just say.' Oddly, this last issue was never a problem. Perhaps they all thought like one of my informants, who stated: 'As far as I'm concerned, when you're with me you can come to anything. I suppose I think, if he's prepared to come to —— then it's up to him.

The first issue was, however, more problematic. When sergeants assigned me to specific officers it was difficult to know whether having me along constituted an order. This was particularly the case with probationers, who may have felt that to raise an objection to my presence would put them in a bad light with their sergeants or inspectors. But, as the study progressed, this became much less of an issue. People would ask me if I wanted to ride with them and, if I was in the canteen when a good call came out, would often come and find me to see if I wanted to attend.

If the principle of informed consent was fudged in terms of the police, it was completely disregarded for the public. I made no attempt to seek the permission of the public with whom I daily came into contact in my role as a researcher. This was a purely pragmatic decision. When I arrived at the scene of a fight, for instance, suddenly to declare to all those present that I was a researcher would have been impossible. However, such incidents are the exception rather than the rule, and in many routine stops, domestic disputes, and the like it would have been possible to state the purpose of my presence. Nevertheless, I decided that to do so would be to create problems of 'observer effect'. I thought that people might play up to the presence of the researcher or, worse still, might try and get me to act as a witness and give testimony against officers in cases of possible wrongdoing. If this did happen I would be breaking the promise of anonymity which I had given to the officers whom I accompanied. As a rule, I remained silent about my role and let people assume what they wanted.

However, although I did not declare the nature of my role, occasionally this was done by police officers. Often they would ask me on our first meeting how I would like to be introduced, and I would reply with my stock formula: 'It's very much up to you. If you want to say: "This is Mr Norris from the University of Surrey engaged in a research project", that's fine. But, if it's a bit tricky the last thing you want is for someone to start playing up to me so I'll leave it up to you.' In consequence, I have been introduced as Special Branch, CID, the Investigating Officer, Plain Clothes, or simply as a colleague. However, in most situations I was not introduced at all. In general, the more relaxed and friendly a situation, the more likely it was that I would be introduced as a researcher, whereas in more hostile or tricky ones I might be introduced as a police officer.

Privacy

The foregoing raises a number of issues other than those relating to informed consent. As Bulmer has written: 'To insinuate oneself into a particular setting on false pretences in order to gather material for research violates the rights of the individual to be let alone, to control his personal space, and information about himself' (1982, p. 219).

Both by default and design, the public often believed or were led to believe that I was a police officer. Under such pretences, I entered their houses and witnessed the most private of scenes: a husband-and-wife quarrel; a woman reporting she had just been raped; or an attempted suicide victim, semi-conscious and covered with blood. And, in spite of the fact that they were providing core data for my thesis, they were not granted the right to control information about themselves.

Furthermore, this invasion of privacy extended from the public to the police. Although the police were aware of my research in the terms that I had constructed for them, I became party to private information about people's domestic lives, their marital problems, their divorces, and so forth. Although much of this information was never recorded, occasionally it provided useful insights into the nature of the job and the constraints of being a police officer.

Deceit and Trust

The practice of participant observation is, inevitably, interactionally deceitful. Researchers have to cultivate informants and lessen the distance between themselves and those they are studying. In this sense, one's aims are to make the research role invisible in the field and to emphasize similarity at the expense of difference. For instance, I would dress in the in-house CID style: grey flannels, blue blazer, white shirt, and formal tie. In this way, officers who did not know of my research role often took me for another CID officer. But this deception would move from the accoutrements of my projected image to areas nearer to self, especially language. As I became familiar with the police argot, I would use police talk to indicate a sense of shared perspective. For example, after I had just started work in a different station for purposes of comparison:

Other PCs had joined the table and gradually the conversation turned into a joint interview — the whole relief interviewing me.

'Has your opinion changed since you've been doing this job? You've been in —— you must have seen a lot there.'

'Yeah, I used to think that you were a bunch of fascist pigs!', I quipped light heartedly.

'We are', he replied with a smile.

'Oh I know that — you know the only time I'd ever come into contact with the police before starting this was being stopped on the way home, late at night. I thought you were a pain but nothing else really. I used to think, probably from watching too many American Cop shows, that it was all crime stuff. But it's not like that, is it? You know, all the "rubbish", "domestics", "process" — that changed my opinion.'

'Do you see our side now, see us as people? What do you say when people ask you what you think of us?'

'I tell them about the work, what it's like—you know, you go into a situation with bottles flying — a pub fight. It's rough and tough in somewhere like ——. Perhaps the police go in a bit strong but then, I think, what would I do? If you've got to deal with it quickly you just get people out and ask questions later.'

This sort of question and answer game went on for about twenty minutes.

'Has this changed you? I was listening to you and you sound just like a policeman, using all the words', intervened one of the older PCs.

'Yeah, my friends say that, "You're getting more and more like a policeman every day" — I've got more cynical.'

This strategy certainly seemed to pay off. Generally, my face is now known and, in specific terms, as I walked into the front office later that evening, a PC came up to me immediately and said, 'If Andy's not going out for a bit why don't you come and see how the front desk works?' Two nights later, I was invited to a goodbye drink for one of the officers who was leaving the relief. It was held in the station, at 4 a.m., when everyone should have been on duty.

As Punch has rightly questioned (1986, p. 72): 'if the latent aim of the field worker is to create trust then what is the aim of that trust?' The concept of trust implies mutuality of interest and an equality of dependency. To a major degree, this is inherently absent in the field-worker role and, therefore, has to be manufactured. In the police setting this is even more apparent since, as many commentators have noted, police officers are very reluctant to share information with each other, let alone outsiders (Ericson 1982; Chibnal 1977; Bittner 1970; Rubinstein 1973; Manning 1977 and 1980).

However, the manufacture of trust requires getting one's hands dirty, since it is not something that can be promised with declarations of confidentiality and anonymity. These are distant and far-off concepts. Trust in the police world is more commonplace and mundane. Trust is about keeping your mouth shut when others are being called to account. It is about not letting slip in front of senior officers that you were not where you were supposed to be. Trust is an action, often marked by absence rather than presence. As such, it involves 'not doing' rather than 'doing'. It is gained and earned, shown in the day-to-day realities of the police world and, as such, it cannot be promised. It has to be displayed and, only after it has been seen to exist, will it be assumed. Until then, all promises are empty.

None the less, there were times when the dependence was mutual and such mutuality created a bond of personal friendship and loyalty which did not fit easily into the general notions of professional ethics.

An officer asked me to indicate to him when the road was clear so he could pull out onto a particularly busy road. I made a mistake and the consequence was that the police van collided with an oncoming car. Thankfully, the driver was well disposed to the police and unconcerned with the damage to his company car which, although quite serious, was hardly noticeable. The matter was effectively forgotten. However, in so doing, the officer was guilty of committing two offences: failure to report damage to a police vehicle and, more importantly, failure to report an accident. Had he reported the accident, I would have felt obliged to have taken a major proportion of the blame which would have, undoubtedly, threatened my continuing research role. By staying silent, he was protecting me and laying himself open to more serious charges.

Like police-work, field-work is not a polite occupation. I promised people anonymity, put officers at their ease with all the interactional devices at my command, and let them know that I understood that police-work was not always performed according to the rules and that I wanted to see how it was really done. In both word and deed, I indicated that I could be trusted not to report back misconduct that I witnessed to senior officers or to their peers. Having done all this, I undoubtedly got what I deserved—a case of 'I've made my own bed, now I've got to lie on it'.

The Dilemma

In the following extract I illustrate some of the possible consequences and dilemmas a researcher may face once intimate access has been obtained. Two brothers have just been arrested for being drunk and disorderly. They have been brought to the station and are about to be charged.

All of a sudden, Brown, one of the brothers, leaps from the bench at the station sergeant. (Why, I do not know). He is thrashing and flailing, kicking and scratching. He is felled onto the desk and the five or six officers in the charge room rush to hold him. Hearing the fracas, other officers rush in from the front office to lend a hand. They join the mêlée despite the five officers already holding him. The man is still thrashing violently. One officer has Brown's arm pushed up behind his back, other officers are holding his legs and his middle. He is pinned to the table. Gary is holding his face and, with the palm of his hand, hitting the side of his jaw. 'Let's get him in a cell.' Someone rushes and opens the cell door. Brown is picked up and carried by the officers to the cell and thrown in. The door is hurriedly slammed shut.

The other man, Blondie, has now started to go berserk. (I have missed this because I was watching the other scene.) Several officers are restraining him. He is screaming and shouting. He is surrounded, picked up, and thrown into another cell. John and Gary follow him in. There are six or seven officers around the door. Sounds of a beating, screaming and swearing emanate from the cell.

The other prisoner has started to thump his cell door. The cacophony of screams, blows, swearing and pounding is electrifying. The other officers are trying to get into Blondie's cell but keep pulling back. The inspector is at the door. 'Gary,' he orders sharply, 'take it easy.' But the sounds of the beating continue. 'Gary! Take it easy', he commands again. John drags Gary out of the cell. The door is slammed shut. John's shirt and hands are covered in blood.

From inside the cell, the screams are getting louder. They are ignored as the ten or so officers in the charge-room try to recover their composure. The inspector turns to Gary, 'This is going down as more than a D.D.' (Drunk and Disorderly).

LATER: In the canteen someone starts to recount the night's events to Dave and Mel who missed it all. John walks in, his shirt still covered in blood. 'Fucking Hell, I want words with that Smith (Gary). That was over the top!' He slumps down angrily in the chair.

Gary walks in. John follows him with his eyes for a moment. 'Can't you keep your fucking temper . . . Didn't you hear the Guv'nor calling you off?' Gary laughs it off. Everyone gets on with eating. More stories are swapped and the night's events are turned into amusements.

About twenty minutes pass and then John and Gary are ordered downstairs by the guv'nor. When they come back they are clutching some incident forms. Roger starts to sing the theme tune of a popular children's

TV programme — *Jackanory* (Jackanory tell a story). He is told to shut up. Peter, John, and Gary go off with their incident forms to the collator's office so they can get their story straight in peace and quiet.

STILL LATER: Back in the canteen Dave, Gary, John, and Peter are sitting down drinking tea. The phone rings. John and Gary are ordered downstairs again. When they come back, it appears that the doctor has seen the prisoners. One has a 'suspected fractured jaw', the other has 'suspected broken ribs'. They are to be taken down to the hospital. The guv'nor wants a better cover story. Mindful of my presence, Peter and Gary go outside. They come back in and everyone attentively waits for the conclusion. Someone is going to have to bear the evidence of an 'Assault on an Officer'. John and Gary are the candidates. The problem is which of them shall it be. Gary says it should be him, but fair play dictates that they toss for it. John loses. Peter, Gary, John, and Jock go outside again. There is the sound of scuffling and laughter. They re-enter—John's 'bottled out'. Peter and Jock are laughing. Peter turns to Jock: 'You'd have jumped on his fucking head.' Jock gives a wicked smile: 'That's right!'

'I'll do it if you don't want to volunteer', Gary says again.

'No,' John is adamant. 'But look', he says, playing to the gallery in an exaggerated hero role, 'I've just bought my house. I'm already going into hospital next week and I don't want to land there tonight. What would my wife say?'

EVEN LATER STILL: John has been hit below the eye. A bruise is starting to come out.

For me, this incident posed, in very explicit terms, a serious dilemma. To what extent did my duty as a citizen override my duty as a researcher? Here he had an individual who had been the recipient of the gross misuse of force and, rather than being compensated for such, was liable to bear the brunt of his own misfortune by having false charges laid against him. True, he was not blameless. However, if it should reach court, he would be liable to receive a heavier penalty and perhaps go to prison on the basis of false evidence.

Discussion

Before embarking upon a detailed analysis of this incident it is necessary to consider in more depth the different responses to the debate on the ethics of field-work practice. There are three broad positions discernable from the literature, the legalistic, the antinomian, and the situational.

The legalists, at one extreme, argue for the adherence to a professional code of conduct (BSA, 1982; ASA 1971; Bulmer 1982) as a solution to the problem of ethical decision-making. Primacy is given to the doctrine of informed consent, respect for privacy, ensuring anonymity and confidentiality, and open and non-deceitful forms of research. Field-work methods in general, and covert observational research in particular, are placed under the microscope, dissected, and then discarded as distasteful.

At the other extreme, the antinomians (Douglas 1976; 1979) or conflict methodologists, as Punch has termed them (Punch 1986), reject all such strictures. The pursuit of knowledge, they argue, is an end in itself and must not be hampered by ethical codes and restrictions which, for the main part, have been erected by the powerful to protect themselves rather than the weak (Douglas 1979).

Between these polarized positions there are an increasing number of accounts from practising field-workers which stress the complexity of ethical decisions faced by the researcher (see Punch 1986; Holdaway 1983; Fielding 1982; Van Maanen 1978). Collectively, these researchers have opted for a situational view of ethics. Following Fletcher, they argue that 'the situationalist enters into every decision making situation fully armed with the ethical maxims of his community and its heritage and treats them with respect as illuminators of his problem. Just the same as he is prepared in any situation to compromise them or set them aside in the situation . . .' (1966, p. 17).

As I have argued, field-work methods, whether covert or overt, can, and do, lead the researcher into a quagmire of ethical considerations. Inevitably, one is faced with contradictory and competing choices and it is impossible to satisfy them all. The legalist position ignores the complexity of the construction of a research role. It tries to substitute the inevitable ambiguity of the ethnographic research enterprise with codes and inviolable rules enshrined in a professional code of ethics, strict adherence to which would have made my own research and most ethnographic field-work impossible.

On the other hand, the antinomians, by rejecting any consideration of ethics in favour of the simplistic notion of 'whose side are we on', reduce any dilemmas to a crude value position—the exposure of the powerful. However, they do not tell us whether it is permissible, in this pursuit, to sacrifice the interests of some of the powerless in order to expose the powerful, or what to do when there is a conflict between the two or between long- and short-term goals. Since these questions are inevitably raised in the process of ethnographic research, particularly that which tries to expose the practices of powerful groups, they are merely avoiding the issue.

In contrast to the legalists and antinomians, the situationalists acknowledge the reality of ethnographic research. Each situation *is* different; individual conscience *does* have its own parameters and field-workers ultimately have to make their own decisions. For Punch, one of the principle mechanisms for guiding such decision-making is through academic convention and peer control. However, as we have seen there is no academic consensus as to the correct response to such issues, and the reality of doctoral field-work is that, more often than not, it is carried out by lone graduates distanced from their supervisors and unlikely to be integrated into an academic community.

This problem is highlighted in relation to the above incident. The literature, as I have already noted, offered little advice. If the literature was not much help, neither were my professional colleagues (in whom Punch places so much faith). In the months that followed, I discussed this incident with over half-a-dozen senior British and American police researchers (to whom I grant the same anonymity as to my research subjects). I received the following advice. I should:

- have immediately reported the action to a higher-ranking authority;
- have lodged an official complaint;
- have done nothing but, if called to a disciplinary hearing, lie on behalf of my police contacts and therefore establish greater legitimacy in their eyes;
- refrain from publishing such material as it is 'unhelpful';
- have reminded all those involved in the incident that a researcher was present and thus allowed them the chance to alter their behaviour in that light.

Although I have my quibbles with these responses, each one has some merit. However, this advice was given with the benefit of hindsight and from the luxury of not being personally compromised.

Furthermore, it is clearly contradictory and this seems to encapsulate the dilemma—if I satisfied one ethical maxim, I was guilty of abandoning another. In retrospect it seems to me that there were six courses of action available to me. I could:

- unofficially report their actions to a senior officer;
- officially lodge a complaint;
- go for the expose mode, publishing quickly and damningly;
- abandon the study;
- neither write up nor publish the data;
- write it up and use the data like any other—in other words, publish normally.

However each of these has to be weighed against a number of ethical considerations:

- does it undermine the principle of informed consent?
- does it cause direct harm to the research subjects?
- does it break the promise of anonymity?
- does it involve manipulating the data?
- does it potentially spoil the field for other researchers?
- does it necessitate having to leave the field and therefore abandon the study?

The first three options, to complain either unofficially or officially about the action or to publish quicky or damningly are all versions of the 'expose mode'. Clearly they all undermine the principle of informed consent, the promise of anonymity, and cause harm to the officers to whom one has granted such guarantees. To use information for the purpose of instigating disciplinary procedures would breach the principle of informed consent, since the basis of the research bargain was that information would only be used for research purposes. Further, anonymity had been guaranteed and therefore to disclose information on named individuals would also breach the bargain. To disclose such information would also lay me open to the charge of deception, since I had insinuated myself as trustworthy and used presentational and interactional strategies to bolster such an image.

There are other considerations, which have less to do with one's responsibilities to those researched than with the academic community to which, however marginally, one belongs. One obligation to this community is that one should publish one's findings honestly and truthfully, and not manipulate the data to serve other ends. Nor should one 'spoil the field' so that other researchers are denied access. Finally, where the research is being supported by funds from a grant-awarding body such as the ESRC, there is an obligation that such funding should result in a tangible end-product, in my case a doctoral thesis. To report the actions or to publish them in the expose mode, may not have laid me open to charges of manipulating the data, but would have spoilt the field, since future researchers would be viewed, quite correctly, as untrustworthy. Finally, to adopt the expose mode would undoubtedly, have put an end to the research and, given that only about half the envisaged field-work had been undertaken, would probably have resulted in my having to abandon the study.

The fourth and fifth options, of abandoning the study or continuing the study but not using the material, would stay true to the research bargaining negotiated with individual police officers, since they do not breach the promise of informed consent or anonymity. But abandoning the study would have meant letting down my sponsors and would have undermined my own career-prospects which were dependent on obtaining a Ph.D. Of course, I could have refrained from writing up or using the material in any way. This would not have endangered the continuation of the research but would have meant that I was guilty of manipulating the data.

The final option, and the one which I favour, is to treat the data like any other and publish normally. It does not break any of the promises implied in the research bargain, the principles of anonymity and informed consent are adhered to, the research subjects are not harmed, it does not require tampering with the data, and does not require leaving or spoiling the field. It does, however, mean that a person who was subject to police brutality has no redress and may even suffer a criminal conviction and possible prison sentence on the basis of false statements made by the officers. Therefore, I could be accused of knowingly conniving with officers to pervert the course of justice. I think there are three responses to this position.

First, I had no ongoing relationship with the public who had, unwittingly perhaps, become part of my research project. In contrast, the relationship with the police officers with whom I worked was built on the promise of confidentiality, anonymity, and the display of trust. In short, members of the public were not involved in a research bargain. They were not promised anything and therefore no trust could be broken except that of some abstract principle of 'public duty'.

This leads directly to the second issue. What is the 'public duty' of the researcher? To my mind, the aim of sociological research should be to uncover structural regularities. By adopting the 'expose' option of either informing disciplinary authorities or publishing damningly and naming names, the episode could be written off as another case of 'rotten apples'. In other words, it could be dismissed as individual deviance rather than structurally located within the police organization. It is only by staying in the field and witnessing a number of similar events that generalizations can be made and structural causes addressed. Thus, if one believes that police brutality is not the result of pathological individuals but is structurally enabled by the nature of the police organization, then exposing a few individuals will make little difference and may, indeed, perpetuate brutality. It is, therefore, necessary to demonstrate the ways in which the problem is bound up with the organizational structure in order to effect policies that may ameliorate the problem.

The third response relates back to the promises of anonymity, confidentiality, and informed consent. In view of the fact that the sociological literature on policing includes well-documented cases of police deviance and some documentation of excessive use of force, if I had not contemplated having to face such an issue I would, indeed, have been naïve. Given that I had expected to encounter police deviance but had, none the less, still made promises of anonymity and been sensitive to the issue of informed consent, then I had no right to change my mind when confronted with such behaviour. To do so would be to abandon sociology for either a moral crusade or cheque-book journalism.

I have considered, from the benefit of hindsight and the retrospective comfort of my armchair, what I believe to be the consequences and dilemmas of my field-work role. I have done so in the belief that moral sensitivity and maturity can only occur through debate, dialogue, and reflection. Therefore, the important issue is to encourage field-workers to become more aware and sensitive to the moral and ethical dimensions of their enterprise. Of course, we may never be able to agree on what constitutes the right decision in a particular case. However, we can insist that researchers consider the consequences of their actions and are publicly prepared to defend their own choice. Hopefully, such reflection will lead to a more honest and relevant debate about field-work practice. There is, of course, a danger that such armchair moralizing merely provides an over-rationalistic gloss on what was a confused, ambivalent, and arbitrary decision. I therefore give the last word to my field-notes, written up the day after the incident.

I was apprehensive about going in tonight. Last night's events have left me confused and a little paranoid. Fear, violence, emotion, disgust have all mingled . . . When the two prisoners went berserk I felt the rush of adrenalin, smelt fear and then anger and sensed the inevitability of the events that followed. I felt frightened by the thought that I had witnessed what I should not have seen. Would I be called to account? What would I say? Would I now be frozen out as being potentially too dangerous to have around any more? How much did they think I could be relied on not to spill the beans? — Whose side was I on?

Such thoughts went through my mind as I boarded my bus. — Was it wise to go in at all? In fact, I let two buses go past. But I had decided that the most important thing was to be seen, to be part of the process, to be in view, to be one of them, to be normal and to go to work and carry on as though nothing had happened. If such a ploy were successful then, hopefully, it would facilitate an even greater depth to my access. I would have demonstrated that I could be trusted.

References

American Sociological Association (1971). *Code of Ethics*.

Banton, M. (1964). *The Policeman in the Community* (London: Tavistock).

Becker, H. (1963). *Outsiders* (New York: Free Press).

—— (1970). *Sociological Work* (Chicago: Aldine).

Bittner, E. (1970). *The Function of the Police in Modern Society* (Cherry Close, Md.: National Institute of Mental Health).

British Sociological Association (1982). *Statement of Ethical Principles and their Application to Sociological Research* (London: BSA, Mimeo).

Bronfenbrenner, U. (1952). 'Principles of Professional Ethics: Cornell Studies in Social Growth', 7 (8) *American Psychologist*, 452–5.

Bulmer, M. (1982). (ed.). *Social Research Ethics* (London: Macmillan).

Cain, M. (1971). 'On the Beat', in S. Cohen (ed.), *Images of Deviance* (London: Tavistock).

—— (1979). 'Trends in the Sociology of Police Work', 7 (2) *International Journal of the Sociology of Law*.

Chatterton, M. R. (1978). 'From Participant to Observer', 25 (6) *Sociologische Gids*, 502–16.

Chibnal, S. (1977). *Law-and-Order News: An Analysis of Crime Reporting in the British Press* (London: Tavistock).

Clarke, M. (1990). *Business Crime: Its Nature and Control* (Cambridge: Polity Press).

Ditton, J. (1977). *Part-time Crime: An Ethnography of Fiddling and Pilferage* (London: Macmillan).

Douglas, J. D. (1976). (ed.). *Investigative Social Research* (Beverly Hills, Calif.: Sage).

—— (1979). 'Living Morality versus Bureaucratic Fiat', in C. B. Klockars and F. W. O'Connor (eds.), *Deviance and Decency* (Beverly Hills, Calif.: Sage), 13–33.

Ericson, R. V. (1981). *Making Crime: A Study of Detective Work* (Toronto/Vancouver: Butterworth).

—— (1982). *Reproducing Order: A Study of Police Patrol Work* (Toronto: University of Toronto Press).

Fielding, N. (1982). 'Observational Research on the National Front' (in Bulmer 1982), 80–104.

Fletcher, J. (1966). *Situation Ethics* (London: SCM Press).

Gold, R. (1958). 'Roles in Sociological Field Observation', 36 (3) *Social Forces*, 217–23.

Holdaway, S. (1983). *Inside the British Police* (Oxford: Basil Blackwell).

Humphreys, L. (1970). *Tea Room Trade* (Chicago, Ill.: Aldine).

Klockars, C. B. (1975). *The Professional Fence* (London: Tavistock).

—— (1979). 'Dirty Hands and Deviant Subjects', in C. B. Klockars and F. W. O'Connor (eds.) *Deviance and Decency* (Beverly Hills, Calif.: Sage).

Manning, P. K. (1977). *Police Work* (Cambridge, Mass.: MIT Press).

—— (1980). *The Narcs' Game* (Cambridge, Mass.: MIT Press).

—— and Van Maanen, J. (1978). (eds.). *Policing: A View From the Street* (Santa Monica, Calif.: Goodyear).

Mars, G. (1982). *Cheats at Work* (London: Allen and Unwin).

Patrick, J. (1973). *A Glasgow Gang Observed* (London: Eyre Methuen).

Punch, M. (1979). *Policing the Inner City* (London: Macmillan).

—— (1985). *Conduct Unbecoming* (London: Tavistock).

—— (1986). *The Politics and Ethics of Fieldwork* (Beverly Hills, Calif.: Sage).

—— (1989). 'Researching Police Deviance: A Personal Encounter with the Limitations and Liabilities of Field Work', 40 (2) *British Journal of Sociology*.

Rainwater, L. and Pittman (1967). 'Ethical Problems in Studying a Politically Sensitive and Deviant Community', 14 *Social Problems*, 357–66.

Reuss-Ianni, E. (1983). *Two Cultures of Policing* (New Brunswick, NJ: Transaction Books).

Rubinstein, J. (1973). *City Police* (New York: Ballantine).

Shearing, C. D. (1981) (ed.). *Organisational Police Deviance: Its Structure and Control*, Toronto: Butterworth.

Skolnick, J. (1966). *Justice Without Trial* (New York: Wiley).

Smith, D. and J. Gray (1983). *Police and People in London*, vol. IV, *The Police in Action* (London: Policy Studies Institute).

Van Maanen, J. (1974). 'Working the Street', in H. Jacob, (ed.), *Annual Review of Criminal Justice*, Vol. 3, *The Potential for Reform* (Beverly Hills, Calif.: Sage).

—— (1978). 'On Watching the Watchers' (in Manning and Van Maanen 1978), 309–49.

—— (1981). 'The Informant Game', 9 (4) *Urban Life*, 469–94.

Westley, W. (1970). *Violence and the Police* (Cambridge, Mass.: MIT Press).

6

Dealing with Data

JANE FOUNTAIN*

This chapter will discuss the strategies I devised to collect and analyse data whilst attempting to relate to the orthodoxy of research methodology texts. The study—my Ph.D. thesis—was of the social and economic organization of a network of sixty-four cannabis dealers, whose operations ranged from selling several pounds of the drug a week for a profit to passing on one-sixteenth of an ounce to a friend occasionally, as a favour. I identified five levels of distribution: wholesaler, middleperson, retailer, and regular and occasional supplier.

It is surprising that there is little information available about the contemporary cannabis scene in Britain, given the drug's estimated one million users per years (ISDD 1990, p. 10), and the cost to the criminal-justice system of, in 1988 for instance, processing 26,111 individuals who were found guilty of offences involving it (Home Office 1989, Table 1.1). Sociologists might reasonably be expected to have taken advantage of such a massive example of deviant behaviour, but this has not been the case, with the result that the existing knowledge about cannabis users and dealers is dependent on outdated, theoretical, and anecdotal information. In the absence of more recent work, Becker (1963) and Young (1971) are too often regarded by social scientists as having provided the classic descriptions of an unchanged situation, yet since their studies, cannabis has gained a relative respectability as other illegal drugs became the focus of moral panics.

The behaviour of the dealers was described and analysed using combinations of explanations offered for it by the interactionist concepts of labelling, deviancy amplification, and the deviant career; subcultural theory; control theory; anomie-based theories; and by the dealers themselves. The research methodology illustrates the

* Jane Fountain is a writer and researcher working in London.

integration between what Jupp (1989, p. 178) calls the 'warring and intransigent fortresses' of the various theories of deviance, and also between theory and research methods, as the interactionist perspective also provided a major contribution to the methodology of the study: as Downes and Rock (1988, p. 186) say, interactionism is 'hesitant about planning and exposition, arguing that such work blinds one to the possibility of learning in the field . . . Interactionists would preserve their openness to the social world, being educated as they pursue research.'

Access

Getting In

As a working-class, tabloid-reading, politically right-wing, full-time housewife and mother from a small town, I had never seen an illegal drug, and had learnt to consider that people who used them were 'weirdos', 'hippies', and 'drop-outs'. I was 30 years old before I actually saw people smoking cannabis, and was very surprised that the stereotypes could not be applied to them. I shed my naïvety and ceased to be shocked when joints were passed round with the same nonchalance that I passed round my home-made cakes. Then I moved to a city, got a job in further education teaching unemployed teenagers, and began to lead an increasingly middle-class, left-wing, life-style. When I was 36 I abandoned teaching to become a sociology undergraduate. *En route*, I met more cannabis users, very few of whom were weird, hippies, or had dropped out.

I met Chris and Sally at the home of a mutual friend, and soon discovered they were cannabis retailers. Initially, the 'evil pusher' image dominated my perceptions of them, but the more I got to know them, the more their deviations from it became apparent. Our friendship developed, and in the following two years I met some of their customers and other dealers. I had just completed a sociology degree and, still in academic mode, began to wonder whether there was potential in these contacts for a study of cannabis dealers, with the couple as my gatekeepers. I formulated a vague plan for this and asked them what they thought. They agreed to co-operate, and from the beginning were familiar with my aims and what I intended to do with the data.

I sat in Chris and Sally's house, where they did most of their trading, and observed the comings and goings of their contacts, asking questions, with their help, when we judged it appropriate; I accompanied the couple when they visited the dealers they bought from; I ate with them; I made good use of their spare bedroom; and joined them on many social occasions, too. My involvement in their lives led to varying degrees of contact with sixty-two other cannabis dealers at several distribution levels, and about seventy of the couple's non-dealing customers.

As I was not deceiving my gatekeepers about what I was researching and why, and particularly as they were both familiar with 'warts and all' sociological investigations, many of the problems of gatekeepers' control over access, chronicled by Hammersley and Atkinson (1983, pp. 63–76) were overcome. For example, the authors give illustrations of gatekeepers who wanted researchers present only when there was something 'normal' happening. However, dealers cannot predict when there will be run-of-the-mill buying and selling of cannabis and when something extraordinary will occur. Similarly unpredictable are what Hammersley and Atkinson call 'troublesome' and 'sensitive things', away from which the gatekeepers may wish to steer the researcher but in which the researcher may be most interested. If I happened to be with my gatekeepers when there was an extraordinary, troublesome, or sensitive incident, my friendship with them, and the lack of deception, meant that I was not steered away and, once I had shared such an experience with them, the gate was left open for further sharing. To illustrate: I was at Chris and Sally's one evening when it appeared that business was going to be slow, and we were discussing whether or not to go out for a drink. Chris said that before we did he would make a quick phone-call to Brian, a dealer who had been collecting fresh supplies for the couple. Brian's flatmate answered the phone, and told Chris that Brian had been arrested. Therefore I was present as the couple panicked and discussed what do do, was with them while they did it, and was party to their discussions in the following weeks about how to minimize the risk of their own arrests.

Access to the rest of the network of dealers of which Chris and Sally were part was unproblematic: my gatekeepers made sure that I met every individual they did business with. I did not experience the problems Hammersley and Atkinson (pp. 78–88) discuss concerning 'blending in', because in the dealing world, if someone brings a friend along then their presence is unquestioned, as the newcomer is presumed to have been vetted before their introduction to the dealer. As Adler (1985, p. 14) comments when two marijuana smugglers wrongly assumed she and her husband knew that their friend Dave was also a smuggler: 'They thought that anybody as close to Dave as we seemed to be undoubtedly knew the nature of his business.'

Getting Along

Many studies have involved field relations which go beyond a formal researcher–gatekeeper association: Klockars (1974, pp. 219–20), for instance, says of his relationship with his principal informant on fencing: 'I came to like Vincent and he knew it. As time went on we became good friends.' In a study closely comparable to my own in terms of field relations and subject-matter, Adler discusses the friend–researcher–gatekeeper relationship (1985, pp. 11–28), believing that access to a group with something to hide (in her study, marijuana and cocaine traffickers) must of necessity be based on friendship. That basis enabled Adler 'to trade my friendship for their knowledge' (p. 27), and she gave her gatekeepers practical, as well as moral, support.

Polsky (1967) lays down often-quoted firm guide-lines for avoiding the moral, legal, and research dilemmas which he sees arising from such relationships, but in the field I found it difficult to 'draw the line' he advocates between myself and those I was studying. Consequently, one drawback of my relationship with Chris and Sally, and with other dealers I came to know well and like, was that I had to be constantly on my guard against ignoring or excusing aspects of my friends' behaviour that I considered immoral. Conversely, I met some dealers I did not like, and had to be on my guard again interpreting their behaviour in a negative way.

Warning of the dire effects of over-identification with the group being studied abound in the literature on participant observation, with the researcher exhorted to blend in with the setting to see things the way 'the natives' do, but not so much so as to lose their objectivity as an investigative outsider. In treading this fine line, researchers can deliberately employ empathy or an 'appreciative stance' when negotiating access to a group with which they have previously had little or no contact. This tactic, however, does not completely insulate them from their subjects: Fielding (1982, p. 90) found that the growth of his relationship with his primary contact in the 'unlovable' National Front 'caused me much reflection on the subject of my own politics and friendships'. I did not have the luxury of being able to consider how much empathy towards dealers and dealing I should display, because when I began the study I had been involved in Chris and Sally's lives for two years, and through them had got to know many other dealers. Some researchers are even closer to their field: Hobbs (1988, p. 7), for instance, used his status as an East Ender to give an insider account of the trading culture there, and says: 'Because of my background, I found nothing immoral or even unusual in the dealing and trading that I encountered.'

Sharrock and Anderson (1980, p. 22) have a solution to the problems of ethnographers' field-work practices, problems which they say stem from the 'illusory dilemma' of concentration on the separation of the worlds of the researcher and those being researched, where researchers begin with the premiss that their subjects' world is inaccessible to outsiders, but that members themselves are able to explain it. They propose a shift in focus which can be applied to my relationship with those dealers who knew the nature of the study and were my key informants: to treat the subject 'as regarding his [*sic*] own actions as objects of investigation by both himself and the researcher'. In this way, researchers and their subjects 'co-produce' the field-work: both have to discover what is going on and the meaning of events and activities they do not share. To approach dealers as a culture which had nothing in common with my own would not, I feel, have led to as full an explanation of their world as co-production of data did.

However, as I was attempting to 'co-produce' data with those dealers with whom I was most friendly, it was often difficult to distinguish between the 'friend' and 'respondent' roles in each of them, and the 'friend' and 'researcher' roles in myself, particularly as dealing is often a sociable activity. I envied, for example, Klatch (1988) at her Moral Majority conference and Van Maanen (1982) with his police officers, as they had constant reminders (respectively items on the agenda and a uniform) that, although they might be adopting a participant role (and in Van Maanen's case this included training as an officer and wearing the uniform), the field was clearly labelled as such. Sitting cosily watching television with Chris and Sally and another dealer who was a good friend of theirs, or spending the weekend camping with the couple and Brian at the Glastonbury

Festival, where they sold cannabis for only a few hours a day, was hardly conducive to role-differentiation, although an aid to it was one which Van Maanen (p. 145) pinpoints: I did not have to live with the consequence of their actions as my informants did.

Gatekeeper Influence

Because I was not a novice in the setting, I could not employ any of the criteria for choosing my informants, as suggested by, for instance, Tremblay (1957), Dean *et al.* (1967), and Burgess (1982, p. 77), who warns that 'the "best" informants may be marginal to the setting under study'. However, it did not seem sensible, given my friendship with Chris and Sally and their willingness to help, to leave them in search of 'better' gatekeepers, so I deliberately made them the centre of the setting—the contacts all the other dealers in the study shared. Thus, as Liebow (1967) acknowledges Tally's influence on his study of the street-corner, I must also acknowledge that my gatekeepers were central to the account of the network I studied. Any other member could have been my gatekeeper to a different branch of it: in the extreme case, if the first co-operative dealer I had met had been an unemployed Hell's Angel, living in a squat, then I would probably have been researching a different group of people within a different culture, for as Blum *et al.* (1972, p. 155) discovered in their study of drug dealers, there is a 'strong tendency' for them to sell to those 'close to them in socioeconomic or life-style conditions'.

My gatekeepers influenced my methodology and the ethical consideration of how much I revealed to any individual (which I discuss in more detail later). Chris, Sally, and I debated whether I should reveal the reason for my presence to some of the people I was deceiving, but we decided to err on the side of caution. If dealers objected to being researched, then they might refuse to do business with the couple, or insist that I was not present. If I carried on the deception, then at least I had a chance of getting *some* data. A further influence on my methodology was that the almost constant presence of Chris and/or Sally during the data-gathering period meant that certain things I wanted to know could never be asked directly. For instance, if I wanted to know how much profit a wholesaler made when selling to retailers, it was unlikely they would tell me in front of the very people from whom they were making the profit. Such data had to be obtained by waiting for snippets of information to come up of their own accord and piecing them together with the aid of a calculator.

In time, I came to regard Chris and Sally as my research assistants rather than as my gatekeepers, for during my periods in the field we were collaborators, like Whyte (1955) and the famous Doc.

Researcher Influence

I influenced what happened in the field, too—sometimes deliberately. For example, if my gatekeepers had little contact with a particular dealer, I would encourage the couple to contact them in order for me to meet the person. However, once we were in the presence of that dealer, I do not believe my influence on the subsequent behaviour was any more (or less) than that of any researcher employing what Adler (1985, p. 27) aptly calls the 'delicate combination of overt and covert roles', and which is discussed thoroughly in the many texts on participant observation (such as Burgess 1982; Hammersley and Atkinson 1983; Lofland and Lofland 1984).

I also made some dealers more aware of aspects of dealing they had only vaguely considered previously. When I monitored the time Chris and Sally spent with customers and the profit they made from each deal, for instance, Chris commented that he had never given much thought to the amount of time spent on a transaction and the surrounding cultural niceties. He also became obsessed with the daily profits, constantly asking me the amount and how it compared with that of previous days. If he thought profits were declining he would make proposals about how to increase them—by devising tactics to attract more customers, for instance. Similarly, when I discussed the risk of arrest with Squeezer, he commented: 'You've made me really paranoid now', perhaps leading to a change in his behaviour regarding the precautions he took against arrest.

As field-work progressed and I became increasingly familiar with the dealers and the way they ran their operations, opportunities to use my influence abounded and I had to guard against it. For instance, Bill and Squeezer both began selling cannabis during the study, and I monitored their progress closely. However, I also took an interest in them in an almost maternal way (discussing them with Chris and Sally, I referred to them as 'my boys'), and, as such, was tempted to offer Squeezer, particularly, advice on how to run his operation more efficiently and profitably.

Research Methods and Design

My research design followed that suggested by grounded theory (Glaser and Strauss 1967). After a year of writing down anything and everything which happened in the field, and filing and cross-referencing it under various headings, I devised an interview schedule to help me to identify patterns in the data, suggest further lines of inquiry, and organize and present it systematically. However, while the interview schedule could be labelled 'unstructured', the techniques I employed for soliciting answers to the questions are not so neatly defined. Even 'interviews' with the same individual were carried out both overtly and covertly, and some were completed by asking respondents a few questions at every meeting over the entire field-work period. I also used an eclectic combination of subsidiary methods: these were primarily observation and the subsequent data from field-notes; monitoring of some aspects of some dealers' operations; and information gathered from people who knew the respondent (but which I did not use unless it was possible to check it with another source, or, preferably, the respondent themselves). I also referred to relevant documents, literature, and statistics where appropriate.

The complete interview schedule consists of twelve sections, running to twenty-six pages: Table 6.1 illustrates just one section of it. The schedule is consistent with the data matrices system of Miles and Huberman (1984), and designed to cope with data-gathering often in small units, from various sources, over a period of time until a response is recorded to as many questions as possible. Even in the overt interview situation it was not usually completed in the presence of the respondent, but filled in from recall later, when 'answers' often took up several pages.

During the early stages of field-work, I divided the respondents into three groups: those who knew I was researching aspects of cannabis distribution and had agreed to co-operate (although how much each individual knew varied considerably); those who did not know I was doing research on anything at all; and those whom I told I was doing research on 'Enterpise Culture', and gave the following cover-story:

I'm doing a Ph.D. on Enterprise Culture in Thatcher's Britain, where people like Richard Branson, Anita Roddick of *The Body Shop*, and the

TABLE 6.1 *Extract from interview schedule*

Interview guide 3: lifestyle

---

a.   *How much time do you reckon you spend on dealing in a week?*
PROMPT: collecting or delivering cannabis, seeing customers, weighing and wrapping.

PROMPT FURTHER ONLY IF NECESSARY, AND MAKE A NOTE IF I DO:
I kept records for a month of how much time Chris and Sally spent. It came to about 50 hours. Do you think you spend more or less time than that?

To what extent do you make yourself available to customers?
PROMPT: Do you, for instance, stay in at certain times of the day when they are likely to phone or visit? Not go on long holidays?

What do you do regularly that isn't at all connected with dealing and drugs?
PROMPT IF NECESSARY: work, cinema, the pub, sport, hobbies, holidays.

What proportion of your friends are not cannabis users, your customers, other dealers?

★★★   Steer conversation, using Chris and Sally—eg: 'We reckon we spend X hours a week on dealing'; 'We would have liked to have gone away at Christmas, but we'd have missed a lot of business, so we didn't'; 'Have you seen such-and-such a film/play/exhibition; read such-and-such a book'; 'We went to X's for supper'; 'We think most of our friends smoke dope.'

Note: Although it may be possible to get dealers' *impressions* on the above, systematic monitoring is needed. I will assess the possibility of getting some dealers to do this.

★★★   Technique for obtaining data covertly.

---

b.   *How do you think dealing is different from a 'normal' job?*
PROMPT IF NECESSARY: illegality; more profitable; insecurity; more, or less, time-consuming; more independence.

Do you find any of the things you mentioned stressful?

IF YES:
How do you dope with that?
PROMPT: make sure you have some time off; take long holidays; unplug the phone; not answer the door; take drugs.

TABLE 6.1 (*cont.*)

★★★   Steer conversation with Chris and Sally talking about their experiences of the positive and negative aspects of dealing compared with legal occupations.

---

c.   *Are there people you have regular contact with, such as workmates, friends, family, neighbours, who don't know you are a dealer?*

IF YES:
Why haven't you told them?

★★★   Chris and Sally could use their own experiences to steer conversation—eg: Sally not telling her sister because of the image of dealers she thought Kate would have; the couple not telling some of their acquaintances who live nearby, even though these people are cannabis users, because they do not want to become known as dealers in their own neighbourhood.

---

woman who started *The Sock Shop* chain, are held up as fine examples of people who saw a gap in the market, and used their entrepreneurial skills to make money out of it—an inspiration to us all.

I've been looking at people operating on a much smaller scale: for instance, I've talked to a woman who does all the cooking for your dinner party, and a man who has set himself up as a gardener. I've looked at some people who are on the Enterprise Allowance Scheme, and are seriously trying to get an idea to make money off the ground—such as a jewellery-maker and a photographer.

I've also found some people who are on the Scheme but not really serious about starting a business—they're just doing it to keep the DHSS off their backs for a year: for example, I met someone who's got an Enterprise Allowance to be a music promoter, but all he's doing is getting bookings for his own band, which he was doing anyway.

I've looked at the enterprises of people who are on the fiddle, like minicab drivers who are moonlighting from another job, and not declaring the income from their driving, and people who are signing on but doing something like window-cleaning, or mending cars, or wheeling and dealing in something, as well. I've talked to a couple of people on the game, and a woman who runs an 'intimate telephone conversation' service.

Finally, I'm talking to dealers—like Chris and Sally—and I hoped you'd help me by telling me a few things about the way the dealing business operates. You don't have to worry about what I'm going to write about you—I shan't be saying anything which will lead to anyone being able to find out who you are.

Observation

I spent two-and-a-half years in the field, where contact with the majority of dealers took place in Chris and Sally's house, although occasionally I met dealers in their own homes, in public places, and on social occasions. My gatekeepers never prevented me from accompanying them wherever I wished, but when, where, and how often I met dealers depended to a large extent on when, where, and how often Chris and Sally met them. This limitation applied particularly to the middlepersons and wholesalers whom the couple met only when they needed fresh supplies: I saw some dealers at these levels only once every six to eight weeks, but other retailers and suppliers were in more frequent contact with my gatekeepers— weekly or fortnightly—and therefore with me. These meetings often lasted an hour or so and, over the field-work period, enabled me to get to know some participants very well.

The network was based on trading relationships, not friendship, and Chris and Sally, and therefore I, lost contact with some dealers—sometimes temporarily, sometimes permanently—and a few dealers had only sporadic contact with Chris and Sally because the couple were not their usual suppliers. An ever-present threat to access was that any dealer could be arrested at any time and stop dealing. In the event, however, this only happened to one dealer, Brian, who served a prison sentence for the offence. As he is an old friend of Chris's, though, it was possible to remain in contact with him.

For three thirty-day periods I closely monitored Chris and Sally's dealing activities. I was able to do this by staying at their house, so that I could record who visited them to buy and sell cannabis; how long each visitor stayed; the time spent on weighing-up and wrapping the drug; how much was bought and sold; and the profit made or amount spent on every deal. During these monitoring periods I also accompanied the couple when they left the house on cannabis business and recorded details of those transactions too. I was also able to monitor, in less detail, the amount sold and the profit made by several other retailers.

Overt Interviewing

I had not foreseen any major problems in getting information from those dealers who knew the nature of my rsearch and had agreed to co-operate: they had been enthusiastic about 'telling it like it is', and had appeared reassured that they would remain anonymous, not least because the individuals I selected for this category were, generally, those with whom I had become most friendly. However, when I began to ask questions from the interview schedule it became clear that it was going to be difficult for me, and for them, to make the transition from friends to formal interviewer/respondent.

I piloted the interview schedule with Chris. It was not a complete success: while he had been more than happy to tell me informally anything I wished to know about himself and about dealing, he became very flippant when I sat with him with pen and paper in hand. For instance, when I asked him how he worked out the price he charged for cannabis, he replied that he charged 'whatever I think I can get away with', which I knew from previous conversations and observation was not the way he operated. During the interview Chris began to read a newspaper and complained that the interview was taking too long, even though we had agreed to set the time aside for it.

After my experience with Chris I decided that I would try a pilot of just one section of it with Squeezer, who knew about the research in much less detail than Chris and who, I suspected, would not treat it in such a cavalier fashion. This second pilot presented different problems. Squeezer, who had been keen to co-operate when I was planning the project, was clearly uncomfortable when he saw I was writing the answers down, and became anxious about what I was going to do with the answers and whether he would be able to be identified from them. Yet he, like Chris, had always been happy to talk to me about dealing previously; had suggested aspects of cannabis buying and selling for investigation; and had even offered to 'write something about it' for me.

I became worried that I would be unable to get useful data by the overt interviewing method, and that dealers would stop talking even informally to me. I decided to abandon interviewing with the schedule in my hand, and writing down the answers in front of the respondent. Instead, I isolated sections of the interview schedule which I could not complete by observation and casual conversation, and made lists of what I needed to know or what I needed to confirm from my observations. Every time I saw the dealer I would check the list beforehand, and ask a few specific questions or steer the conversation to get the information I wanted. Once I had the answers I would make a comment such as: 'You realize I'm going to write this down when you've gone, don't you?' No dealer in this group ever objected; often, they would say something along the lines of 'you may as well ask me a few more questions then', and I could openly consult my list.

This method was clearly more acceptable than the formal interview to those dealers with whom I had formed friendly relationships: answers could be seen by them to be part of general friend-to-friend conversation, over which they felt they had some control, and I felt that it led to more spontaneous answers as the influence of my researcher role was minimized. Okely (1983, p. 45) found a similar solution when formal interviews with travellers failed to get her the data she needed:

It was more informative to merge into the surroundings than alter them as an inquisitor . . . Towards the end of the fieldwork I pushed myself to ask questions, but invariably the response was unproductive, except among a few close associates. Even then, answers dried up, once it appeared that my questions no longer arose from spontaneous puzzlement and that I was making other forms of discussion impossible.

Covert Interviewing

During the compilation of the interview schedule I had planned 'to steer the conversation with Chris and Sally's help'. Often this strategy worked well, but when it did not I felt I should abandon that particular question until a much later contact, rather than risk 'blowing my cover' by being obsessively interested in a particular aspect of their life or dealing activities. As Agar (1980, p. 456) says:

. . . you should not have to ask. To be accepted in the streets is to hip; to be hip is to be knowledgeable; to be knowledgeable is to be capable of understanding what is going on on the basis of minimal cues. So to ask a question is to show that you are not acceptable and this creates problems in a relationship when you have just been introduced to somebody.

In the field, however, I was saved from being grossly unhip, unknowledgeable and unacceptable by several factors:

- dealers enjoyed 'talking shop' with other dealers;
- the majority of the dealers in the covert interviewing category were those at middleperson and wholesaler level. Chris and Sally were retailers, and the higher-level dealers often passed on

advice and related anecdotes to the 'lower orders' with little prompting;
- the middlepersons and wholesalers in the network were men. Sally and I exploited their paternalism by displaying wide-eyed naivety which flattered them and enabled us to ask very unhip questions (Easterday *et al.* 1977, usefully discuss the roles of female researchers in predominantly male fields);
- some dealers were my friends before I began the research, and I met most of the others in the network many times: therefore, it was not necessary for me to ask questions when we had just been introduced, nor even tell them I was a researcher.

Consequently, it was only certain sensitive questions, such as finances or ciminal records (other than for drug offences, which no dealer seemed to mind talking about) which presented difficulties in covert interviewing. If all my attempts to solicit such data failed, I had to accept that some dealers' interview schedules were never going to be completely filled in, or that data I had obtained about an individual from another source could not be checked by asking the dealers themselves.

Initially, some of the data I had imagined would be easy to obtain covertly presented difficulties. For example, as part of the background picture I wanted to build up of each individual, there was a question in the schedule about education. When appropriate I would chat about my own, or Chris and/or Sally about theirs, and often the respondent would react as I had planned. Bryn, however, with whom I piloted covert interviewing, did not, and I felt I could not keep returning to the subject and cause him to wonder why I was displaying such an intense interest in his educational background. Later I realized that I had entered into my spy persona too wholeheartedly—in the course of an 'ordinary' conversation it would not have been unusual to have asked him outright whether he had been to a university. Incidents such as this improved my technique in later covert interviews.

Interviews using the Enterprise Culture Cover-Story

The dealer with whom I chose to pilot this strategy was Frenchie. It was only partly successful. He displayed only a very mild interest in enterprise culture and in Chris and Sally's co-operation with me, and I felt it was inappropriate to ask for his. 'Interviews' with him then became a combination of using the cover-story and the covert strategy. A further problem was that Frenchie used a variety of illegal drugs, and the level of his participation in, and response to, what was going on around him, fluctuated wildly. The influence of drug-use by respondents on the collection of data was not a major problem in this study, however.

I persevered with the cover-story and had more success with other dealers. When I talked about 'people who are on the fiddle' and prostitution—or before—some dealers suggested that I included cannabis dealing in the Ph.D. too. If this happened I would say admiringly 'that's a good idea', and ask them for suggestions for themes, which usually led to the dealers revealing something of their own activities. This strategy worked well. If dealers did not respond in this way, and depending on the reaction I thought I would get, I continued the cover-story by saying I wanted to include enterprises such as dealing. Chris and/or Sally were able to confirm my credentials, and that I was trustworthy, by telling the dealer that they were helping me with my research. Even if I felt it was inappropriate to ask the dealer to help personally, they often would comment at this point that they 'could tell me a thing or two', and so I could proceed to ask them questions of a general nature whenever I had contact with them: they would invariably illustrate the answers with their own experiences. I used the cover-story with about a dozen dealers, and even if I decided not to ask for their co-operation, the route to asking specific questions about dealing was smoother and faster than the 'steering the conversation' technique I employed in totally covert interviewing.

Thus, while in theory I had neatly categorized strategies for soliciting information from each dealer, in the field the edges between the categories were somewhat blurred. A further complication was that, as field-work progressed, I had to remember at what stage in which category each dealer was, because this changed: as I got to know some individuals better, I was able (after consultation with Chris and Sally) to reveal more about the study to them.

Because I was afraid I would lose access to the network of dealers, I had begun field-work using the methods just described while waiting for my Ph.D. proposals to be accepted by the Economic and Social Research Council and the University of Surrey. Initially my knowledge of research methods was somewhat sketchy, and my main concern was to get everything that happened written down. However, once I officially began the study, attended lectures on research methods, and read textbooks on research methodology, I realized that whichever method was used to gather data, its validity and my interpretation of it had to be assessed, particularly as there are no other studies of British cannabis dealers with which to compare it.

Validity of Data and Interpretation

Fielding and Fielding (1986, p. 24) say: 'when pressed about validity and reliability, qualitative researchers ultimately resort to their own estimation of the strength of the cited data or interpretation; we have heard such responses many times. To avoid reliance on this last resort, it is possible to compile a long list of validity checks—from, for example, Burgess (1982) and Hammersley and Atkinson (1983). While I cannot claim to have ticked off every item, I did not often have to resort to the inadequacy of 'the assertion of privileged insight' (Fielding and Fielding, p. 25): the multi-method techniques I used in the two-and-a-half years I spent in the field enabled me to operate a cross-checking procedure when faced with data from solicited and unsolicited accounts, field-notes from observation, and hearsay.

I could discuss proposals which had arisen from the data with several of my informants, and this often led to the generation of further proposals and lines of inquiry. However, asking them to validate my interpretations of specific aspects of their *own* behaviour and accounts of incidents was problematic. As Hammersley and Atkinson (1983, p. 196) point out, the researcher has to recognize 'that it may be in a person's interests to misrepresent or misdescribe his or her own actions, or to counter the interpretations of the ethnographer'.

Where interpretations clashed, I had to be aware of the consequences for my relationship with the dealer concerned, not least because there was a danger that they would withdraw their co-operation. For example, I noted that the first time Phil visited Chris and Sally, he arrived with two friends and a handful of marijuana, and as he walked through the door asked Sally if she had any 'skins' (cigarette papers) so they could smoke it. The trio then sat down as if preparing for a long smoking session, and it was clear that they had already been using the drug before their arrival. In less than two minutes Phil and his friends had unknowingly violated several of Chris and Sally's rules for customer behaviour. Chris tactfully explained that they did not want 'hoards of people trooping through the door' because they were very risk-conscious, and were worried that neighbours may have seen them, the marijuana in Phil's hand, and noticed that the three were under the influence of it. He added that he and Sally were often too busy to spend time smoking cannabis or marijuana with customers—'if we did, we'd never get anything else done.' The trio nodded amicably, bought their cannabis from the couple, and left. On his next visit Phil's behaviour had changed considerably, and he obeyed his new dealers' rules to the letter.

My interpretation of this incident was that on his first visit Phil had behaved as he did because he had learnt from his previous dealers, and from his own experiences selling cannabis and cocaine, that this was what was expected of him, and that he had changed his behaviour according to the expectations of his new dealers. I felt I knew him well enough to ask him if this proposition was correct. However, as his visits to Chris and Sally's house only ever lasted about ten minutes, I had to force the pace and put the question somewhat out of the blue. Even though Phil was aware that I was studying dealing, he misinterpreted what I was saying—or I presented it badly—and thought I was accusing him of being a 'druggie'. He was clearly offended, and it took several weeks for my relationship with him to recover. Chris made it clear he disapproved of what I had done, too: 'He looked really freaked when you suddenly came out with it like that.'

Thereafter, if I suspected offence might be taken, I confined the respondent-validation strategy to asking respondents for comments on other respondents' behaviour and accounts. I hasten to add that I did not intend to rely on data gathered solely by this 'garden-fence' method, but I made use of the normal gossip which occurs amongst friends and acquaintances to back up what I already knew or suspected, and then incorporated it into my observation and questioning of a particular dealer. An illustration of this is when I asked Squeezer how his business was going, at a time when I had calculated that he was making very little profit, and he replied that he was 'doing quite well'. A few days later I casually asked a close friend of his the same question. She replied: 'He says he's not doing very well—he says he smokes most of the profits.' The next time I saw Squeezer I asked him if his cannabis use had increased since he began dealing: it had.

The time I spent with the network of dealers alleviated much of the danger to which one-off and formal interviews and susceptible. As Whyte (1973, pp. 114–16) says, an informant's current emotional state, values, attitudes, sentiments, and opinions may not be consistent and are highly situational, but I was able to check, periodically, the continuing validity of what respondents did or told me, and note any changes, for, as Hammersley and Atkinson (1983, p. 193) warn: 'What people say and do is produced in the context of a developing sequence of interaction. If we ignore what has already occurred or what follows, we are in danger of drawing the wrong conclusions.'

Burgess (1982) and Hammersley and Atkinson also demand consideration of the following for checks on distortion in informants' accounts of incidents: the reliability of the informant; the plausibility of the account; the place of the informant in the setting; and comparison with others' accounts of the same incident.

Checks on the reliability of an informant can be formalized, and for this I found the coding scheme devised by Reuss-Ianni (1983, p. 135—reproduced in Table 6.2) helpful. Where my data did not

TABLE 6.2 *Validity and reliability coding scheme*

Validity score	Reliability score
A Data gathered through observation with direct participation	1 Informant always reliable
B Data gathered through observation but not as direct participant	2 Informant usually reliable
C Interview data checked against documentary or other factual source	3 Reliability of informant unknown
D Interview data corroborated by one or more additional informants	4 Informant unreliable
E Interview data from a single informant	

Source: Reuss-Ianni (1983, p. 135).

score at least D-2, I attempted to better it with information from other sources. If this proved impossible but I still made use of the data, I pointed out its possible invalidity and unreliability.

The plausibility of an account can be checked by the researcher who is established in the setting under study. Here, I believe, 'privileged insight' plays an important—but not the only—part. For example, I found Frenchie's hints that his frequent visits to Spain to work for illegal drug traffickers implausible, not only because his recklessness, heavy drug use, and criminal record for drug offences, would, I thought, deter anyone with a lot to lose from employing him, but also because he was clearly not earning any money there: he once phoned Chris and Sally from Spain to say he had run out of money, and asked for £250 to be sent; on another occasion he phoned from a Spanish airport and asked Chris to organize a return ticket for him; and he once returned with no money, and borrowed £100 from Chris.

The place of the informants in the setting can influence how they give an account of their world. For example, the study identified a five-tier cannabis distribution pyramid, and many of the dealers thought that those above them in it spent all their time using and selling the drug, and were part of a violent, multi-drug-using, criminal, subculture. As I had contact with every level, though, I discovered that this was a false impression.

Some accounts of incidents given by respondents could be confirmed by asking others who were present, but it was not always possible. Bryn, for instance, told me of events which happened up to twenty-five years ago, and which are relevant to current aspects of his dealing operation, but as I did not have contact with anyone who knew him at that time I was unable to check the information. In such cases, if I wanted to use the data I would try to return to the subject at a later date, to see if the respondents' accounts tallied with their previous telling of it.

Ethical Considerations

After I had been collecting data for about nine months, I started to write the methodology chapter of my thesis. Until I came to the 'Ethics' section, I had been only dimly aware of the condemnation covert observation receives from some social scientists. For guidance on research techniques I had been concentrating on participant (or semi-participant) observation studies (such as Fielding 1981; Holdaway 1982; Okely 1983; Adler 1985; Hobbs 1988), and textbooks on ethnography (such as Hammersley and Atkinson 1983; Lofland and Lofland 1984) which, although recognizing the ethical dilemmas of the covert observer, did not condemn the technique. For example, Lofland and Lofland (pp. 43–4), while commenting on the attention ethical considerations have attracted from 'specialists in ethics' and from field-workers 'agonising over their behavior and relationships', say: 'Without in any way denigrating these efforts or belittling the honestly expressed moral anguish of some researchers, it seems to us that too much can be made of the fieldwork setting as involving special and particular ethical problems.'

I was complacent, then, that my methodology (including what I thought were rather clever ways to extract information covertly from dealers) and the checks I had built into it regarding objectivity and validity would result in a faithful representation of the dealers, and would therefore be acceptable to social science. I turned to the ethical guide-lines of the Social Research Association (1983) and the collection of texts on covert participant observation edited by Bulmer (1982), thinking I could dismiss the issue easily. My smugness evaporated when I read of the many horns on the many ethical dilemmas facing social-science researchers generally and semi-covert, semi-participant observers like myself in particular. However, rather than list them all, I will discuss the two aspects of my study with which I was especially concerned: that my varying degrees of deception often left me feeling guilty—not because of the condemnation the lack of informed consent receives from some social scientists, but because I was deceiving the dealers; and that by exposing hitherto unresearched aspects of the distribution of cannabis, I might harm not only the sixty-four dealers I was researching, but also all the others in Britain.

Feeling Guilty

Although by the end of the study only half-a-dozen of the sixty-four dealers remained unaware that I was doing any sort of research at all, only my two gatekeepers had enough information about the study for them to be able to gauge whether or not co-operating with me could harm them. The others were at best misinformed, and at worst lied to. My initial reaction on learning that this was unacceptable to some social scientists was a defiant: 'Well, social science knows almost nothing about cannabis dealers, and this was the only way I could tell them,.' Ultimately, this remains the justification for my methodology, but this does not mean that all was therefore plain sailing, as Bulmer (1982, p. 246) recognizes: 'Dilemmas and choices will continue to face the field researcher that dogmatic statements of "should" and "must" will not eliminate. The complexity of practical decision-making will continue to dog the steps of the sociologist using observational methods.'

Consequently, even the strongest critics of covert research rarely suggest that a phenomenon should not be studied if deception of subjects is involved. For example, Bulmer (pp. 235–6) sums up the contributions to the collection on the merits and demerits of covert participant observation thus: 'Complete concealment of the research . . . may rarely if ever be justified, but the converse—that total openness is in all circumstances desirable or possible—does not follow.'

I examined the justifications for the ethical compromises made by other covert researchers and the literature cataloguing the issues, and discovered that the majority of commentators ultimately conclude (although they reach that conclusion by different routes) that the ethical dilemmas of an ethnographer will require compromise to 'solve', much of it dependent on decisions made by the individual researcher. Reynolds (1982, p. 213) pinpoints the issue as I saw it:

To conform to the highest standards of individual morality in temporary personal exchanges at the expense of examining important, critical scientific and societal problems may not be the choice preferred by a number of investigators. It is for each social scientist to decide how they wish to serve society: as a personal moral exemplar or as a source of useful and valued information.

Nonetheless, placing myself firmly in the latter category did not assuage the guilt I felt. Adler (1985, p. 25) maintains that the covert researcher's role in the field makes such encounters with ethical dilemmas and 'pangs of guilt' necessary because:

They can never fully align themselves with their subjects while maintaining their identity and personal commitments to the scientific [I would substitute 'academic'] community. Ethical dilemmas, then, are directly related to the amount of deception researchers use in gathering the data, and the degree to which they have accepted such acts as necessary and therefore neutralized them.

Adler (p. 26) found that despite the 'universal presence of covert behavior' throughout her setting, she and her husband still 'felt a sense of betrayal every time we ran home to write research notes on observations we had made under the guise of innocent participants'. Like Adler's, the setting I studied also operated on a basis of secrecy, and like her gatekeepers, my own sometimes advocated and condoned my covert approach, because of the possible effect on their business if one of their buyers or sellers objected. Even though I gradually revealed more about the study to some of the dealers, I was hindered by the reluctance of even some willing respondents to be formally reminded at every contact that they were being studied (Squeezer, for instance, as detailed earlier). Despite these justifications, I could not escape feeling like a betrayer sometimes, too.

Often, I felt like the head of MI5 on an assignment with two of my staff. The planning and execution of such missions was exciting but, particularly if they were successful, I was sometimes left feeling guilty. For example, Chris, Sally, and I spent several hours at Bryn's flat one day, during which he made us lunch and gave us, without too much prompting, many details about himself and his dealing activities, unaware that I was researching the subject. When we left, we gleefully hurried off to the nearest café, and wrote it all down. After the euphoria over all the information we had obtained died down, however, I felt that we had abused the hospitality of this friendly man, who had so clearly enjoyed our company. We agreed that we would not have spent so long with him, listening to his long, rambling tales, if they had not been so useful for research purposes. We did it again, though.

I also felt guilty because I was pleased when dealers had negative experiences. For instance, my first thought on hearing that Brian had been arrested; that there was a severe shortage of cannabis; that Chris and Sally had been sold some cannabis of inferior quality; and that Bill had been badly beaten up and his stocks of cannabis and cash stolen, was 'what a brilliant research opportunity!'

Bulmer (1982, pp. 232–3) says that one of the situations where covert methods can be justified is 'retrospective participant observation', based on the researcher's own experiences as a member of the field: he cites the studies of Becker the dance musician, and Polsky the pool hustler as examples. Lofland and Lofland (1984, p. 22), say that such researchers do seem to suffer less guilt, too: 'if the research project arises after you have become part of the setting—a frequent corollary of "starting where you are"—the moral onus seems less severe.' Certainly, the guilt I felt was not overwhelming—indeed, I often felt guilty for *not* feeling guilty, at, for example, simulating friendship when talking to Brian about his arrest, attending his trial, and visiting him in prison.

Another justification for covert observation methods comes from Shils (1982, p. 271), who, although a strong critic of the method, says that it is necessary where those being studied are crminals, although he adds: 'Their necessity on behalf of social order does not diminish their morally objectionable character; it simply outweighs it.' I considered hiding behind the motive of helping society to control cannabis dealers in order to justify my methodology. But this would not have been true. The seeds of the study, as described at the beginning of this chapter, were sown because the cannabis users and dealers I met did not conform to the popular stereotype, and sociology had done little to investigate its accuracy.

Publish and Be Damned?

Whilst Bulmer (1982, p. 241) says that researchers using observational techniques should not model themselves on secret agents or investigative journalists, such research reveals the identities of the subjects, whereas I gave considerable thought to disguising them. This involved more than merely using pseudonyms and not revealing the name of the city where the dealers operate. I did not write dates, times, nor place-names in my field-notes; I confined my field-note headings to 'Week 4: in Brian's flat', to indicate temporal and situational context; I wrote up most field-notes within twenty-four hours of collecting them, destroyed some of the originals, and stored many of the write-ups at the house of a trusted friend; when compiling frequency counts (on, for example, the dealers' ages, housing situations, legitimate occupations, and education history), I made sure that a profile of a particular individual could not be built up from them; and when discussing the precautions dealers take against arrest and a dealing conviction, I omitted those which I thought were particularly ingenious. These precautions meant that some highly relevant data was omitted—often at the expense of emphasizing a particular point or providing a 'good' story. They also meant that I became very anxious in case I had included details which might lead to the identification of the dealers by outsiders. My anxiety knew no bounds: for instance, I quoted Sally saying that her profits from selling cannabis meant that she could make impulse buys without worrying about the cost. She gave an example: 'I'm going through Marks and Sparks and I fancy some prawns, and I can buy loads.' I became obsessed with the prawns that were usually in her fridge, and that if she was arrested, her relationship with me would be revealed; my thesis scrutinized by the police; the quote and the prawns in her fridge connected; everything I had written about 'Sally' used against her; and the whole network traced—all because of those dratted prawns.

I discouraged dealers from writing down my phone-number and address, and I did not write down theirs. I did this because I was aware that if any dealer was under surveillance by the police, and I, because of my association with them, was arrested, my data would be an aid to the collection of evidence against them. A further reason for removing evidence was that I was aware of the potential an arrested dealer might see in a defence of helping *me* with *my* enquiries, so I was also protecting myself by this tactic. Whilst Whyte (1955), Becker (1963), Polsky (1967), and Adler (1985) are among those who have found illegal actions by themselves to be 'a necessary or helpful component of the research' (Adler, p. 24), like them, I did not imagine that this made me immune from charges of witnessing crimes and withholding information. To avoid police attention on myself as someone who knew many dealers, I therefore did not publicize the nature of my research any more than necessary, and used the cover-story with some of my acquintances—including police officers I met at criminology conferences.

That said, most of the dealers will recognize themselves and others if they read the study. I find Adler's comment—'I hope I cause them no embarrassment' (1985, a chapter note, p. 158)—too optimistic an apology, and feel the issue merits further consideration than many ethnographers give to it, for anonymity also serves to protect them from recriminations. The respondents who were most aware that I was studying them included those with whom I was, and remain, most friendly: with some, I hope that I will be able to rely on that friendship to avoid their long-term wrath, but Brian may not forgive me for pretending friendship, even though he knew I was carrying out the study. Of those who knew I was researching something, but were vague about the details, Frenchie will very probably object to being used throughout the study as an example of an inefficient and risk-taking dealer. The reaction of the half-dozen respondents whom I never told I was doing research on anything at all, but who would recognize themselves in the study, worries me considerably.

While the study sits on a library shelf, with access to it restricted, I am confident that those dealers who did not know I was studying them will not see it. Several of the others have begun to ask me if they can read it, though, and the time is rapidly approaching when I can no longer put them off by saying 'when it's finished', or by giving them verbal edited highlights. Some will find not only considerable details about themselves, but also that they have contributed to data on, for example, the sort of people who distribute cannabis; their motivation for doing so; how they operate; the profits they make; the precautions they take against arrest; and the effect of their own and/or other dealers' arrests on themselves, and on the network of which they are part. On the library shelf, I am confident that it will not harm them or other cannabis dealers, but if it is published I envisage having to face up to the responsibility of having provided the law-enforcement agencies and policy-makers with useful information which could contribute to their arrests.

Dilemmas continue to dog me, then. If I decide to attempt to have the study published—and I probably shall—I risk harming the dealers and losing some of my friends. Jupp (1989, pp. 157–8) advises that I should have a academic and professional commitment to publication, and 'as a general rule, provided the researcher has taken whatever steps as are reasonable to ensure anonymity there is no reason to refrain from publication'. I may be exaggerating the harm I will cause: interviews with police officers by Campbell (1990) and Graef (1990) show that those who have some experience of dealers at the levels of this study are aware of the inaccuracy of the stereotypical 'drug barons' and 'evil pushers', in spite of government policy statements which perpetuate the images. The effect on my personal relationships may be more severe. I wish I could believe Lofland and Lofland (1984, pp. 157–8) who recognize the dilemma, but say: 'Most people do not seem to care very much about scholarly analyses that are written about them. Many don't get around to reading them even when they are published . . . The use of psuedonyms and a scholarly mode of writing tend to minimise the participants' interest . . .'

I fear Hughes (1960, p. xii) has identified the more likely

outcome of the publication of my research: 'hatred . . . is visited almost daily upon the person who reports on the behavior of people he [*sic*] has lived among; and it is not so much the writing of the report, as the very act of thinking in such objective terms that disturbs the people observed.'

References

Adler, P. A. (1985). *Wheeling and Dealing: An Ethnography of an Upper-Level Drug Dealing and Smuggling Community* (Washington DC: Columbia University Press).

Agar, M. (1980). *Professional Stranger* (New York: Academic Press).

Becker, H. S. (1963). *Outsiders: Studies in the Sociology of Deviance* (Glencoe: The Free Press).

Blum, R. H. *et al.* (1972). *The Dream Sellers: Perspectives on drug dealers* (New York: Jossey-Bass).

Bulmer, M. (1982). (ed.), *Social Research Ethics: An Examination of the Merits of Covert Participant Observation* (London: Macmillan).

Burgess, R. G. (1982). (ed.), *Field Research: A Sourcebook and Field Manual* (London: Allen & Unwin).

Campbell, D. (1990). *That was Business, This is Personal: The Changing Faces of Professional Crime* (London: Secker & Warburg).

Dean, J. P., Eichorn, R. L., and Dean, L. R. (1967). 'Fruitful Informants for Intensive Interviewing' in J. T. Doby, (ed.) *An Introduction to Social Research* (2nd edn., New York: Appleton-Century-Crofts).

Downes, D. and Rock, P. (1988). *Understanding Deviance: A Guide to the Sociology of Crime and Rule-Breaking* (2nd edn., Oxford: Oxford University Press).

Easterday, L., Papademas, D., Schorr, L., and Valentine, C. (1977). 'The Making of a Female Researcher: Role problems in fieldwork' (in Burgess 1982).

Fielding, N. G. (1981). *The National Front* (London: Routledge & Kegan Paul).

—— (1982). 'Observational Research on the National Front' (in Bulmer 1982).

—— and Fielding, J. L. (1986). *Linking Data*, Sage University Paper Series on Qualitative Research Methods, vol. 4 (Beverly Hills, Calif.: Sage).

Glaser, B. G. and Strauss, A. L. (1967). *The Discovery of Grounded Theory: Strategies for Qualitative Research* (New York: Aldine).

Graef, R. (1990). *Talking Blues: The Police in Their Own Words* (London: Fontana).

Hammersley, M. and Atkinson, P. (1983). *Ethnography: Principles in practice* (London: Tavistock).

Hobbs, D. (1988). *Doing the Business: Entrepreneurship, the Working Class, and Detectives in the East End of London* (Oxford: Oxford University Press).

Holdaway, S. (1982). 'An Inside Job: A Case study of Covert Research on the Police' (in Bulmer 1982).

Home Office (1989). *Home office Statistical Bulletin*, Issue 30/89. *Statistics on the Misuse of Drugs: Seizures and Offenders Dealt With, United Kingdom, 1988* (London: Government Statistical Service).

Hughes, E. C. (1960). 'Introduction: The Place of Field-Work in Social Science', in B. Junker (eds.), *Field Work: An Introduction to Social Sciences* (Chicago, Ill.: University of Chicago Press).

Institute for the Study of Drug Dependence (1990). *Drug Misuse in Britain: National Audit of Drug Misuse Statistics* (London: ISDD).

Jupp, V. (1989). *Methods of Criminological Research*, Comtemporary Social Research Series 19 (London: Unwin Hyman).

Klatch, R. E. (1988). 'The Methodological Problems of Studying a Politically Resistant Community', *Studies in Qualitative Methodology*, *1*.

Klockars, C. B. (1974). *The Professional Fence* (London: Tavistock).

Liebow, E. (1967). *Tally's Corner* (London: Routledge & Kegan Paul).

Lofland, J. and Lofland, L. H. (1984). *Analysing Social Settings: A guide to Qualitative Observation and Analysis* (2nd edn., Belmont, Calif.: Wadsworth).

Miles, M. B. and Huberman, A. M. (1984). *Qualitative Data Analysis* (London: Sage).

Okely, J. (1983). *The Traveller-Gypsies* (Cambridge: Cambridge University Press).

Polsky, N. (1967). *Hustlers, Beats, and Others* (Harmondsworth: Penguin (1971) edn.).

Reuss-Ianni, E. (1983). *Two Cultures of Policing* (London: Transaction).

Reynolds, P. D. (1982). 'Moral Judgements: Strategies for Analysis with Application to Covert Participant Observation' (in Bulmer 1982).

Sharrock, W. W. and Anderson, R. J. (1980). *On the Demise of the Native: Some Observations on and a Proposal for Ethnography* (University of Manchester Department of Sociology: Occasional Paper No. 5).

Shils, E. (1982). 'Social Inquiry and the Autonomy of the Individual' (in Bulmer 1982).

Social Research Association (1983). *Directory of Members Handbook 1983/4* (London: Social Research Association).

Tremblay, M.-A. (1957). 'The Key Informant Technique: A Non-Ethno graphic approach' (in Burgess 1982).

Van Maanen, J. (1982). 'Fieldwork on the Beat', In J. Van Maanen, J. M. Dabbs, and R. R. Faulkner, *Varieties of Qualitative Research. Studying Organizations*, Innovations in Methodology 5 (Beverly Hills, Calif.: Sage).

Whyte, W. F. (1955). *Street Corner Society* (Chicago, Ill.: University of Chicago Press).
—— (1973). 'Interviewing in Field Research' (in Burgess 1982).
Young, J. (1971). *The Drugtakers: The Social Meaning of Drug Use* (London, Paladin).

PART IV

Women and Ethnography

7

Greenham Revisited: Researching Myself and My Sisters

SASHA ROSENEIL*

When, along with 30 000 other women, I first visited the Women's Peace Camp at Greenham Common in December 1982, I had no idea that a year later I would be living there, let alone that six years on I'd be writing a Ph.D. thesis about the place. A 16-year-old sixth-former, I knew that something momentous was afoot and that I wanted to be part of it, but I certainly could not articulate the importance of what was happening outside that United States Air-Force base in Berkshire. So it was that my doctoral thesis set out to explore the sociological significance of Greenham on both a micro-level, to the tens of thousands whose lives were changed by the experience of involvement, and on a macro-level, to the social structures and institutions of a hetero-patriarchal society.

In this article I discuss the process of carrying out research on a social–political movement and community of which I have been a part. Locating my research in the newly established tradition of post-positivist feminist methodology, I focus particularly on how I have used my own experience and how being an 'insider' has impacted on the research process.

This chapter consists of five closely connected parts. First, I set out the methodological principles of feminist research practice that have guided my work. Then I go on to explore the autobiographical background to the research, how and why I came to undertake the project. Thirdly, I discuss specific methodological issues arising from my status as an insider and the retrospective nature of the research. Fourthly, I elucidate how I actually carried out the research, making strategic use of my own experience of living at Greenham. Finally, I identify a number of ethical–political issues

* Department of Sociology, University of Leeds.

which have been of particular concern to me in the course of the research.

Three Guiding Principles of Feminist Methodology

As a member of a second generation of 'second wave' feminist scholars, I came to a sociology in which there was already a substantial literature on the theory and practice of feminist research. This work, with the exception of a few early 'feminist empiricists' (Harding, 1986, pp. 24–6), is part of a wider post-positivist tradition in the social sciences, and has excited me with the possibility of doing research as my feminism indicates I should.[1] Using a framework developed by Harding (1987) to synthesize the work of a number of writers of feminist methodology, there are three basic principles which have guided my research practice.

1. *Focusing on Women's Experiences*

The first principle of feminist research is that it formulates research questions from women's experiences, since traditional social science has derived its research questions solely from the perspective of men.[2] Stanley and Wise (1983) are perhaps the strongest proponents of the centrality of women's experience to feminist research. Their work re-emphasizes the importance of the aphorism 'the personal is political', and establishes the significance of women's consciousness and everyday life experiences as the material of research.

In this spirit, my research is based on questions which have arisen from women's experiences of feminist political struggle, particularly from sociological reflections on my own experiences of Greenham. I have used women's accounts of their time at Greenham, as well as my own, as the primary data for my research. Whilst studying a social–political movement operating in the public sphere and concerned with 'public sphere' issues of militarism and violence, my research is equally concerned with 'private' and 'personal' experiences of friendship, sexuality, feelings, and emotions at Greenham. These, I believe, are of great political and sociological significance.

[1] On feminist methodology see e.g. Bowles and Duelli Klein (1983); Cook and Fonow (1986); Harding (1986; 1987); Millman and Kanter (1975); Nielsen (1990); Smith (1987); Stanley (1990); Stanley & Wise (1983; 1990); Westkott (1979).

[2] This argument is made by Bernard (1973); Millman and Kanter (1975); Du Bois (1983); Smith (1974). This does not mean that feminist research is only that which is *on* women. Stanley and Wise (1983, p. 18) point out that feminist research can and

2. *Research for Women*

Almost all discussions of feminist methodology emphasize that feminist research is carried out *for women*, to contribute to the understanding of women's oppression and to further the struggle for women's liberation.[3] As Harding points out: 'The questions about women that men have wanted answered have all too often arisen from desires to pacify, control, exploit or manipulate women. Traditional social research has been *for men*' (1987, p. 8). Feminist research, on the other hand, should aim to improve women's lives (Duelli Klein 1983) and to change the patriarchal *status quo*. The obvious corollary of this liberatory purpose for feminist research is that 'value-neutrality', the *sine qua non* of positivism, is abandoned.

My research adheres firmly to this principle of feminist research. I intend my work to be a contribution to the growing record of the history of women's collective resistance to male power, as well as to the theorization of our oppression. I hope that it will be inspiring and empowering for future generations of feminists, as well as interesting and perhaps illuminating for women who have been involved in Greenham themselves. The research is certainly 'passionate' and politically engaged; as a Greenham woman myself, I am as passionate and politically engaged as the women I have interviewed. I have no qualms about rejecting 'value-neutrality' and taking sides.

Flowing from the commitment to produce sociology for women as a collectivity, there has been a deep concern amongst feminist researchers about the ethics of the treatment of the individual women on whom research is 'done'.[4] As Wise (1987) points out, for feminists the ethical dilemmas of research are also political dilemmas, since the research relationship is fundamentally a relationship of unequal power between researcher and researched. Given that women have long been exploited and objectified in social-science research by men, there is a general belief that feminist research should confront the hierarchical nature of the research relationship

must be conducted on all aspects of social life, and on men; Walby (1988) makes a similar point. Research on men can have much to say about women's oppression.

[3] See e.g. Weskott (1979); Acker *et al.* (1983); Mies (1983); Stanley and Wise (1983); Duelli Klein (1983); Finch (1984); Harding (1987); Smith (1987).

[4] See e.g. Acker *et al.* (1983); Finch (1984); Oakley (1981); Stacey (1988); Stanley and Wise (1983); Wise (1987). My discussion will focus on the ethical–political issues which arise when feminists research other women; when feminists carry out research on men very different problems seem to arise (Scott, 1984).

head-on. Probably the most important principle of feminist research ethics is that the researcher and the research product should not objectify the researched. Feminism and the broader post-positivist paradigm declare that those being studied are subjects in their own right, actively constructing their own lives. People are not just acted upon, as the more structuralist tendencies in sociology would suggest. Indeed, the researched 'are also avid students of human relations; they too have their social theories and conduct investigations' (Gouldner, 1970, p. 496).[5] Stanley (1990) demands that feminist researchers 'leave on one side the ridiculous assumption of positivist deductivist theoreticians that people merely experience while theorising is the prerogative of a special class or group' (1990, p. 157).

As a member of the social group that I have studied, I have been acutely aware of ethical–political issues of the researcher–researched relationship. The agency and self-conscious theorizing of the women I have interviewed have been apparent to me throughout, and I will discuss later how I have sought to use this, rather than to suppress it.

3. *Locating the Researcher on the Same Critical Plane as the Researched*

Linked to the rejection of 'value-neutrality' is the third distinguishing feature of feminist methodology: a commitment to reflexivity. Feminist research rejects the self-obscuring and alienating methodologies which are rooted in the knower–known, subject–object dichotomies of traditional positivist epistemology. In contrast, feminist methodology aims to highlight and examine the role of the researcher, and demands that research work be unalienated labour (Reinharz 1984; Stanley 1990). Based on an epistemology that considers all knowledge to be socially constructed, it begins with the acknowledgement that the identity of the researcher matters. She is unavoidably present in the research process, and her work is shaped by her social location and personal experiences.[6] As Gadamer (1976) argues, 'prejudice' is the ontological condition of human existence in society, and thus, no researcher comes to her research a *tabula rasa*. Rather than seeking to 'bracket' our 'prejudgements' (our existing

---

[5] This argument is made by Gouldner (1970), Smith (1987), Stanley (1990), and Stanley and Wise (1983).

[6] For a discussion of feminist epistemologies, see Harding (1986).

values and experiences), which is impossible, we should make ourselves aware of them, and expose them to the prejudgements of others. Feminist methodologists suggest that we *exploit* our subjectivities and personal experiences and locate ourselves and our research practices on the same critical plane as the overt subject of study.[7]

Because the basis of all research is a relationship, this necessarily involves the presence of the researcher as a *person*. Personhood cannot be left behind, cannot be left out of the research process. And so we insist it must be capitalised upon, it must be made full use of. If we can't do research in any other way than by using ourselves as the medium through which research is carried out, then we must fully explore this' (Stanley and Wise 1983, p. 162).

To this end, Stanley (1985) proposes that researchers explore their 'intellectual autobiographies', and the traditionally unacknowledged role of their emotions and feelings in the research process (Stanley and Wise 1983; see also May in this volume).[8] It has been noted, however, that this means exposing oneself to public scrutiny and that this often demands considerable courage (Stanley and Wise 1983; Reinharz 1984).

The methodological injunction to place oneself as researcher on the same critical plane as the researched has made possible my study of Greenham. Greenham was so important to me personally that without this space opened up by feminist writers, legitimizing, and indeed demanding, the discussion of the researcher's subjectivity, for me to have attempted to research Greenham would have been impossible. As it is, inspired by this third principle of feminist research, I have sought to examine my experiences in the way that I have those of the women I have interviewed, and I have attempted fully to acknowledge and explore the role of my subjectivity in constructing the research product. A vital part of this is the writing of an intellectual autobiography, which lays out my pre-existing values and experiences in relation to the research.

---

[7] See e.g. Smith (1974); Stanley and Wise (1983); Du Bois (1983); Reinharz (1984); Harding (1987).
[8] This injunction has been taken up by the 'Manchester School of feminist research', which is published in the Studies in Sexual Politics series (e.g. Farran *et al.* 1985; Griffiths *et al.* 1987).

The Background to the Research: My Intellectual Autobiography

To traditional methodologists what follows may seem, at best, irrelevant, a self-indulgent excursion into adolescent *angst*; at worst, it will be seen as indicative of complete failure at the enterprise of social-scientific research. I would disagree. Working within the post-positivist, feminist epistemology discussed above, I believe that my intellectual autobiography, the story of who I am and how I came to do this research (including my adolescent *angst!*), is crucially relevant.

Brought up in a left-wing Jewish vegetarian household in middle England, I attended an independent Church of England girls' day-school. There I spent my early teens happily rebellious, enjoying the role of the rather eccentric critic and debunker of the middle class, Christian conservatism which predominated. I had been passionately interested in politics for as long as I can remember, and grew up accustomed to long, intense political debates over dinner. My family had a tradition of involvement in anti-nuclear campaigns. My grandmother, a member of the Committee of a Hundred in the late 1950s, spent several spells in prison during my mother's childhood. My parents (who divorced when I was 9) had met at an international peace conference in Moscow, where my father was arrested for protesting against Soviet nuclear weapons. My early political consciousness was formed in an environment in which politics were always connected to personal experience. I cannot remember not knowing about the pogroms that forced my grandparents to flee to Britain in 1919, or about the Holocaust in which most of our relatives were murdered. I clearly recall my mother telling me, when I was very young, of the terror of living through the Cuban missile crisis, and my maternal grandmother describing the poverty of her childhood in rural Ireland. I had always 'known' that racism, fascism, war, nuclear weapons, and poverty were wrong, and that I must struggle for social change and for peace.

It was, however, watching a television programme about the government's 'Protect and Survive' civil-defence scheme (take the door off its hinges to make a shelter, whitewash the windows, and put a paper bag over your head), that captured my imagination and fuelled my nightmares of nuclear war. *Détente* was dead, hostilities between the superpowers were escalating, and NATO was about to site a new generation of nuclear missiles thirty miles from where we lived. In the autumn of 1980, while in London on our weekend access visit, I persuaded my mother that we should go on the first large demonstration of the rejuvenating peace movement. I remember the exhilaration of being part of a collective statement of opposition to the arms build-up, and afterwards I began to feel all the more intensely the isolation of my position at school, the lone anti-nuclear voice in my form. I joined national CND and subscribed to *Peace News*, but longed to do more.

When we moved into Northampton in 1982, having lived 15 miles away in a tiny hamlet ill-served by public transport, I immediately joined the local CND group. I set up a youth CND group and organized coaches to demos, leafletings, fly-postings, and benefit gigs. In the 'adult' group I became part of a dissatisfied caucus of non-Labour Party members who disliked the bureaucracy of the meetings and their control by a handful of male Labour hacks. I felt frustrated by their unwillingness to do anything other than hold public meetings and collect signatures for petitions. Increasingly I thought of myself as an anarchist rather than as a socialist, and, with others who felt similarly, formed an alternative 'affinity group'. We had wider concerns than the CND group, embracing environmentalism and animal liberation, and we prepared ourselves to take direct action by discussing at length the philosophy and practice of non-violence. In many ways this group was much more satisfying to my political concerns. It was a small group, in which decision-making was by consensus, not by majority vote, and we shared a deep sense of urgency in the struggle to save the world. But I still felt marginal, an outsider. Slowly I came to realize that it was because I was a woman. There were only three women in the group, and just as in the CND group it was the men who set the agenda, directed and dominated the discussion, and listened to each other. We women certainly weren't the tea-makers—that would have been far too overt a form of sexism for this group of anti-sexist new men; rather, we were just completely peripheral. It was at about this time that I started to read the early feminist articles and pamphlets which connected militarism with male domination, and I heard about plans for the 'Embrace the Base' demonstration at Greenham.

In December 1982 my mother, my sister, and I travelled down to Greenham from London on one of the four or five coaches organized by Balham Women for Peace. The event was incredible; over 30,000 women gathered to protest against cruise missiles. I couldn't believe that there were so many women there, and I had never experienced an atmosphere like it before. We sang, danced, shouted, and I felt strong and powerful. I began to believe that there was something I could do to save the world.

I wanted to stay that night and take part in the blockade of the base on the Monday morning to prevent the entrance of construction vehicles to work on the missile silos. But I had no bedding with me and anyway I had to be in school. I didn't know it at the time, but that trip to Greenham was to sound the death knell to my school career; for the next eleven months, until I finally left school, my attention was elsewhere. Although I had loved academic work, school came to seem irrelevant, a diversion from what really mattered. The world was on the eve of destruction, and yet I was supposed to do prose translations and churn out essays. In June 1983 I was arrested for the first time, along with several other members of the affinity group, at a blockade of the USAF base at Upper Heyford. I had taken time off school to go to the demonstration, and afterwards was absent in order to make court appearances.

That autumn, as the date of deployment of cruise drew nearer, the conflict between school and my political involvements intensified. I was entered for the Cambridge entrance exams in early November, but spent the last weekend of October at Greenham with thousands of other women, cutting the fence and getting arrested. In spite of our protests the first missiles arrived in November, and my double-life reached a critical moment. I had passed my exams, but there were still an intolerable seven more months until 'A' levels. By the second week in December, exactly a year after my first visit, I had left school and moved to Greenham.

The last thing on my mind during the ten months I spent living at Greenham was the thesis I am now writing. I had been forced to choose between academic work and my political life, and I chose politics; there was no contest, really. But by summer 1985 I was ready to go back to studying and embarked on a sociology degree.

That is the 'public' account of how I came to be involved in Greenham and ended up, eventually, researching Greenham. It is an account that would probably be recognized by my family, my history teacher at school, and my friends in anti-nuclear groups in Northampton. But there is another strand to the autobiography of this period of my life, one that was intensely private at the time. If it goes against the grain to include the above account in a piece of sociological research, to write what follows is surely beyond the pale. That I should choose to reveal the following despite warnings that it may harm my prospects of an academic career is indicative of the methodological importance I attach to the demand that the researcher place herself on the same critical plane as those she is researching. Reflexivity can be a frightening demand.

Early in 1982, alongside the sense of being different which I had always cherished (there weren't many other Jewish vegetarian daughters of socialist acupuncturists at my school!), I became aware of an altogether more disturbingly 'different' part of myself. I fell in love and started a relationship with another young woman, a year above me at school.

Becoming aware of my lesbianism was both an exciting and a deeply painful experience. The joys of exploring my sexuality and the delights of sharing my political passions with someone else for the first time thrilled me to the core, and I wanted to tell everyone. But very soon most of my form had stopped talking to me, the room would fall silent when I walked in, and then the whispering would begin. Many of my friends no longer wanted to know me. I started to feel that I could never be happy as a lesbian, that in choosing to love a woman I was choosing a life of isolation and loneliness. The pressure took its toll on our relationship, and during the year-and-a-half of its duration we broke up and got back together many times. Everything was made even worse by the fact that my lover became seriously ill during this time, and was forbidden by her parents (who knew of our relationship) to come on demonstrations with me or to invite me to her house.

In effect I was leading three different lives; there was my school and home life, my political life, and my lesbian life. I felt torn in different directions and tormented by the impossibility of integrating the three different 'me's. For the first two there were role models, and I could be socially acceptable in both of those two very different worlds. But my lesbianism seemed to bring only exile and hatred, and I gradually came to despise 'Sasha the lesbian', and my lover. Not surprisingly, we eventually split up for good. I busied myself in my politics, but never once told my political friends, afraid that I would be cast out of that circle in the same way that I had been by my school-friends.

It was Greenham that changed things. A visit to Northampton by a Greenham woman to tell women involved in CND about the first mass 'criminal damage' planned for Halloween prompted a decision by the women in the affinity group. We left the group, which we had been finding increasingly unsatisfactory, and the three of us went to Greenham together for a long weekend. It was my third visit, but the first time that I became aware of what it was, besides the feeling of 'actually doing something', that so attracted me. It was the sense that women can do things with each other, without men, that are important and exciting, and it was the realization that many of the women there were proud, defiant, self-confident lesbians. Greenham offered me a way of committing myself fully to opposing nuclear weapons, and the possibility that it was all right to be a lesbian, that I could be happy with who I was. At Greenham I could integrate my 'political-self' and my 'lesbian-self'.

That only left my 'academic-self'. In many ways she was irrevocably changed by Greenham, by an intense period of confrontation with the state, by living outside the norms of society, by going to prison, and by becoming a lesbian feminist. I chose sociology as the subject most likely to offer me the sort of explanations I sought for the issues that concerned me, but I didn't have high expectations of what I already knew was the world of 'men's studies'. Because the feminist sociology and the chance to explore theories of women's oppression were largely left to the final year, I was far from ready to stop when I reached what I'd been waiting for. Hence the Ph.D.

Writing my thesis on Greenham has been, in part, an attempt to finally reunite those three parts of myself that I had believed were irreconcilable. The project has been the antithesis of alienated labour, a labour of love, motivated by an impulse to explore systematically and rigorously the sociological significance of Greenham. My subjectivity, my feelings, and my experiences, public and private, could not be wrenched from it because they provide both the motivation and much of the material for it. Rather than 'bracketing' my involvement in Greenham for the purposes of the research, I have self-consciously exploited it.

I lived at Greenham for ten months. During this period I had the whole gamut of 'Greenham experiences'. I lived, at different times, in a bender or a tent, or just under the stars, with one rucksack of possessions and a roll of bedding, through rain, snow, drizzle, and hail, as well as in the scorching summer heat. Except when I woke to find my sleeping bag soaking wet and that there was no dry wood for the fire, the weather didn't really bother me. I washed under a tree from a kettle of boiling water, and did my share of cooking for everyone over an open fire. From April 1984 we experienced evictions once a day or more. I often awoke to policemen shining torches in my face, or vigilantes shouting abuse and throwing rocks. I have been beaten up, thrown off lorries, and dragged through barbed wire by soldiers, and pushed into mud up to my chest by policemen. We have blockaded convoys of military vehicles carrying cruise missiles on exercise, and have been herded into pens by soldiers. Night after night we crawled through the undergrowth to cut down fences, enter the base, and occupy buildings. I have lost count of the number of times I was arrested and appeared in court, but I remember very clearly my two spells in prison.

Lest living at Greenham reads as sacrifice and misery, I must explain that, above all, Greenham was exhilarating, liberating, and great fun. Living with an ever-changing group of women from all over the world, global sisterhood was our everyday experience. There was a great feeling of community, and I formed deep, long-lasting friendships. We experimented with non-hierarchical, collective ways of decision-making about actions and money, and did heavy manual work that many of us had never tried before—mending and maintaining vehicles, chopping wood, building shelters. We wrote songs about things that happened to us, and we laughed a lot, at ourselves, and at the police and soldiers. From it all I developed a profound sense of our collective agency and our power to challenge the state, the military, the police, the courts, and the patriarchal alliances of local citizenry. In short, Greenham provided me with immense resources to find joy amidst struggles against a patriarchal system.

It is hard to write of this in the first-person singular. I have moved deliberately between the singular and plural voices in order to emphasize that much of what I have described are collective experiences. None the less, this intellectual autobiography is uniquely mine, mediated by my pre-existing subjectivity and prior life experiences, and it is this that has shaped my research project.

Methodological Issues

Two distinctive methodological features of my research become apparent in the context of this account of my intellectual auto-biography—first, that it is 'insider research', and secondly, that it is largely retrospective. Both of these depart from customary ethnographic research practice and deserve further discussion.

Insider Research

Whilst 'insider research' is rarely discussed in textbooks on research methods and does not appear in Gold's (1958) classic fourfold typology of field-work roles, I am certainly not the first sociologist to use her personal experience and unique life-history for research purposes. Long before feminists were advocating this, Mills argued that the sociological imagination thrives on inward reflection: 'you must learn to use your life experience in your intellectual work, continually to examine and interpret it. In this sense craftmanship (*sic*) is the centre of yourself and you are personally involved in every intellectual product upon which you work' (Mills 1958 196).

More recently several sociologists have coined different terms for what I choose, for simplicity's sake, to call 'insider research'. Riemer claims that 'opportunistic research strategies' (1977, p. 467), using one's own 'at hand' knowledge, unique biographies, and situational familiarities as sources of research ideas and data, can be sociologically profitable: 'Adoption of an opportunistic research strategy enables the researcher to use familiar situations or convenient events to their advantage. They *know* rather than *know about* their area of study. They are insiders' (p. 469). Adler and Adler, in a discussion of different field-work roles, identify the 'complete-member-researcher role' (1987, p. 67). Within this role, they distinguish between the 'opportunistic researcher', who studies settings with which she is already familiar, and the 'convert', who becomes the phenomenon which she is studying. Hayano (1983), who conducted a study of poker rooms where he was already a regular player, calls the former type of research 'auto-ethnography', the study of 'one's own people' (p. 150). Greed (1990), a surveyor who researched women in her profession, names the method 'retrospective ethnography', because it involves drawing on one's past experience: 'I have already lived what I am researching . . . The idea is that I look back on events from my past life and observe and analyze them, giving them the same research treatment as the events that happen today, almost like an action replay' (p. 147).

A number of writers argue that the best qualitative researchers are those who are already 'empirically literate', that is, already familiar with the phenomenon and setting under study. If the investigator already 'fits' into a particular environment and is familiar with its social organization, there is a certain level of 'in-built, face-level trust' between researcher and researched (Riemer, 1977, p. 474). They have a shared language and set of experiences which can be taken for granted: 'The researcher knows the language and symbolic meanings of those being studied. This enables the researcher to avoid meaningless and irrelevant questions, and to probe sensitive areas with greater ease' (Riemer 1977, p. 474). In addition, as Riemer points out, being an insider 'acts as a built-in truth check' (p. 474), a form of triangulation. The researcher is more able to discount misinformation, whether deliberate or not, and can evaluate informants' accounts in relation to her own experience. Prior in-depth knowledge of the subject of research also means that the researcher has greater control over choice of respondents and can achieve a more representative sample.

In comparison, 'strangers' are more easily misled and distracted, and find it hard to get beyond 'the superficial or the merely salient' (Miles and Huberman, 1984, p. 48). It is more likely that they will attempt to lay inappropriate conceptual frameworks on to situations. Moreover, there are many social settings which would be inaccessible to an 'outsider' researcher, even one who was trying very hard to participate fully. Krieger's (1983, 1984) study of a Midwestern lesbian community was only possible because of the trust she had by virtue of her prior membership. Another example is Dornbusch's (1955) study of the Coast Guard Academy, which was based perforce on retrospective material from his time there as a cadet, since cadets were forbidden to criticize the institution to outsiders.

I believe that in conducting this research project, it was strongly advantageous for me to have been involved in Greenham myself. In effect, the research began with my first visit to the camp, and although I stopped living there in October 1984, I still know women who live there now, and I have been back for a number of periods of up to a week over the last seven years. This means that I had a large amount of background knowledge on which to draw, and many initial ideas and hunches about what it would be sociologically interesting to focus on.

For example, my familiarity with everyday life at Greenham, and its routines and vocabulary, meant that I didn't commit the social solecism of the questioners who are described, in affectionate exasperation, in the following Greenham song:

> *At the Peace Camp, Newbury, Berkshire*
> (to the tune of 'English Country Garden')
>
> What are the questions visitors will ask us
> At the Peace Camp, Newbury, Berkshire?
> I'll tell you now of some that I know,
> And the rest, you'll surely ask them.
> 'Are there many of you here?'
> 'Is it cold, and are you queer?'
> 'Where do you get your water from?'
> 'Would you die for the cause?'
> 'Do you shit in the gorse?
> At the Peace Camp, Newbury, Berkshire.
>
> What are the questions the media will ask us
> At the Peace Camp, Newbury, Berkshire?
> I'll tell you now of some that I know,
> And the rest, you'll read them later.
> 'Why did you make this sacrifice?'
> 'Can I talk to someone nice?'
> 'How does it feel now you have failed?'
> 'Can you pose by the gate?'
> 'Hurry up, it's getting late.'
> At the Peace Camp, Newbury, Berkshire
> . . .

Having been on the receiving-end many times, I was all-too aware of how intrusive were the battery of questions of a well-meaning researcher, whether visitor, journalist, or sociologist (we did not differentiate). Particularly between 1982 and 1985, living at Greenham was often like being in a goldfish bowl. Many were the times I staggered blearily to the fire to make my first cup of coffee of the day, only to be greeted by a microphone-wielding reporter or questionnaire-toting undergraduate. Persistent inquirers into the minutiae of daily life at Greenham, if men, would be told to visit the mixed peace camp at Molesworth, and if women, would usually be invited to stay a few days and experience Greenham for themselves.

Fortunately I avoided finding myself in this situation, since I had already experienced Greenham for myself, voluntarily.

I also made a decision, based on my experience of living at Greenham, not to attempt to interview women actually at the camp. I knew that the logistics of a three-hour interview, probing personal histories, would be impossible outdoors, sitting on the ground, a log, or a crate, with a tape-recorder on one knee. Undoubtedly, if we sat in the public space by the fire we would be repeatedly interrupted, or if we found somewhere quiet away from the fire, we would freeze (eight months of the year).

Perhaps even more importantly though, I simply would not have been able to interview most of the women I did, had I not been a Greenham woman myself. Greenham was an extremely intense, 'life-changing' experience which many of my interviewees said they would never have agreed to talk about to someone who hadn't shared it. Greenham was a community, with its own history, vocabulary, and set of reference-points, knowledge of which indicated member-ship, and elicited an extraordinary amount of trust and openness. I am convinced that the degree of intimacy between myself and the women I interviewed was the product of our shared experiences, and was only possible because they knew that I was a Greenham woman and a feminist first, both temporally and in allegiance, and a sociologist second. It would not have been the same had I gone as a researcher to live at Greenham as a 'complete-member' and become a 'convert' (Adler and Adler 1987, pp. 67–9), which is the more usual participant–observer role. My membership of Greenham friendship networks also made it possible for me to interview many women whom an outsider would not have 'found'; for example, women without a high profile in the media, and those whose involvement was largely in local support groups, rather than at the camp.

My method of insider research is certainly open to criticism for more traditional methodologists. It departs radically, not only from the standards of positivist research, but also from those of mainstream interpretive qualitative research. It blatantly eschews the 'bracketing' of personal experience, as advocated by Schutz (1967), and is based on what ethnographers have traditionally most warned against: 'going native' (Bryman 1988; Miles and Huberman 1984). As a Greenham woman researching Greenham, I did not fulfil the role of 'marginal native' advocated for ethnographers by Freilich (1977); I was already a 'native'. I am deeply emotionally involved with the subject of my study, and this undoubtedly shaped the questions I asked and the nature of my sociological interest in the topic. Because my self-hood is implicated so strongly in the research process, replication in the same form by another researcher would be impossible. However, as I have argued earlier, the social location and experiences of a researcher inevitably shape research, and the difference between insider research and other forms of qualitative, and indeed quantitative, research is only a matter of degree. I claim a high level of validity for my findings *because of*, not in spite of, my own involvement in Greenham. I do not claim that the research product is in anyway definitive, but I do believe that it is better than that produced by an outsider could have been.

This said, I should acknowledge that even within a post-positivist, feminist framework, insider research is not without problems. The most obvious of these is the danger of being too close to the subject-matter either to see the sociological significance of that which appears completely normal, or to be able to frame criticisms. Had I started researching Greenham very soon after living there, with little time for reflection, the problem of desensitization through familiarity might have been more serious. As it was, beginning four years after Greenham had last been my home, I came back to the subject-matter refreshed. Throughout the formal period of the research I made a conscious effort to 'make the familiar strange', to attempt to see things as if for the first time and then to compare these observations with my immediate 'gut feelings'. As far as criticizing Greenham is concerned, having overcome the initial barrier of anxiety about undertaking the research (discussed later), I have been determined to tell 'the truth' about Greenham as I have seen it. And here again the length of time between my living at Greenham and formally beginning the research, and my subsequent engagement with individual feminists and a feminist literature hostile to Greenham have, I believe, afforded me a certain degree of critical distance.

Retrospective Research

My study of Greenham is also, unavoidably, largely retrospective. I was only 16 when Greenham surged into public consciousness as an important new social–political movement. Even if I had been older, and a trained sociologist, I doubt whether I would have been able to conduct a research project on the camp contemporaneously with its peak. The emotional impact of involvement and the life-changes it brought about were so great that I would have had little time for getting on with the research, and probably little inclination to do so. Certainly had I, or anyone else, tried to do so, the product would have been very different: more immediate, possibly more descriptive, but lacking a long-term perspective and overview. Had it been based on participant observation rather than complete membership (which I doubt the women would have agreed to), I think the data would have been less rich. Interviews were held anything up to ten years after the events they describe, and my recollections are of events and experiences of up to nine years ago. The problem usually highlighted in relation to retrospective data is the possibility of distortions in memory, due either to memory failure or influenced by subsequent changes in values and norms, which may unconsciously alter perceptions. Thompson (1988) discusses the nature of oral history evidence and evaluates the social–psychological literature on memory. His conclusion is that by far the most significant loss of material from the memory occurs very shortly after the event (within minutes). The process of discarding continues over time, but for the first thirty-four years is insignificant compared with the immediate phase of loss (Thompson 1988, pp. 110–13). Thus, there seems to be a 'curve of forgetfulness' which inevitably affects even contemporary reporting and participant observers. The research on remembering also appears to show that the memory process depends, to a large extent, on interest: 'Reliability depends partly on whether the question interests an informant. It is lack of any intrinsic interest which vitiates many of the early laboratory experiments with memory . . . (Thompson 1988, p. 113). Recalling is an active process; a story may be retold in different forms to different audiences, and memory can be aided by prompting and context and hindered by an unwillingness to recall distasteful events and experiences (p. 114).

I believe that the retrospective nature of my interview data does not constitute a serious problem of reliability. As the most distant events of which anyone was asked to speak took place ten years previously, recall was probably little worse than it would have been had I been interviewing a day or two after the event in question. All the interviewees said that the experience of involvement in Greenham had been extremely important in their lives, and they were all very willing to talk. Thus, their memories were probably aided by their interest and the significance of the experience in their life-histories.

It is, of course, possible that unhappy and disturbing experiences were not recalled as readily as more positive ones, and this must be taken into consideration. For example, few women volunteered memories of loneliness or isolation during their first few days at Greenham. But on prompting with a question, several went on to remember such feelings, which I assume had been selectively pushed aside because their overall memory of Greenham was positive. Similarly, when asked explicitly about police harassment a number of women recalled incidents that had not appeared in their unprompted recollections. Certainly many women were nostalgic about their time at Greenham, but no-one was so nostalgic as to be unable to remember disputes and conflicts or to frame criticisms.

Another possibility is that memories have been selectively organized to fit in with changed values and political beliefs, so that perhaps an interviewee reinterprets her life before Greenham in the light of her new political consciousness. Indeed, I am sure that this had happened with women I interviewed, but I do not think it is particularly problematic. Recognizing that *all* recalling is influenced by current beliefs, my interest has been more in the (current) social meanings of particular events and part experiences to the women, and less in reconstructing 'factual' accounts of events. The retrospective nature of the interviews is, in itself, interesting. When recalling events a few women telescoped two separate events into one. Here the usefulness of having been involved myself and having a large amount of historical background knowledge became apparent. When it was important to try to separate out particular events, I would probe and prompt, so that usually the interviewee began to disentangle them herself. On other occasions, where this did not seem important, I just noted the significance of the reorganization of memory that appeared to have taken place and let it be.

My conclusion is that the retrospective character of my research was actually advantageous. It gave me and my respondents more perspective on the importance of Greenham. It allowed for a longitudinal element in the study, and focused both my attention and that of my interviewees on changes at an individual and a societal level. As Morgan (1977) has noted, it is only really possible to grasp the meanings of our actions and changes in our consciousness retrospectively.

The Strategic Use of Self in the Research Process

I now move on to look at how I made strategic use of my insider status at each stage in the actual process of carrying out the research.

Sampling

As a loosely structured social–political movement, Greenham has no membership, no list of subscribers, no ready-made sampling frame, and hence no possibility of probability sampling. So, I had to rely on my own knowledge of the social organization of Greenham by gate-based networks.[9] I started with my own network of friends, who largely lived at Greenham between 1982 and 1985, and I worked outwards, using what has been called the 'snowball sampling' method (Coleman 1958). Greenham did not work on a rota basis, and has no clearly defined cohorts of activists. Thus, a woman whom I knew from my time living at the camp might know women who were there before or after me, as well as women who were there at the same time as me but whom I never met. Networks of friends overlapped considerably, and so I was able very quickly to move beyond women already of my acquaintance, by asking each woman I interviewed to suggest further possible interviewees. Of the thirty-five women I interviewed, twenty-five were not known to me prior to the interview, although in some cases I knew of particular women through mutual friends.

From the outset I was extremely concerned to maximize the variety of women I interviewed, in order to move beyond the popular stereotypes of Greenham women (the *Guardian* stereotype of the middle-class, middle-aged, southern England mother of four; the *Sun* stereotype of the teenager with a crew-cut). Based on my knowledge of hundreds of women I had met at Greenham, I drew up a list of characteristics of those involved with Greenham which I hypothesized were important variables. This process is often called 'judgement sampling' (Burgess 1984) or 'strategic sampling'

---

[9] From January 1983 onwards there have always been camps outside the Main Gate and at least one other gate to the base (and at times between the gates as well). The gates had been given names by Greenham women (the colours of the rainbow) early in the history of Greenham, and the camps came to be referred to as 'gates'; e.g. Blue Gate is the camp outside the gate which women had given the name Blue. (Interestingly the Ministry of Defence Police long ago adopted our naming system).

(Thompson 1988). These variables were: age when first involved; length of involvement; dates of first involvement and withdrawal; gate of association; level of involvement—'camper', 'stayer', or 'visitor'; place of residence before involvement; occupation before involvement; sexuality identification before involvement; mother-hood status (age and number of children) before involvement; education before involvement; sexuality identification now; occupa-tion now; class identification; racial/ethnic origin; nationality. I entered these on a matrix-style chart, which I then filled in for the first few interviewees (who came from my own network of friends). Then I began to sample with these variables in mind, attempting to achieve as much variety as possible across the range of characteristics, and continuing to fill in the chart. I was concerned particularly to focus on women who had not been in the public eye as media-chosen 'spokespeople'.[10] While I do not claim statistical representativeness for my final sample, I do believe that it covered a very broad cross-section of the sorts of women who were involved with Greenham, in different ways and at different periods in the camp's history.

The biggest problem I encountered was deciding when to stop, and whom not to interview. By the end of the field-work period I had collected the names and addresses of several hundred women, each of whom would have had her own fascinating account of her experiences of Greenham. It was difficult to decide which contacts to follow up and which not, often just based on snippets of biographical information and how these fitted into my schema for maximizing diversity. On a number of occasions my imagination was simply caught by something I was told about an individual, and I felt that I had to interview her whatever the state of my variables matrix. As Thompson notes: 'One of the deepest lessons of oral history is the uniqueness, as well as the representativeness, of every life story. There are some so rare and vivid that they demand recording, whatever the plan' (Thompson 1988, p. 131).

---

[10] The danger of 'élite bias' is much commented upon in the literature on various form of qualitative research (e.g. Lofland 1971; Miles and Huberman 1984; Zimmerman and Wieder 1977). The feminist literature on biographies emphasizes the importance of challenging the 'great individual' approach to feminist history, which is a self-perpetuating cycle in which once particular people have been singled out for mention in a study, they come up again and again in future studies. This perpetuates the belief that only a few individuals had any influence (Hannam 1985; Stanley 1985).

The Dialogic Interview

I discovered very quickly that whenever I had a telephone-number for a woman it was best to make initial contact by telephone rather than by letter. Explaining the research over the telephone proved to be much more successful than in writing because it allowed women to ask questions and voice their doubts immediately. I was then able to respond to them as an embodied woman rather than an unknown correspondent. I always began by telling the woman who had given me her name, and by explaining that I was doing some research about Greenham for a Ph.D. and a book (forthcoming). I would then say that I had been involved with the camp myself. At this point every woman I contacted by phone expressed interest in the project and needed little, if any, persuasion to agree to take part. Those who did need some persuasion were a handful of women who had only visited the camp and who thought that I should talk to 'real' Greenham women. When I explained that I thought it important to interview women who had been involved in all sorts of ways, they all agreed.

Several of the interviews of women I did not already know were arranged by the women who put me in touch with them, and I found this problematic. Because I had not made the initial contact myself, these women did not really know what to expect, in terms of the sort of things that I would be interested in, how long the interview would last, and that I would like it to be on a one-to-one basis. These interviews tended to be terminated before I felt everything had been covered, usually because the woman had another engagement. In the majority of cases, however, where I had negotiated the interview myself (which I soon realized was essential), the interviews would run their course generally unhindered by time-constraints; they lasted between two and four hours, and were remarkably free of interruptions (a number of women left phones unanswered).

The interviews, which were all tape-recorded, were loosely structured around a guide that I had drawn up before the first interview, based on what I considered likely to provide data for the questions and issues that lay behind the research. After the first four interviews, all with women already known to me, I revised the guide slightly. The 'guide' was just that, a point of reference for me to ensure that I covered everything I wished to and that I covered the same topics in each interview. In most interviews I referred to it very little until close to the end, finding that most of the questions arose 'spontaneously' in the course of our conversation.

I was particularly interested in understanding the relative significance to the women I interviewed of different events and aspects of life at Greenham and of the issues with which Greenham was concerned. I wanted the women's own weighting of issues to become apparent through the interviews. So I asked questions about nuclear weapons near the beginning of interviews, and I refrained from bringing up issues of feminism and sexuality until later. I believe that this strategy was largely successful, and that I have achieved an insight into the importance attached to different experiences and issues by the women themselves. I cannot claim, however, that they were not at all influenced by my interests and emphases which, unavoidably, became more and more apparent as the interview proceeded. It is possible that women whom I knew prior to the interview were more likely to be influenced in this way. However, as must by now be clear, I do not believe it is possible for any researchers to absent themselves from the research, in the manner traditionally advocated. I believe that the impact I had on the weightings given by the interviewees to different issues would have been no greater than that of a stranger. Indeed, it is possible that I had less impact because impression management and the 'good name' of Greenham would be much less important when interviewed by an insider.[11]

The term 'rapport' does not accurately describe the intense, passionate connections established between myself and the majority of the women I interviewed. Very quickly our talking about Greenham seemed to recapture some of the energy and excitement of our periods of involvement. I found that as soon as it was established that we had a shared experience of actions and daily life at the camp, and a shared vocabulary for discussing them, women seemed to open up and were prepared to expose their thoughts and feelings quite boldly. Although the interview is an inherently 'unnatural' situation, I found that almost all of them proceeded smoothly, much like a long, intense conversation. Like Oakley (1981) and Finch (1984), I frequently found myself asked for my opinions and about my experience of particular events or issues; the interviews typically

---

[11] The work of Goffman (1959) has shown how people seek to manage impressions of themselves and of the settings with which they are associated.

became dialogic. I answered as fully and honestly as I could, and often the divergence or similarity of our opinions and experiences became a topic of discussion in itself. This sort of mutual exchange of stories was not only ethically and politically desirable for me as a feminist, but I believe it added to the richness of the interview material, and prompted my memory of particular incidents. Many of the interviews covered deeply 'personal' matters, such as sexuality, and when asked similarly 'personal' questions I felt it absolutely proper to respond. By the end of almost all the interviews I felt warmly towards the woman, and I think in most of these cases this was reciprocal. I left the majority of interviews with hugs and kisses, and often invitations to make social calls in the future. This is not really surprising when it is considered that I was interviewing women who have been involved in the same social–political movement and networks as myself and who share a number of important experiences, beliefs, values, and friends with me. However, none of this is standard interview practice, and would be frowned upon by those adhering to methodologies that emphasize objectivity, inter-subjective reliability, and replicability, and which do not seek to locate the researcher on the same critical plane as the researched.

At this point I must acknowledge the exceptions to this description of the interviewing process. There were two interviews which did not happen like this, where I felt a low level of 'rapport' and personal engagement with the women concerned. In both these cases there was a distinct absence of mutual liking. These women were the least feminist of all of those I interviewed, and they both expressed the opinion that I was asking too many questions about 'women's issues' (although, as I have already said, I was deliberately holding back from doing this). Their concern was exclusively with Greenham as a site of opposition to nuclear weapons, and they objected to its 'hijacking' by 'militant feminists'. Neither woman wanted to talk about her feelings about Greenham; they both wished to restrict the discussion to 'public' political issues and matters of 'fact' about Greenham. They were not the oldest women I interviewed, nor were they, by any means, the only heterosexual women, nor the only women who never actually lived at the camp, or who had different politics from me. Greenham was a place of coalition and extraordinary diversity, and I interviewed many other women who were unlike me in all these respects. However, these two were the only women who did not share a basic set of Greenham beliefs, who were anti-feminist, anti-lesbian, and who thought of going to Greenham as a sacrifice rather than as an enjoyable, exciting political action. What all this meant was that the basis of the easy 'rapport' that I had with everyone else, whatever her age, sexuality, or political background, did not exist.

After the first of these women volunteered a number of anti-lesbian remarks, I felt unable to ask her any of the questions that I wished to about sexuality. I felt intimidated and upset by her hostility, and criticized myself for not probing her anti-feminism and anti-lesbianism more. After all, interviewers are not supposed to feel personally attacked by what an interviewee says. But I did feel it, and I am sure she meant me to, having apparently made a number of assumptions about me on the basis of a couple of questions I posed about Greenham being women-only and, I suspect, on the basis of my age and appearance. A few days later, and a little more experienced as an interviewer, I was rather more assertive in probing the other woman's anti-feminism. But again her hostility, which arose as soon as I mentioned 'women', caused a mutual mistrust and formed a barrier to the sort of rapport I achieved with the majority of my interviewees.

Although these interviews left me feeling somewhat demoralized, in retrospect I have come to see the importance of the data they produced. They also made me realize that interviews do not always have to work well as social encounters; they don't have to run smoothly and involve strong 'rapport', in order to produce useful data. However, as the exceptions that proved the rule, they also highlighted the importance of the trust and intimacy that developed between myself and most of the interviewees in getting beyond relatively superficial political statements and elucidating personal experiences.

Analysis and Theorizing

Like most research, my study of Greenham does not conform to either of the ideal typical models of induction or deduction. I did not come to the project with 'an empty head' and a hypothetical 'explanation' of Greenham, as the former tends to suggest. Nor was the agenda of the research entirely pre-set or its products untainted by my own material experiences, as the latter proposes (Stanley and Wise 1990). The method of data analysis that I used owes a debt to

Glaser and Strauss's 'grounded theory' (1967), although I did not follow their injunctions to the letter.[12] What my approach shared with theirs is a commitment to refining and testing ideas and theory throughout the process of data-collection, so that the collection of data could be guided by my emerging theoretical ideas.[13]

I began the study with a large number of ideas and hypotheses at various levels of development. These were derived from reflections on my own period of involvement and an engagement with the literatures on social movements, women and politics, and feminist theory. From there I formulated a set of research questions, which helped to focus and bound the data-collection. I set out to put these ideas and tentative hypotheses to the test of the experiences of a broad sample of women, of as wide a range of backgrounds and standpoints as possible. From my interviews with these women many more hypotheses arose, which I noted in the form of memos (Strauss 1987). I then sought to test these out in subsequent interviews by asking women directly what they thought of a particular idea or theory. The virtue of the loosely structured, in-depth interview was that it was possible, throughout the year-and-a-half of my field-work, continually to test my latest thoughts on other women and incorporate their feedback into my evolving analysis.

This practice acted as a form of triangulation, the 'respondent validation' (Hammersley and Atkinson, 1983; Miles and Huberman, 1984) of my interpretations of data derived both from my own experience and from earlier interviews. But more importantly, it was vital to my research design, as a practice which recognizes the agency of human individuals. It acknowledges and utilizes the fact that theorizing is not an exclusively academic enterprise, only conducted

---

[12] Strict adherence to grounded theory is recognized as problematic by a number of writers; for example, Hammersley (1984) argues that it is impossible because of the time needed for transcription of interview data (and I certainly found this), and Bulmer (1979) questions whether it is possible to suspend awareness of relevant theories and concepts until a late stage in the process. Bryman (1988) points out that very few researchers have actually made use of the approach in the exact form advocated by Glaser and Strauss.

[13] Since Glaser and Strauss's 'Discovery of Grounded Theory', most writers on qualitative research have advocated the simultaneous collection and analysis of data, recognizing that data analysis actually begins even before the field-work; see e.g. Burgess (1984); Miles and Huberman (1984); Hammersley and Atkinson (1983).

in the isolation of the scholar's study. Theorizing, particularly feminist theorizing, is, and must be, as collective an activity as possible, closely intertwined with political praxis. Ethically and politically I did not want to theorize *about* Greenham women, as some strange foreign species, in the way that ethnographers often do; I wanted to theorize *with* Greenham women, my sisters. Perhaps the ideal situation would have been to do this in group meetings when Greenham was at its height. But given that this was no longer possible, and that the women now live scattered all over Britain and beyond, the process of analysis that I adopted seemed like a reasonable compromise. Many women I interviewed volunteered their own theories about much that happened at Greenham and about the reactions of the men as a group, and of the various agencies of the state, as well as about the methodology of my research. Texts on ethnography traditionally regard the 'theorizing informant' as problematic, but I found such informants absolutely invaluable.[14] In some ways interviewing Greenham women was like having a large, diverse research team with whom to mull over findings and hunches, and the final analysis I developed draws heavily on the theoretical contributions of the women I interviewed.

I transcribed in full the first third of the interviews using a word-processing package, while pressures of time (and concern for my sanity!) meant that I transcribed the remainder more selectively, in order to draw out similarities to and differences from the first set. Then, making use of the memos I had kept, I 'coded' each interview for significant categories and concepts, teasing out of the data important themes. The 'codes' acted as abbreviations or labels to classify segments of the interview texts, pulling together large amounts of material into meaningful units of analysis. I then entered the codes against the transcribed text by means of the qualitative data analysis package: *The Ethnograph*. This facilitated the retrieval of all instances of particular categories across the thirty-five cases. The process of transcription and coding took place, as much as possible, throughout the period of field-work, as well as afterwards, and I continually incorporated new categories that arose from the data into the coding scheme.

---

[14] For example, Hammersley and Atkinson warn against the 'more "sophisticated" interviewee' who moves away from description into analysis, as this means that 'the data base has been eroded' (1983, p. 189).

I then used the coding scheme to trawl other data sources. These included my own retrospective accounts of Greenham, written during the field-work period, newspaper cuttings, journals (my own from my time at Greenham, a collective gate journal, and journals of a number of women I interviewed), and Greenham newsletters and leaflets.

Ethical–Political Issues

Having been a Greenham woman myself, the ethics and politics that guided my research originated more in Greenham's values and politics than in the sociological literature on ethics. In particular, there was at Greenham a strong opposition to hierarchies and inequalities of power, and a concomitant emphasis on individual self-determination and autonomy. Researching my friends and my sisters has demanded the highest ethical–political practice; if I slipped up, I have no doubt that it would have been pointed out to me in no uncertain terms. The anti-hierarchical impulse of Greenham actually made me very dubious about doing research on Greenham at all. Greenham women, myself included, have always been very critical of anyone setting themselves up as an expert on the camp. For many months I grappled with anxieties about starting a project which would inevitably set me apart from my friends, and possibly make me enemies. But eventually I decided to take the plunge. I really did want to do the research and was prepared to risk criticism from women whose opinions matter to me.

Thus, it was clear from the outset that I would have to grapple with issues of power in the research relationship. I was extremely concerned not to objectify and exploit the women I was researching in the way that the media had so often done, removing all control over what was said about us. To this end, as I have discussed, I attempted to involve the women I interviewed in the process of theorizing about Greenham. The dialogic nature of the interviews, and the fact that I was also researching myself and my experiences, both helped to mitigate the inherent power-imbalance of the researcher–researched relationship.

Ultimately, though, much as feminist researchers may wish it, and myself as much as any, the problems of objectification and exploitation do not just disappear because of the researcher and the researched's shared experiences.[15] Indeed, it is probable that my insider status, which encouraged women to be exceptionally open with me, has given me much more power to exploit and manipulate the women whom I have interviewed than an outsider could ever have achieved.[16] Moreover, sometimes during dinner or drinks with friends when the conversation turned to Greenham, I would suddenly feel like a spy, secretly gathering snippets of information for later use. Of course, in theory my friends knew about my research, but I certainly didn't remind them every time I saw them that anything they said might be taken down in writing and used as data.[17] Similarly, I found myself acutely socially uncomfortable on my three or four trips to Greenham for 'reunions' during the period of the research. I made an effort to tell as many women as possible that I was doing the research, because I felt an ethical–political obligation to do so, even though I would have been there if my thesis had been about the decline of the Roman empire. Doing research in which one's own life and one's friends and acquaintances are always potential sources of hunches, theories, and data can be socially and ethically–politically extremely problematic, and means that one is never really off-duty.

However much I sought to involve the women in the research process, I have not conducted a truly *collective* piece of research. I have *exploited* and 'used' the women I have interviewed (and probably also unsuspecting women I have not interviewed), extracting their words to illustrate points of my choosing. When women did not validate my ideas and theories about Greenham, when 'interpretive asymmetry' became apparent, I sometimes chose to ignore the interpretations of the women who proffered them. In the final analysis, it has been *my* analysis that has triumphed; I have retained the power of authorship. It is my version of Greenham, albeit based on interviews with three-dozen other women, that will be published as authoritative. Although I hope very much that women collectively

[15] Oakley (1981) suggests that the problems of objectification and exploitation disappear for feminists researching women, because of the shared social structural position of the researcher and the researched. Wise (1987) and Bowles and Duelli Klein (1983) challenge this, and point out that women researchers tend to occupy more privileged social locations than the women they research.

[16] Finch (1984) and Stacey (1988) both suggest that the greater the intimacy and identification of the researcher and the researched, the greater the potential for exploitation.

[17] A similar experience is noted by Ditton (1977), Wise (1987), and Hobbs (1988).

will gain from its publication, and that the recording of Greenham and my analysis will prove empowering, it is I who profits as an individual (even if not financially).

As this is so, my most important ethical–political concern has been not to abuse the power of authorship. I felt obliged to point out to the women I was interviewing that I had designed and focused the research largely according to my interests, and that I retained the power of authorship. I promised to send them a transcript of, at the very least, any sections of their interview that I was planning to quote, in order to check for recording inaccuracies, but pointed out that I would, in the end, interpret it. Getting their agreement to this was a vital part of establishing 'informed consent' to the research. In addition, my awareness of the power of the written word in constructing history has committed me to ensuring that the research-product would reflect the variety of women who have been involved. I have aimed not to erase lesbians, working-class women, younger and older women, and women from minority ethnic groups, in the way that much that has been written about Greenham and other women's political mobilizations has done. I have also sought to give an important place in my narratives and analysis of Greenham to the voices of women who disagree with me. At the end of the day, though, all textual products of the research must be read with the accounts I have given of my experiences and subjectivity firmly in mind.

Conclusion

While doing feminist research as an insider may not be short on ethical and political dilemmas, my experience has been extremely rewarding. As an exercise in reflexive, unalienated labour, involving the 'unity of hand, brain and heart', as Rose (1983) proposes feminist research should, it has demonstrated the possibility of integrating 'the personal' and 'the sociological' within the confines of a doctoral thesis. Moreover, it has shown that there are numerous methodological advantages for feminists from the strategic use of insider knowledge and status, which far outweigh the traditionally emphasized problems. To conclude, I can but advocate that more sociologists look to their own unique life-histories and experiences for the inspiration of their research.

References

Acker, J., Barry, K. and Esseveld, J. (1983). 'Objectivity and Truth: Problems in Doing Feminist Research', 6 (4) *Women's Studies International Forum*, 423–35.

Adler, P. and Adler, P. (1987). *Membership Roles in Field Research* (Beverley Hills, Calif.: Sage).

Bernard, J. (1973). 'My Four Revolutions: An Autobiographical History of the ASA' in J. Huber (ed.), *Changing Woman in a Changing Society* (Chicago, Ill.: University of Chicago Press).

Bowles, G. and Duelli Klein, R. (1983). (eds.). *Theories of Women's Studies* (London: Routledge & Kegan Paul).

Bryman, A. (1988). *Quantity and Quality in Social Research* (London: Unwin Hyman).

Bulmer, M. (1979). 'Concepts in the Analysis of Qualitative Data', 27 (4) *Sociological Review*, 651–77.

Burgess, R. (1984). *In the Field: An Introduction to Field Research* (London: Unwin Hyman).

Coleman, J. (1958). 'Relational Analysis: The Study of Social Organizations with Survey Methods', 16 (4) *Human Organization*, 28–36.

Cook, J. and Fonow, M. (1986). 'Knowledge and Women's Interests: Issues of Epistemology and Methodology in Feminist Sociological Research', 56 *Sociological Inquiry*, 2–29.

Ditton, J. (1977). *Part-time Crime* (London: Macmillan).

Dornbusch, J. (1955). 'The Military Academy as an Assimilating Institution', 33 *Social Forces*, 316–21.

Du Bois, B. (1983). 'Passionate Scholarship: Notes on Values, Knowing and Method in Feminist Social Science' (in Bowles and Duelli Klein 1983).

Duelli Klein, R. (1983). 'How to Do What We Want to Do: Thoughts about Feminist Methodology' (in Bowles and Duelli Klein 1983).

Farran, D. *et al.* (1985). (eds.), *Writing Feminist Biography*, Studies in Sexual Politics, Nos. 13/14 (University of Manchester).

Finch, J. (1984). ' "It's great to have someone to talk to": The Ethics and Politics of Interviewing Women', in C. Bell and H. Roberts (eds.), *Social Researching: Politics, Problems, Practice* (London: Routledge & Kegan Paul).

Freilich, M. (1977). *Marginal Natives At Work: Anthropologists in the Field* (Cambridge, Mass.: Schenkman).

Gadamer, H. (1976). *Philosophical Hermeneutics* (Berkeley, Calif.: University of California Press).

Glaser, B. and Strauss, A. (1967). *The Discovery of Grounded Theory: Strategies for Qualitative Research* (Chicago, Ill.: Aldine).

Goffman, E. (1959). *The Presentation of Self in Everyday Life* (New York: Anchor Books).

Gold, R. (1958). 'Roles in Sociological Field Observation', 36 (3) *Social Forces*, 217–23.

Gouldner, A. (1970). *The Coming Crisis of Western Sociology* (New York: Basic Books).

Greed, C. (1990). 'The Professional and the Personal: A Study of Women Quantity Surveyors', in L. Stanley (ed.), *Feminist Praxis: Research, Theory and Epistemology in Feminist Sociology* (London: Routledge).

Griffiths, V. *et al.* (1987). (eds.), *Writing Feminist Biography 2: The Use of Life Histories*, Studies in Sexual Politics, No. 19 (University of Manchester).

Hammersley, M. (1984). 'The Researcher Exposed: A Natural History', in R. Burgess (ed.), *The Research Process in Educational Settings: Ten Case Studies* (London: Falmer Press).

Hammersley, M. and Atkinson, P. (1983). *Ethnography: Principles in Practice* (London: Tavistock).

Hannam, J. (1985). 'Usually Neglected in Standard Histories' (in Farran *et al.* 1985).

Harding, S. (1986). *The Science Question in Feminism* (Milton Keynes: Open University Press).

—— (1987). 'Is there a Feminist Method?', in S. Harding (ed.), *Feminism and Methodology* (Milton Keynes: Open University Press).

Hayano, D. (1983). *Poker Faces: The Life and Work of Professional Card Players* (London: University of California Press).

Hobbs, D. (1988). *Doing the Business: Entrepreneurship, the Working Class, and Detectives in the East End of London* (Oxford: Oxford University Press).

Krieger, S. (1983). *The Mirror Dance: Identity in a Women's Community* (Philadelphia, Penn.: Temple University Press).

—— (1985). 'Beyond "Subjectivity": The Use of Self in Social Science', 8 *Qualitative Sociology*, 309–24.

Lofland, J. (1971). *Analysing Social Settings* (New York: Wadsworth).

Mies, M. (1983). 'Towards a Methodology for Feminist Research' (in Bowles and Duelli Klein 1983).

Miles, M. B. and Huberman, A. M. (1984). *Qualitative Data Analysis: A Sourcebook of New Methods* (London: Sage).

Millman, M. and Moss Kanter, R. (1975). (eds.), *Another Voice: Feminist Perspectives on Social Life and Social Science* (New York: Anchor Books).

Mills, C. W. (1958). *The Sociological Imagination* (New York: Oxford University Press).

Morgan, R. (1977). *Going Too Far: The Personal Chronicle of a Feminist* (New York: Random House).

Nielsen, J. M. (1990). *Feminist Research Methods* (Boulder, Colo.: Westview Press).

Oakley, A. (1981). 'Interviewing Women: A Contradiction in Terms', in H. Roberts (ed.), *Doing Feminist Research* (London: Routledge & Kegan Paul).

Reinharz, S. (1984). *On Becoming a Social Scientist* (San Francisco, Calif.: Jossey-Bass).

Riemer, J. (1977). 'Varieties of Opportunistic Research', 5 (4) *Urban Life*, 467–77.

Rose, H. (1983). 'Hand, Brain and Heart: A Feminist Epistemology for the Natural Sciences', 1 (1) *Signs*.

Schutz, A. (1967). *The Phenomenology of the Social World* (Evanston, Ill.: Northwestern University Press).

Scott, S. (1984). 'The Personable and the Powerful: Gender and Status in Sociological Research', in C. Bell and H. Roberts (eds.), *Social Researching: Politics, Problems, Practice* (London: Routledge & Kegan Paul).

Smith, D. (1974). 'Women's Perspective as a Radical Critique of Sociology,' 44 *Sociological Inquiry*.

—— (1987). *The Everyday World as Problematic: A Feminist Sociology* (Milton Keynes: Open University Press).

Stacey, J. (1988). 'Can There Be a Feminist Ethnography?' 11 (1) *Women's Studies International Forum*, 21–7.

Stanley, L. (1985). 'Biography as Microscope or Kaleidoscope?' (in Farran *et al.* 1985).

—— (1990). 'Feminist Praxis and the Academic Mode of Production: An Editorial Introduction', in L. Stanley (ed.), *Feminist Praxis: Research, Theory and Epistemology in Feminist Sociology* (London: Routledge).

—— and S. Wise (1983). *Breaking Out: Feminist Consciousness and Feminist Research* (London: Routledge & Kegan Paul).

—— (1990). 'Method, Methodology and Epistemology in Feminist Research', in L. Stanley (ed.), *Feminist Praxis: Research, Theory and Epistemology in Feminist Sociology* (London: Routledge).

Strauss, A. (1987). *Qualitative Analysis for Social Scientists* (Cambridge: Cambridge University Press).

Thompson, P. (1988). *The Voice of the Past: Oral History* (Oxford: Oxford University Press).

Walby, S. (1988). 'Gender Politics and Social Theory', 22 (2) *Sociology*.

Westkott, M. (1979). 'Feminist Criticism of the Social Sciences', *Harvard Educational Review*, 49: 4, 422–30.

Wise, S. (1987). 'A Framework for Discussing Ethical Issues in Feminist Research: A Review of the Literature', *Writing Feminist Biography 2: Studies in Sexual Politics*, 19 (University of Manchester), 47–88.

Zimmerman, D. H. and Wieder, D. L. (1977). 'The Diary: Diary Interview Method', *Urban Life*, 54.

8

Racism, Sexuality, and the Process of Ethnographic Research

H. L. ACKERS*

This chapter is essentially concerned with reflections on my experiences of ethnographic research as a feminist. The research itself was neither consciously feminist nor primarily concerned with women's experiences. It was a study of racism and political marginalization in Britain and focused upon institutional racism within the Labour Party. In practice, much of the research took place in predominantly male contexts. Reflecting on this scenario some five years later, from a feminist perspective, reveals the determining influence of gender and sexuality throughout the research process from its inception to its conclusion.

Introduction: Gender, Racism, and Social Research

Liz Stanley (1990) argues that 'good' research is that which accounts for the conditions of its own production, thereby resulting in 'unalienated knowledge'. The production of such 'honest' knowledge, however, requires a degree of conscious self-awareness. The ability to recognize in fullness the conditions under which a body of knowledge is produced may develop throughout and beyond the research process. Indeed, it may be that once the researcher is extracted from the ethnographic process it is possible to reflect with a heightened circumspection on the parameters of experience.

Unalienated knowledge, then, is a necessary pre-condition for the exploration of a feminist ontology, or 'way of being in the world' (Stanley 1990, p. 14). It is our 'way of being', whether conscious or subconscious, that determines how we act upon and react to particular social contexts and how one experiences and perceives the

* Department of Applied Social Science, University of Plymouth.

research process. Stanley further argues that: 'it is the experience of and acting against perceived oppression that gives rise to a distinctive feminist ontology' (1990, p. 14). Such a contention is complicated by the intervention of racism, however, which requires that women at once act against oppression and, in the process, acknowledge their role as oppressors, or the beneficiaries of racism.

Racism is also fundamentally a social construction; it is a product of wider power relations within society and of associated ideological forces. The failure of feminism to recognize the complex position of white women in relation to both black women and men and of their relationship to each other, obstructs the realization of 'unalienated knowledge' and the adequacy of a feminist ontology. This is not to suggest that we can merely tack on an awareness of our structural position in relation to black people, and its implications for the research process, for the relationship between racism and sexuality is both dialectical and mysterious. It represents the hidden taboo— almost too personal even for feminist debate. It is this web of power relations and the mechanisms through which the dominant groups construct the parameters of acceptable sexuality that forms the focus for this chapter, with specific reference to the implications of this for ethnographers.

In a chapter entitled, 'The Sexualisation of Race', Calvin Hernton refers to the interconnectedness of racism and sexuality: 'there is a sexual involvement, at once real and vicarious, connecting white and black people in America that spans the history of this country from the era of slavery to the present, an involvement so immaculate and yet so perverse, so ethereal and yet so concrete, that all race relations tend to be, however, subtle, sex relations' (1988, p. xi). For the young white woman beginning ethnographic research on racism this 'link' is particularly powerful. Precisely because it is rooted so deeply in the personal, it may remain concealed and thereby unchallenged in the course of traditional methodological enquiry and may not be rendered explicit in the ethnographic 'write-up'.

Sexuality, and more specifically attitudes towards inter-racial sexuality, represent perhaps the most dangerous and powerful of racial stereotypes reinforcing essentialist explanations of racial inequality such that: 'black people are experienced and perceived as threats to white racial purity, as well as to the white power structure itself' (Hernton 1988, p. xii). To research racism as a white woman, then, is to become involved in a complex weave of power relations in which one's badge of whiteness and gender creates its own inter-subjective dynamic. To develop an awareness of these relations and to begin to attempt to understand them is to move in the direction of unalienated knowledge.

This chapter is concerned to examine and discuss some of the issues that this raises in relation to ethnography by means of retrospective analysis in a specific research context. It does not attempt to impose any *post-hoc* rationality on what was in fact a very 'chaotic' period of my life, but aims to evaluate it, in hindsight, as it was. Issues concerning my role as a middle-class, white person involved in anti-racist research formed a constant theme running throughout my research and are discussed in great detail in the final thesis. The object here is to focus on those aspects of the work which, whilst I was clearly aware of their impact on the research, were not rendered explicit nor subjected to any systematic evaluation. In particular, the discussion raises questions concerning the role of academic culture in restricting the awareness of such issues and looks at how we might offer better guidance and support to researchers in dealing with them.

The discussion begins with some background to the research in terms of its specific focus and the methodology employed. It then considers the effect of gender and sexuality on the research process, focusing on the twin concerns of access and support and presents a series of 'scenarios' which occurred during the research. This is followed by a broad discussion of sexuality and racism and the implications of the discussion for ethnographic research.

The Research Context

The research was funded by the ESRC by means of the now extinct 'linked' awards scheme. The project was supervised by a professor of geography who had some experience of ethnography and of 'cultural studies'. The title of the project which ostensibly provided the 'link' was: 'Ethnic Minorities and the Role of Institutions'.

I had just completed my undergraduate degree at the same university in the field of geography and was concerned that much of the research in the area of 'race' had involved often-empiricist studies of the outcomes of racism (that is, measuring racial disadvantage), with relatively little attention given to the causes of such disadvantage.

It became evident from the literature that the white dominated policy-making process was actually compounding racial inequality. I was therefore, concerned to examine the policy-making process and in particular the representation of black people. This led to a focus on the process of political marginalization in Britain. The Labour Party was selected as a case study as it has long purported to represent the interests of black people and has received considerable electoral support from the black community. In practice the research was much broader than that, and it is perhaps useful to think in terms of the 'formal' and 'informal' contexts (this division is particularly important in the context of the present discussion).

The 'formal' component of the research involved my attendance at and observation of the Labour Party 'in action' in a variety of spheres. I was involved at the national level in my role as secretary of the Labour Party Race Action Group (LPRAG). This included discussions with the National Executive Committee (NEC) over black representation, a research exercise to determine levels of black involvement in the Party, and with newsletters and consultation. I was also closely involved with the campaign for a national black section. At the local level, the research included an in-depth case-study of a constituency Labour Party in South East London and its relationship with the local black community. This involved ongoing participation in political meetings at all levels, interviews with community and political 'leaders', some questionnaire work with ward parties, and liaison with anti-racist and black groups. This constituted the 'formal' component of my research and these were the issues that I was able to discuss with my supervisors, family, and friends.

The 'informal' component formed the living context of my work; much of it was intensely personal and concerned my relationships with people within the political groups, with my flat-mates, and local community, and my family. I lived 'in the field' and became involved in youth and community work in the local area, partly as a result of my concern over the very low levels of poltical involvement of young black people and also in relation to anti-racist work in general. Reflections on these experiences were dutifully written up in the form of a diary—I never really saw them as field-notes as such. The process of writing about them, however, helped me to rationalize what often seemed like cruel personal attacks as I transgressed the boundaries of social groups and threatened accepted notions of race, gender, and sexuality. My thesis is devoid of any of these experiences and represents a 'clinicized' selection of material which I deemed fit for academic consumption and which I hoped would neither compromise myself nor damage the cause of anti-racism. Yet many of these, formally unarticulated, experiences were central to the development of the research and largely steered its direction.

In terms of methodology this separation of the 'formal' and 'informal' components was further reinforced. The selection of an appropriate methodology for the former was carefully considered and discussed with my supervisors. The tension between the demand of traditional 'objective' enquiry and those of anti-racism led to the development of an 'action-research' framework defined by Mathieson as: 'The gathering of information that primarily constitutes an attempt to realise given practical or political values. It is a conscious attempt to combine activities that have traditionally been kept separate in the realisation that research cannot be value-free' (1974, p. 36). The research was triangulated, involving a postal questionnaire, structured interviews, and participant observation; the observation work was conducted overtly with no attempt to conceal my role as a researcher or anti-racist.

The 'informal' component, however, was less pre-determined. I cannot say that the observation was entirely overt, nor indeed when I was and was not 'observing'. The casual observance of behaviour in local pubs or conversations between friends and neighbours is rarely prefixed by statements of one's role and objectives. It could, therefore, be argued that 'data' gleaned from such contexts is inadmissible on the grounds of ethics. Indeed, when I did begin to discuss my 'research' with two youth-workers whom I had come to know well, they were apparently 'affronted that I might abuse our friendship by making them part of the research' (field-notes). There is also a tendency in this type of situation to 'note the remarkable' and not the mundane, which can give a false impression of everyday life in field-notes.

It is with this in mind, and with the clarity which comes from being in a different place with five years experience between myself and the research and with a clearer feminist vision, that it is now possible to explore some of these concerns. The questions I would like to address concern the effect of this relationship between racism, gender, and sexuality on the research process. In particular:

- How did it affect the degree of *access* that was made available to me and at what cost to myself?
- How did it restrict the the amount of support available, and my ability to *retreat* from the research?
- How did the knowledge gained from these broader experiences determine the ethical and other decisions which I took in the decision of which material to use and which to hold back?

To some extent these issues would arise in relation to any in-depth piece of research on 'topics' of such sensitivity. They are rarified in the case of ethnographic research, however, where the researcher is immersed in the research process.

Access to the Field

Access is a central issue in any research exercise; in ethnographic research it is crucial. The negotiation of access often takes a covert form. It is not simply a matter of writing a formal letter to cover a questionnaire or request for a formal interview. In ethnographic research, access is an ongoing process of negotiation: of building and retaining trust and reassuring people of the legitimacy of this form of enquiry. The degree and scope of access achieved largely determines the scope, quality, and effectiveness of the research. Initial readings of Foote-Whyte (1943), Pryce (1979), and Rex and Moore (1967) gave the impression that typical ethnographers, having identified their broad area of interest, should then physically move into the field in order to gain and retain access.

I was already living in south-east London and the precise location of the 'field' was more a question of the availability of short-life housing than anything else. However, the implications are the same; the dividing line between 'home' and 'work' which exists for most researchers, enabling one to reflect on the day's events and resume 'normal' life in the evenings and at weekends, simply does not exist. I remember reading with some concern Pryce's justification for what might be seen as unethical steps to promote and authenticize his 'cover': 'What I was discovering was that to learn more about the church from the standpoint of ordinary members, I needed to be on the inside as a fully-fledged believer. I had no choice but to give in one Sunday morning when I and other unsaved persons like myself were called to the alter [*sic*] and asked if we were ready to be baptised' (1979, p. 285). My research was not covert, so I had no great pretences to keep up. The very visibility of my presence and of an entirely different life-style with different consumption patterns, social activities, household circumstances, gender relations, and apparent freedoms did in itself generate problems, however.

I lived in a large, hard-to-let property with four other students (all males initially). By middle-class standards we were all living on very low wages (student grants!), but like many students, although we were not materially affluent we managed to live quite well and spent a lot of time in the pub, at parties, and going on holiday. We were not 'conspicuous consumers', however, and spent relatively little on clothes and furnishings. To many of the local people these facts made us something of a curiosity in an area where fashion (particularly in terms of clothing and vehicles) was apparently a mark of one's standing in the community.

Language was also a constant symbol of our 'difference'. On one occasion my neighbour, a white working-class woman, questioned me about the use of language in our house, referring to it as 'solicitor's talk', which made her feel like a 'silly little girl' (field-notes). She felt that such talk was unnecessary and added that many young black people would find it irritating. John Greve refers to the extent to which 'social researchers have been handicapped by their approach, manner, accent, vocabulary and image' (1975, p. 164). In reality, there is very little you can do to overcome some of these problems; although it could be argued that the demands of the academic context which defines articulacy in terms of 'acquiring middle class research skills or communication skills which equip you to do bourgeois sociology' (John, 1981, p. 340) actually accentuates the tension!

Somewhat surprisingly I had little difficulty in obtaining access to a wide variety of formal and informal contexts in the course of the research. I say surprisingly, because at the time it never occurred to me to question the ease with which I slipped into the 'field'. On reflection I can see that being a young, single white woman in predominantly male contexts had a significant impact on the access opportunities available to me. I can see also that this access did not come without its bitter fee.

What then were the implications, in research terms, of being young, white, female, and middle class? (I shall consider the role of the academic community in raising awareness of such issues on research later on.) I think these were threefold and included the effect of sexuality on the research process, the effect of role stereotyping and perceptions of women in the power structure. The most significant issue was the issue of sexuality, which proved to be an instrumental advantage but had its personal and political costs.

Sexuality and Access: Choice or Constraint?

My motives were often construed solely in sexual terms, and as such my research intentions were often not taken seriously, nor were they seen to constitute a threat. My involvement with the members of the black section, for example, went largely unquestioned, so that I was on many occasions the only white person (and often the only woman) in attendance at meetings of the national black section and in local black groups (this also reflected to some extent the recognition of the amount of campaigning work I had undertaken during the formative period). During that time, however, I was often invited out to dinner, to the pub, and to parties by colleagues, both black and white, ostensibly to discuss strategies and chat informally about black participation. These meetings frequently ended up in compromising and often deeply insulting scenarios where I had to avoid injury to male egos in order to retain good working relations *and* access: for example, on many occasions I was propositioned by men in their fifties and in some cases made to feel under serious threat in the process.

The vulnerability of women to sexual advances is nothing new. My experiences in this research, however, suggest that access in these contexts had a lot to do with the intermeshing of racism and sexuality and the mythologies which exist to glorify the sexual prowess of black men. Hernton refers to the construction of black male sexuality such that black men are seen by white people and may come to see themselves as 'walking phalluses; the object of white women's desires' (1984, p. 84).

In practice this meant that what I would now identify as sexual harassment was a commonplace event. It was once related to me, some time after the research, that the members of the then black section all assumed that I was having a relationship with one of them, but no one knew exactly who. Who needs a better cover?

Colleagues could discuss my sexual motives and activities amongst themselves without ever considering my political or research object-ives. This, coupled with a fairly realistic appraisal of the position of white women within the power structure, considerably reduced any perception of threat which might otherwise have affected my access. The following 'scenarios' give some impression of the type of situations I faced in the course of the research and illustrate the tension between the 'quest for knowledge' on the one hand and the preservation of self on the other.

During my involvement in the local community as a youth-worker I met up with a group of Rastafarians who apparantly shared a much stronger sense of political efficacy than many of the other young black people. Rastas regularly came to the youth-club to talk to the young people and attempt to influence them in the teachings of their religion. In much the same way as the Jehovah's Witnesses whom I encountered (and who were recruiting a large number of young black people at the time), the Rastas were opposed to any form of participation in the formal political process (including voting). I was very interested in discussing these issues, particularly as they effect-ively disenfranchized young black people. I therefore spent some time building up a relationship with one of the leaders of 'The Twelve Tribes', and was consequently able to attend various functions and talk with quite a few members of the Tribe.

On one of my earlier meetings with the Rasta leader, however, I was placed in a situation which threatened both my access and my person. I had spent some time talking to the man, who also worked part-time in the club, after which he offerred me a lift home which I accepted. He then suggested to me, *en route*, that he 'could make me sweat' (field-notes), and that I should come home with him. I was concerned not to offend him in the hopes both that I could get safely home and that my relationship would not be damaged.

Such perceptions of my role in sexual terms were not restricted to black men. On one occasion I had arranged to meet a white man of some considerable stature in the local community, to discuss the relationship between the Community Relations Council and the Borough Council. The discussion progressed fairly well until we began to talk about the political attitudes of young black people. I was then informed that he knew of many white female youth-workers who had sexual relationships with black men. In my diary I pondered over this. Was he concerned about the professionalism of these women, or 'was he as entwined in this sex/racism web as everyone else; are stereotypical white male attitudes primarily a reflection of sexual jealousy?' I subsequently returned to the man's house 'for a coffee', after which I was promised a lift home. Coffee finished, I ventured to ask for the lift. He replied: 'Oh! I assumed you were staying the night' (field-notes). Again I was faced with the 'options' of challenging his behaviour and risking an important channel of access while possibly also putting myself at risk, or politely 'getting out of the situation'. I took the latter route and made a conscious decision not to make contact with this man again.

A similar situation arose during a discussion about our work with a black youth leader when he ventured to ask me: 'What would you do if one of them [a young black man] wanted to screw you?' This man (my boss) was himself in his fifties. He had continually sexually harassed me and other female workers, in some cases with extreme violence. One of his 'tactics' was to stress that, although the young men were about the same age as me, 'they were world's apart from me' (field-notes), inferring perhaps that he was a more appropriate match by virtue of his social status (not race). I made the following note in my diary: 'Exactly what are these people trying to prove by pointing out the "sexual beast" in young black people—when they themselves continually approach me sexually?' In the examples referred to, I had the 'option' of 'using' misconceptions regarding my sexuality instrumentally in order to maximize access (by failing to challenge sexism) or of making an outright challenge. In practice I felt that I had little choice but to let many of the comments 'slip', particularly when I felt that they were 'personal', in order to preserve the channels of discourse which I had built up so that I might more fully understand the processes of racism.

In other senses the sexual mythology which permeates the psyche of us all in a racially and gender-structured society actually restricted my access and the accuracy of the research, perhaps with more painful results.

At the political level there were very few black women involved. However, on several occasions black women displayed overt hostility towards me and deep suspicion which caused me considerable distress. Indeed in the beginning there were no women in the black section, and at the first national conference held in Birmingham some two years later one of the first women speakers referred to the degree of institutionalized sexism within the movement itself. At the meeting it was a black woman who first questioned my presence, probably rightly so but possibly not for the right reasons (she was unhappy about my representation of her viewpoint in a paper to the NEC). I never attended formal meetings again.

On another occasion I was apprehended by a black woman in the street outside my house. She was threatening to hit me with her stilletos on the grounds that I had insulted her son—a 5-year-old who regularly played in my house. He had just locked me out by accidentally pulling the door to. In my dismay I had accused him of being a 'stupid boy'! The mother's response was that: 'You treat black kids like shit, think they are all thick, don't like black women but only black men—and you only like them for one reason' (field-notes). The incident depressed me considerably, although I tried to rationalize her behaviour. I made the following note in my diary: 'I am finding working in this area more and more taxing and wonder how long I can cope—with everyone focusing their greivances on me.'

These and the following incident illustrate quite vividly the important effect of social distance on the research process and the interlinkages of sexuality and power in society; issues for which I had had very little preparation or guidance.

In my role as a voluntary youth-worker in the local youth-club I undertook to organize an 'educational weekend' away. The idea was that the club members would have the opportunity to get away from South London (for some of them this was their first time out of the area) and to organize informal discussions on issues of interest (policing, sexuality, educational opportunities, benefits, and the like). The event took place at a residential centre on the Thames which offered various outdoor activities. I organized canoing and swimming between the more formal sessions. The black women who came on the course did not take part in these activities, which seemed to offend their notions of acceptable feminine behaviour. They apparently regarded my involvement in them as reflecting sexual promiscuity and particularly an interest in the young black men. Some time after the weekend I was invited to a party at the house of one of the black women who had taken part. That evening the youth leader and the Senior Youth Officer, both black men in their fifties, openly accused me of having had sexual relations with a group of the young men during the residential course.

I formally complained in writing to the Youth Office but received no reply and left the matter there, although my relationship with almost all the local black women was now tarnished as many of these young men were their partners. In retrospect I feel that the distance between myself and local black women was partly a consequence of the sex-racism issue but also a reaction to wider social differences and their perception of these in terms of power. As a single, middle-class woman, with a car and no children and living with a group of male students, I posed something of a threat to these women, the majority of whom were single parents and struggling to make ends meet.

On one occasion it was suggested to me by some of the local black women that I was very wealthy and, as such, attracted the interest of young black men. I seems that there was some relationship here between notions of sexuality and the suspicion that white women are often better able to satisfy the material needs of young black men. Indeed, the rumour concerning my sexual activities during the residential weekend had developed further to the suggestion that I was actually paying the young men for sex! I spent an entire evening convincing the partner of one of these men that this was entirely unfounded. My diary records the following reflection on these events: 'The implications of this whole sex/racism issue has brought home to me the truth in Calvin Hernton's conclusion [1988, p. 175] that, racial acts and ideas cannot be understood without grasping how their motivation is as much sexual as economic.'

It is clear from these scenarios that my existence, in itself, created social contexts and stimulated social behaviour which might not have occured in my absence. Not only was my social background, my 'race' and gender, affecting my analysis of events it was apparently also a stimulus to behaviour.

In her analysis of the social construction of black masculinity, Sally Westwood comments that: 'The issues of masculinity and race are too interwoven to separate at this time' (1990, p. 61). Despite her assertion that 'there is no innocent ethnography', however, and her acknowledgement that being a white, middle-class female with a university background affected her *interpretations* of the lives of young black men, she stops short of exploring the intervention of sexuality on the research process itself. This is not to argue that her research is any less 'objective' as a consequence of her gender, but that the gender, race, and sexuality of researchers may have an important impact on the behaviour under observation—in this case the assertion of black masculinity through the medium of football.

Traditional courses dealing with methods of social investigation had not 'trained' us to recognize and acknowledge the intervention of sexuality on the research process beyond an instrumental consideration of the 'interviewer effect' on questionnaire response-rates.

Women as Administrators

The second issue affecting access opportunities was also related to gender, but in a more 'routine' sense. Feminists have for some time now documented the ways in which women's roles in wider society mirror their 'traditional' roles within the family. The same is true of women's roles in the political sphere. Once again this is an area where the researcher can 'opt' to utilize the assigned role instrumentally, or attempt to challenge such stereotyping.

During the research I became involved in the Labour Party Race Action Group (LPRAG) which had been campaigning methodically for some years but had obtained little influence within the Labour Party nationally and had very few black members. The secretary at the time was a highly committed white woman who more or less ran the group single-handed. She eventually decided to give up the position and I was elected in her place to fill the workhorse-handmaiden role while some more charismatic male took the Chair. This was a great opportunity for me to gain access to the National Executive Committee and Labour Party Conferences and to be able to keep and administrative check on what was going on nationally in the area of black representation, 'ethnic' canvassing, and so on. It also enabled me to support the black-section movement in a more active way, through development of closer links and some initial financial support, and facilitated a better response-rate to the questionnaire on black participation than would otherwise have been the case (it was administered under the auspices of LPRAG).

Once again, secretaries are not perceived as a threat but merely as executors or administrators, thus providing quite a convenient position for a researcher. In this and in other similar voluntary positions which I held (for example, in the Neighbourhood Council's Anti-Racist Group and as a voluntary youth-worker), I was able to trade my time and skills for access. This is certainly not to suggest that I perceived my role in such a mechanistic light. Indeed, the concept of access barely occurred to me at the time (apart from the first few weeks). I was committed to the promotion of anti-racism and to the black-sections strategy, and sought to use whatever influence I could obtain to promote that cause. In research terms the project was an experiment in action-research; I had no notion of non-participant observation.

The 'handmaiden' role, therefore, proved quite useful, both in terms of enabling me to 'prove' my commitment through effort and also to avoid positions which might have proved too publicly confrontational. There was, for example, some concern at the time that white people should not 'front' anti-racist action groups. Some of this concern reflects a tokenistic and marginalizing approach to anti-racism. Nevertheless, for the purposes of the research it was better not to be seen to be taking a stand on this issue (the role of white people in anti-racist strategy was a particular concern of mine which is discussed in detail in my thesis; see Ackers 1985).

It could, however, be argued that by compromising on these points, and permitting the Chair to take the public position while I worked behind the scenes to promote him, and by failing to project my personal views about anti-racist strategy (at least in this instance), I was failing in both my action-research objectives and in not challenging sexual sterotyping. But had I challenged these points I might well not have been elected or benefited from the trust I had established in undertaking this seemingly altruistic role.

Women and 'Power'

The third issue which served to enhance access, particularly in the political arena, is linked to the previous two points. It concerns the position of women within the power structure, and perhaps more specifically male *perceptions* of women and power. In a society which upholds the rationality and reasonableness of man and denigrates the emotions and feelings of women, the prospect of a female researcher-political activist poses less of a challenge, less of a threat. The political system, whatever its persuasion, mirrors society at large; a competetive individualism and blatant pursuit of career accolades form the focus of the political entrepreneur, and men, as in any other sphere of life are greeted as potential competitors. A female political activist-researcher blends more easily into the background; she is presumed to have different motives, is less of a challenge and more of an opportunity—if not to sleep with then to oil the cogs of his machine. She typically takes on the 'everybody's wife/mistress' role.

Such a role is quite useful from a research point of view, where the key to access is often the absence of threat. The question remains, however, of how to reconcile the need to achieve and maintain access, often through collusion with patriarchal values, with the immediate personal (and political) dilemmas of how to deal with sexual demands, assumptions, and compromises, let alone actually working out strategies positively to challenge sexism and promote woman-centred values.

On a day-to-day basis this means deciding on what you let slip, when and how to challenge, how to protect yourself from potential physical and emotional abuse, and primarily, how to retain a sense of pride and personal worth. One of the most worrying aspects of this scenario, particularly when the researcher is working in total isolation, is the ease with which one develops a sense of immobilizing guilt. Did I give him the wrong impression? Could I have avoided the situation? Should I have challenged?

During the research I took part in several racism-awareness training exercises. An important part of this 'training' is to develop self-awareness and learn how to recognize and effectively challenge all racist behaviour. I have since found such a view of racist encounters to be overly simplistic and ignorant of the personal risks involved in such blanket challenging. In some situations such challenges may prove counter-productive, not just to the flow of information but also to anti-racism and feminism in general, where the key to change may lie in the long-term erosion of 'common-sense' notions through discussion and visible praxis, and not in the one-off santioning of behaviour. In other circumstances, to challenge may be to invite personal reprisal. For the ethnographer there are additional issues at stake here in terms of the continuing viability of the project, which may mean that such discourses are relegated to notebooks for the period of the research.

Spheres of Support

The second area which I wish to explore concerns the effect of the intermeshing of racism, sexuality, and gender on the availability of support. Robert Moore, reflecting on his experiences in Sparkbrook, comments: 'I discovered that full-time research is not a job; it is a way of life, and so one's life becomes woven into the research' (1977,

p. 26). Ethnographic research often involves such degrees of immersion (sometimes referred to as 'going native'—a point I shall return to later) and it may cease to be possible to detach oneself from the research process. Without some potential for retreat and support, however, such research saps the self; there is no space to reflect and depersonalize experiences, or to rediscover who you are, as you are constantly defined by those around you according to their perceptions and beliefs. It is, therefore, important, both for the research and the researchers, that they should develop spheres of support.

My experiences of negotiating and retaining access, as described, clearly demonstrate a lack of preparedness and of guidance and support available to the ethnographer. In practice, potential sources of support might include one or several of the following: the academic community; family; or flat-mates and close friends.

The Academic Community

The academic community should, in theory at least, play an important role in supporting research students, and particularly those involved in ethnographic work. It should provide a forum where students and supervisors can openly and honestly discuss and evaluate their experiences of the research and formulate their strategies and courses of action. That this is not the situation comes as no surprise; indeed, the ESRC has attributed the lack of support as a leading factor in the low completion-rates of postgraduate research. There are many possible explanations for the prevalence of overtly competitive, often disinterested or self-interested and uncaring academic environments. I do not intend to rehearse these arguments here, but to examine the specific academic context in which my research took place and the impact of this on the direction of the research and the degree of support available to me. Some of these issues relate to the specific disciplinary base of my research, although similar scenarios have been identified from within sociology and social policy (Hearn 1990; Oakley 1974; Roberts 1981). I have identified three aspects of the discipline of geography as it then was which I feel considerably reduced the support it was able to offer me in avoiding or dealing with my experiences of the research. These include: The representation of women within the discipline both in a supervisory capacity and as fellow research students; the awareness of 'race' and gender issues and the status attributed to feminist critiques within the discipline; the status attached to specific methodological approaches and its reflection in research 'training'.

Women in Geography

Having achieved the status of a full-time postgraduate student in a reputable institution, as a woman you are by definition something of an oddity both within academic life and beyond. Women are very poorly represented amongst teaching staff in geography departments. A survey conducted by the Women and Geography Study Group of the Institute of British Geographers (WGSB), found that, in 1980, women accounted for only 10 per cent of all full-time lecturing staff (in 36 per cent of the departments surveyed there were no full-time women lecturers at all). The geography department in which I was based was no exception to this, despite its focus on human and social geography. There were very few women members of academic staff in the department, and a tiny proportion of the large postgraduate population were female. There was little scope, therefore, to share research experiences and seek guidance, particularly on issues such as sexuality, with other women students or staff. Furthermore, this patriarchal imbalance was reflected in course curricula.

Geography, Gender, and 'Race'

> We might, in fact, be forgiven for thinking that women simply do not exist in the spatial world . . . At present geography remains a male-centred subject, both in terms of the gender of those who structure its content through their research and teaching, and in terms of the nature of that content. (WGSB 1984, p. 20)

My academic background within geography was entirely 'gender-blind'. While issues concerning patterns of regional and local inequality were often raised, the focus was on social class. The question of gender was simply never raised in undergraduate courses. Neither was it raised as an issue or perspective in the research methods component of postgraduate 'training'.

A similar 'colour-blindness' existed in relation to issues of racism. Just as academic work in relation to 'racism' has been cleft by academic disciplines, so too has feminism and methodological awareness. There was, however, a growing awareness amongst the postgraduate student population of the limitations of traditional class reductionist approaches to social inequality, particularly within the

Socialist Geographers Group. One consequence of this was that a certain amount of pressure was put on me from the male students to focus my research on black women. I resented the inference that, because I was a woman, my research should focus on women.

The development of feminist critiques of research methods in other disciplines have to some extent compounded this problem by arguing for more research by women on women, in order to reflect more adequately the experiences of women in society. This focus led Joyce Layland to express concern that her research into the social construction of masculinity by gay men did not fall within the remit of 'feminist' research and that such research might be open to criticism for 'putting energy into men' (1990, p. 38).

A group of feminist geographers who have become active since my research present a different view: 'Feminist geographers are concerned with the structure of social and spatial relations that contributes to women's oppression. Consequently men must be included in the analysis: as oppressors in certain situations and as oppressed in others. Moreover men as well as women can be feminists, concerned about gender roles and inequality' (WGSG 1984).

The debate over whether research should focus on the 'victims' or under-represented social groups, or on the beneficiaries of social inequality also led me to question the inference that my research should not only be 'on women', but 'on' black women. David Silverman criticizes the 'ethnographic tradition' for producing endless accounts of society's 'underdogs' and argues that although this may satisfy 'middle class sociologists with social consciences' (1985, p. 21), additional knowledge is required. More than merely an imbalance, such a focus detracts from a concern with the political *processes* of racism and sexism in society and with the political effectiveness of research.

Apart from these political considerations, the assumptions of my male peer group concerning the unity of interest and concomitant access such research would have afforded me were probably ill-founded (for the reasons discussed above). It is interesting to note that none of these 'pro-feminist' men had evidently considered the gender implications of their specific research topics. Feminist research was a 'job for women'!

Kimmel comments on this tendency of social-science researchers to:

act as if their own gender had nothing to do with [their] work, and treat male scientists as if their being men had nothing to do with the organisation of their experiments, the logic of scientific enquiry, or the questions posed by science itself. And yet when blacks or women, or gays and lesbians do research on blacks or women or gays and lesbians we wonder how come they cannot think of anything else. We assume that their interests in sociology will centre on these topics. Only straight white men get to do abstract universally generalisable science. (1990, p. 95)

My personal struggle to come to terms with the implications of my role as a middle-class white person in anti-racist research and action formed a constant reflection on my work. While in the process of working through these issues, completely unsupported by the academic community, however, I failed to address myself to the impact of gender and sexuality. This was not the 'focus' of my study, and I had no academic background, or supervision, that led me to question their impact. I was sufficiently aware of their intervention to record events in my personal diary, but I did not consciously and systematically reflect upon and 'rationalize' these experiences and their impact on my access and support. I regarded them as autonomous, separate, issues and failed to recognize their role in the race-relations dynamic.

Geography and Method

Perhaps more so than many other branches of social science, geography suffers from a serious problem of identity (partially determined by the government's onslaught on social science and the advantages which accrue to the label 'science'). It is also important to note that, as a social geographer one is working alongside people with interests in river sedimentation and remote sensing! Geographers consequently have taken a long time to develop a critique of positivism. This was reflected in the total absence of qualitative approaches in the research-methods curriculum and in their designation within the discipline as somewhat inferior and un-scientific. In particular, there has been no parallel within geography to the development of feminist research methods in sociology. The Women and Geography Study Group has since argued for changes in approaches to research, although they are largley preoccupied with developing a critique of the social-survey method and not with ethnographic research.

My supervisor was a 'humanistic geographer' and recognized the importance of qualitative data. He had himself some experience of ethnographic work in the 1950s, and frequently recounted stories of his youth-work in Cardiff and of Shirley Bassey who was then a member of the youth-club. My early introduction to ethnography came through his recommendation of Whyte's study (1955) and that of Rex and Moore (1967). I also gained some stimulation from Ken Pryce's book *Endless Pressure* (1979). It never occurred to me at the time that these studies were all undertaken by men and that my experience might be somewhat different! Neither did this occur to my supervisor, a measure of whose naïvety is reflected in his initial suggestion that I undertake an ethnographic study of Rastafarianism. He was clearly unaware of how such an 'exotic' and interesting cultural group was constructed around certain notions of gender roles which could have posed serious problems for a white female ethnographer.

The overall effect of the discipline, then, was to give me a sense that my research was not valued in academic terms and an acute sense of isolation. I had no one with whom I could discuss the process of the research and no support in enabling me to work out effective strategies for dealing with the ensuing dilemmas.

Family Support

Another important source of support might be expected to come from the ethnographer's family and close friends. In a society where racism and sexism are endemic and permeate the fabric of family life, however, notions of gender roles and perceptions of the black population are likely to prove problematic to the young white female ethnographer. Challenging such personal and intimate prejudices within the context of one's own family can prove particularly painful.

Very few people understand what 'geography' as a modern discipline really involves. It is associated with maps, rivers, and minerals and other such 'non-controversial', seemingly impersonal, subject-matter. Geographical research is considered to be a respectable 'scientific' enterprise. As such, my family were unable to reconcile their traditional conceptions of the scope of geographical enquiry with the subject of my research (so too were many geographers!) I did not wish to shatter their illusions of the clinical 'academic' nature of research. Moreover, had I attempted to relate my experiences of the research, particularly in relation to the perceptions of my sexual role, I would have run the risk of causing undue concern and also possibly bolstering stereotypical attitudes about interracial sexuality.

Recent research has pointed to the importance of 'social distance' in explaining racist attitudes in Britain (Chivers and Sharp 1989; Ackers 1991; Hernton 1988). What this means in practice is that white people may feel 'comfortable' or unthreatened with black people at a certain distance, for example as shopkeepers, cleaners, or even in a professional capacity as doctors or lecturers. The perceived threat, however increases as the social distance decreases. The contemplation of black neighbours often marks an important cut-off point at which the black presence ceases to be 'acceptable'. Another important source of support might be expected to come from the ethnographer's family and close friends. Perhaps the most sanctioned form of contact, however, is that which concerns the *prospect* of interracial sexual relations and 'mongrelization'. This concept of social distance is perhaps also useful in the research context; I believed that my parents would feel comfortable with the 'formal' components of my research where my contact with black people was governed by the codes of the traditional interviewer–interviewee relationship, but that they would be unable to understand the need for more informal, personal contact.

Consequently many of the issues which preoccupied my mind were my secrets; home became an important escape to me, and when painful events took place I would often go home for several days, but I became something of a stranger to my family for some time. They were aware that I was often depressed and that I would leave as suddenly as I came, but I was never able to discuss my experiences of the research, particularly those aspects relating to sexuality, with my family.

I also had to cope that what at one time seemed routine prejudices and racist attitudes, both from within my family, as in any other, but more so from their friends and colleagues, taking the form of comments which I felt unable to challenge for the sake of my parents, both of whom had 'respectable' jobs in the local community. I recollect one particularly irritating occasion when I was in an operating theatre having my tonsils removed. The consultant was a colleague of my father and had some inkling of my research. Just as the anaesthetic was beginning to take effect, he said to me: 'I suppose you're going to tell us what we already know; that there are too many of them here.' I was unable to respond at the time due to the anaesthetic. I could, however, have challenged this evident abuse of his professional power the following day, during a ward round. I did not; he had 'done me a favour' in treating me and I was aware that I should not risk offending a colleague of my father's.

On other occasions I had to share a dinner-table with 'intelligent', middle-class folk who had supported the National Front when it was 'respectable', but who now felt comfortable with Margaret Thatcher's commitment to end 'coloured' immigration. Again I failed to challenge. In the minds of these people such comments were not racist. Racism was something they associated with the crude assertion of racial superiority. Such 'educated' people now talk in terms of 'differences' not 'inferiority', and raise the defence of nationality. The 'New Racism' (Barker 1981) is more 'respectable' and hence more pernicious; to question the 'reasonableness' of such assertions, therefore, is typically perceived as a cruel personal attack.

I came to realize that my research was a catalyst for discussion about 'race', and yet I was unable, because of the context, effectively to challenge such racism. Not only could the family not offer me the support to deal with my experiences in London, but the terrain itself generated new and often more frustrating scenarios.

Living in the Field

Another potential source of support was from my immediate friends in London. My flat-mates were all students, mostly postgraduates, studying economics. They were all white, male, and from middle-class backgrounds. Their research was largely library-based and therefore quite different from mine. They probably knew more about my research, however, than anyone else at the time and were aware of some of the dilemmas it was raising. We had known each other for three years while living in halls of residence as undergraduates, but the experience of living together and beginning to map out our various lives revealed great differences of opinion and outlook. In particular, I found that several of them shared quite racist views and that as a group they behaved in a characteristically sexist way. As my research developed these differences were accentuated, particularly when they were faced with increasing contact with the local black community. Although in many ways their friendship constituted an important source of support and distraction, their response to this situation introduced a new site of conflict into the research. To some extent their response manifested itself in a protective reaction; at times when I was under some potential physical threat they would ensure that they always opened the door first, and on occasions actually escorted me home from the youth-club in which I worked. In many ways they treated much as they would have treated a younger sister, albeit within their perceptions of what was in my best interest and what was not!

The following scenarios illustrate some of the conflicts which arose within the house and demonstrate how the interconnectedness of sexuality and racism unfolded in yet another context.

In my role as a youth-worker I obtained British Council funding to facilitate an exchange visit with young Algerians in Montpelier. This caused some excitement to the young people involved, who had never been out of England, and resulted in many of them visiting me at home. It was a warm summer and we often sat on the wall outside my house in the sun. On returning from vacation one of the flatmates decided that this 'lowered the tone of the place' and 'would have to stop' (field-notes). This created some conflict and tension within the household. To make matters worse, while he was away the rest of the household had agreed to let some of the lads paint the inside of the house as part of a scheme for the young unemployed. The worker who had persuaded us to take part in this 'scheme' subsequently failed to pay the lads (I later found that this was commonplace. Indeed, one of the local youth-clubs was decorated under such false pretences and the young people never received any payment.) I was in something of a predicament, as my flat-mates were unable or unwilling to make up the money. As a compromise the lads suggested that we hold a blues party to raise some funds with which to pay them. This was agreed and went very well, but we made no money and the 'doorman', who was black, caused some problems as he mistakenly let all white people in free while charging black people, on the assumption that the former were all our friends.

Several days later my next-door neighbour stopped me to pass on 'confidential' information that a petition was being set up locally, apparently because there were 'too many black people hanging around outside the front' (field-notes). There was also some talk of us running an illegal drinking house. It came to nothing but was designed to convey the sentiment of local white people towards their black neighbours.

On another occasion we had the house broken into and the television taken. The week before we had just taken a new tenant, a black female law student. The first reaction of two of my flat-mates was to question the integrity of this woman (they had opposed her moving in, but were outvoted). The reaction of the police was somewhat different; they pointed to the flats opposite and suggested that the occupants could be the culprits. The occupants were in fact young black men whom I knew well from the youth club. I responded defiantly, but the police were unrepentant.

These scenarios give some indication of the types of issue which arose as a result of living in, and clearly having an impact upon, the field. The research not only involved the observation of events and relationships but itself *created* social situations and relationships. Indeed, it became evident that I could not move in any of my 'social circles' without causing some reaction or effect. The complexity of the issues raised and the personal impact of them, however, together with some misgivings about the 'objectivity' of these 'findings', meant that they were relegated to my personal diary and did not form part of the analysis in my thesis. As such, the material presented for the thesis was incomplete and insufficient as an explanation of racism or as a strategy for action. Any genuine attempt to challenge racism in society must be founded on a clear understanding of how and why the processes of racism operate.

Analysis of the responses of my flat-mates to the research solely in terms of 'race' were clearly inadequate; the perceived threat which underpins such attitudes and behaviour stems not from racial categorization alone but from its part in the construction of masculinity.

My experience of the research has led me to realize that a dangerous mythology does indeed exist concerning the sexual prowess of black men, and this mythology constitutes a threat to white men's sense of sexual adequacy. Their perceptions of black male (and female) sexuality often oscillate from the exotic to the animalistic. Perhaps the most obvious manifestation of this is their curiousity about black men's genitalia. This question often arose, particularly after a few beers when in a jocular mood. The question itself is underpinned by something more sinister, though; it is not the actual size of the penis that is really of concern to white males but its *psychological* size, and their perceptions of their own masculinity and their control over the sexuality of white women. Hernton (1988) comments: 'it is incredible to suddenly realise how thoroughly and constantly aware whites are of black man's sexual existence—an awareness, affirmed and denied, that dominates and sexualises the entire range of race relations' (1984, p. 115).

Kimmel's analysis of the social construction of masculinity begins to unravel this preoccupation with physiology. Kimmel describes masculinity as a social construction, within a dynamic of power relations 'by which the "other" is created and subordinated' (1990, p. 96), and argues that our experience of the erotic is largely a reflection of culture, social context, and patterns of domination. Kimmel further describes the basis of the 'contemporary male sexual script': 'sexuality is not about mutual pleasuring, but the confirmation of masculinity, which is based on physical capacities. And these, in turn, require emotional detachment, a phallocentric world view of sexual pleasure, and self-objectification' (p. 105).

This process of the construction of female sexuality through white male domination was not without its contradictions: white men permitted, by default, the construction of a mythology of black male sexuality which strikes at the very heart of their fragile self-concept and actually threatens their power relation with white women. This acute threat to white masculinity underpinned the hypocrisy of the American South at a time when it was permissible for white men to have sexual relations with black women, but the price of black male sexual interactions with white women was public castration and lynching.

It is perhaps a measure of the inadequacy of the academic mode of production that such issues have rarely been raised in standard social-science texts. The development of interdisciplinary women's-studies courses has, however, enabled the removal of arbitrary interdisciplinary boundaries, facilitating a more holistic analysis of the relationship between sexuality and racism as it is reflected in literature and the arts. Joanna De Groot's analysis of nineteenth-century art, for example, gives a stark illustration of how western society constructed images of oriental sexuality: 'It was, of course, a function of [European male's] power that they could make, use and impose such images to protect sexual and racial privileges, manage their contradictions, and consolidate their dominance' (1989, p. 108).

During the course of the research I began a relationship with a black man who had no links with the research or the local community whatsoever. The response within the house was, on the surface, friendly, but on occasions became extremely hostile. One of the men once asked me what was wrong with white men, adding the ditty: 'once black, never turn back' (field-notes). I was unsure at the time why he felt like this—he was certainly not 'interested' in me personally. With hindsight and more experience, I am sure that he felt his own sexuality was under threat. It was not one white woman that was being violated, but white women as a race, and this constituted a threat to white male hegemony.

Relationships in and around the house in which I lived were not formally a part of the research. They did, however, provide me with a great deal of insight into the deeply intimate attitudes of white people and of the complicating interlinkages of racism and sexuality. It is clear from this discussion, however, that far from being a retreat, my life at home merely constituted a different and more intensely personal arena within which the theatre of racism was daily enacted. One realization which came to me very early in the research was that, despite the literature, ethnography was certainly not about 'going native'; on the contrary, it was a perpetual reminder that I fitted nowhere: neither with my family, in the academic community, with my student colleagues, nor with the people who formed the focus of the research. Such a realization is quite daunting, and brings loneliness and a sense of isolation into one's everyday life.

Selection and Sanitization

'Experiential field-work' or ethnography has been considered a particularly appropriate methodology for feminists and anti-racists, in so far as it can be used to understand the experiences of women and black people which other more 'scientific', methodologies tend to obliterate. Too often, however, concern has focused on the experiences and subjective realities of the research 'subjects', as if the researchers themselves were not a part of the dynamics of sexual and racial oppression and therefore also actors in their own right. Anne Williams, reflecting on her field-notes from a feminist perspective, talks of the 'reflexive' aspect of field-work, 'in the sense of seriously locating myself in my research' (1990, p. 254). She expands the parameters of the 'experiential' to encapsulate her own experiences and feelings about her work and cites the following from her field-notes: 'From the stream of action I encounter, I select bits and pieces . . . Understanding emerges out of the interaction between me as a researcher and the situation within which I find myself—out of the questions that emerge from my response to the situation' p. 254).

The daily anecdotes recorded in my diaries helped me to make some sense out of what was going on around me; they did not form a part of my thesis, however, partly I think because I felt that the academic world would not be interested in my 'personal' life, and more than that, because such details might actually undermine the authenticity of an otherwise 'public' piece of work. I felt that I could not muddy the waters of respectable academic research with my 'subjective' feelings and emotions. I was influenced in this respect by the reflections of Robert Moore on his Sparkbrook study: 'John Rex and I often remarked how we should write our Sparkbrook novel. This was not because either of us had lost faith in sociology; it was rather an expression of our need to communicate something of our response to Sparkbook as a human situation' (Rex and Moore 1977, p. 16). Moore further comments that the data gathered in the ethnographic phases of the research was 'colourful and sociologically rich', but that 'a more objective survey was also important in terms of the public presentation of the research' (p. 99). By failing to communicate their personal responses to their study of human experiences, Rex and Moore arguably omitted the most crucial dimension of their research in order to satisfy the demands of the academic community. I now realize that my *personal* experiences were indeed the core of the *political* problem that I was concerned with, and that the academic end-product of my research was less adequate and more partial for having omitted these concerns.

Another reason for omitting these aspects of my experience concerns the ethical dilemmas I faced in deciding which material to use. These is an important tension here between the demands of the academic mode of production and an ethical commitment to the research subjects and the cause which the research espouses. The Radical Statistics Group (Bhat, Carr-Hill and Ohri 1988) point to some of the dangers and potential abuses of research evidence in the course of anti-racist work, with research in some contexts actually utilized to foster and promote racism (they refer specifically to the production and publication of crime statistics). The debate over the issue of 'ethnic monitoring' and the 'ethnic' question in the census provides another case in point where research evidence may actually prove damaging to the cause of anti-racism. The mass of disparate data collected in the course of ethnographic research, particularly if taken out of context, is open to widespread abuse. There is, then, a tension between the need to 'ply the searchlight of methodic sincerity' (Walinowski, cited in Williams, 1990, p. 256) and a real concern not to expose material which may prove damaging to black people. I therefore selected out that material which I felt might provide fodder for the appetites of hungry racists, eager to pick up scraps to legitimize their distorted, sexualized notions of black people. This process was both conscious and subconscious, and at times, I think, was principally about not raising issues which I did not myself understand and certainly could not offer rational explanations for.

Reflections

I began this chapter by saying that good research is that which accounts for the conditions of its own production and that, in order to achieve this, the researcher must concern herself with how she reacts to and experiences the process of research. I then proceeded to demonstrate how my experiences of actually undertaking a piece of ethnographic research within the constraints of the academic tradition resulted in the presentation of a thesis devoid of personal experiences, and thereby seriously incomplete in its analysis.

More specifically, this 'story' demonstrates how the pressures to produce a publicly acceptable and respectable academic product perpetuate a false dichotomy between the 'formal' or public component of research and the 'informal' or personal. In relation to my research, this resulted in the loss of a whole arena of experiences and insights which, far from being peripheral to the study, were actually pivotal to an understanding of the dynamics of racism. And, on a personal level, it left me isolated and vulnerable.

If we are to be able to encourage future researchers to produce more complete and holistic explanations of social interaction and to avoid the heavy personal costs of working in such isolation, however, we must seek methods of better supporting such a research ethos. Perhaps the most pressing concern here is with the under-representation of women and black people both as lecturers and as research students in academic life, thereby restricting the forums within which such open discussion can take place. The development of interdisciplinary support groups for women staff and students is perhaps one way forward, providing researchers with the necessary support, reassurance, and strategies for dealing with issues which arise both 'in the field' and within academic institutions.

It is also essential that the curricula presented to undergraduate students (particularly in relation to research methods) actually empower them to build upon and develop their awareness of the role of dominant groups in the construction and manipulation of racism, gender, and sexuality. Such an underpinning is essential to enable students not only to locate the 'subjects' of their research within the structure of societal power relations, but also to locate themselves and take account of their own feelings, reactions, and experiences. The increasing popularity of 'skills-based' research training, is, however, unlikely to provide students with a belief in the validity of ethnographic research and with the courage to deconstruct the barriers between the personal and public aspects of their work.

References

Ackers, H. L. (1985). 'Racism and Political Marginalisation in the Metropolis; The Relationship between Black People and the Labour Party in London', Unpublished thesis, London University.

—— (1991). 'Anti-Racist Strategy in Predominantly White Rural Areas; A Case Study in a College of Further Education in West Devon', Conference Paper to West Devon Anti-Racist Group. (Copy of full report available from Education Dept., County Hall, Exeter).

Barker, J. (1981). *The New Racism* (London: Junction Books).

Bhat, A., Carr-Hill, R., and Ohri, S. (1988). *Britain's Black Population*, Radical Statistics Group (Aldershot: Gower).

Buttimer, A. (1974). *Values in Geography*, Commission on College Geography Resource Paper, No. 24 (Association of the Annals of American Geographers, Washington DC).

—— (1976). 'Beyond Sexist Rhetoric: Horizons for Human Becoming', in P. Burnett (ed.), *Women in Society: A New Perspective* (mimeo).

Caplan, P. (1987). (ed.), *The Cultural Construction of Sexuality* (London: Tavistock).

Chivers, T. and Sharp, T. (1989). 'Combating Racism', paper to the British Sociological Association Conference, Polytechnic South-West, Plymouth.

Chung Yuen Kay (1990). 'At the Palace: Researching Gender and Ethnicity in a Chinese Restaurant', in L. Stanley (ed.), *Feminist Praxis* (London: Routledge).

De Groot, J. (1989). ' "Sex" and "Race"; The Construction of Language and Image in the Nineteenth Century', in S. Mendus and J. Rendall, *Sexuality and Subordination* (London: Routledge).

Foote-Whyte, W. (1943). *Street Corner Society* (Chicago: University of Chicago Press).

Greve, J. (1975). 'Research and the Community', in D. Jones and E. Mayo (eds.), *Community Work and Racism* (London: Routledge & Kegan Paul).

Griffiths, M. and Whitford, T. (1988). *Feminist Perspectives in Philosophy* (London: Macmillan).

Harding, S. (1987). *Feminism and Methodology* (Milton Keynes: Open University Press).

Harvey, L. (1990). *Critical Social Research* (London: Unwin Hyman).

Hearn, J. and Morgan, D. (1990). *Men, Masculinities and Social Theory* (London: Unwin Hyman).

Hernton, C. (1988). *Sex and Racism in America* (New York: Grove Weidenford).

Jackson, P. (1987). (ed.), *Race and Racism* (London: Allen Unwin).

John, G. (1981). *In the Service of Black Youth* (Leicester: National Association of Youth Clubs).

Kimmel, M. (1990). 'After Fifteen Years; The Impact of the Sociology of Masculinity on the Masculinity of Sociology' (in Hearn and Morgan 1990).

Layland, J. (1990). 'On the Conflicts of Doing Feminist Research into Masculinity' in L. Stanley (ed.), *Feminist Praxis* (London: Routledge).

Mathieson, T. (1974). 'The Politics of Abolition', 14 *Scandinavian Studies of Criminology*.

Moore, R. (1977). 'Becoming a Sociologist in Sparbrook'. In C. Bell and H. Newby (eds.), *Doing Sociological Research* (London: Allen & Unwin).

Morgan, D. (1981). 'Men, Masculinity and the Process of Sociological Enquiry' (in Roberts 1981).

Oakley, A. (1974). 'The Invisible Woman: Sexism in Sociology', in *The Sociology of Housework* (London: Martin Robertson).

Pettigrew, J. (1981). 'Reminiscences of Fieldwork amongst the Sikhs' (in Roberts 1981).

Pryce, K. (1979). *Endless Pressure* (Harmondsworth: Penguin).

Rex, J. and Moore, R. (1967). *Race, Community and Conflict* (London; Oxford University Press for the Institute of Race Relations).

Roberts, H. (1981). *Doing Feminist Research* (London: Routledge & Kegan Paul).

Silverman, D. (1985). Williams, F. (1989). *Social Policy: A Critical Introduction* (Oxford: Polity Press).

Stanley, L. (1990). 'Feminist Praxis and the Academic Mode of Production; An Editorial Introduction', in L. Stanley (ed.), *Feminist Praxis* (London: Routledge).

Westwood, S. (1990). 'Racism, Black Masculinity and the Politics of Space' (in Hearn and Morgan 1990).

Williams, A. (1990). 'Reading Feminism in Fieldnotes', in L. Stanley (ed.), *Feminist Praxis: Research, Theory and Epistemology in Feminist Sociology* (London: Routledge).

Whyte, W. F. (1943). *Street Corner Society* (Chicago: Chicago University Press).

Women and Geography Study Group of the Institute of British Geographers (1984). *Geography and Gender* (London: Hutchinson).

Index